*For Adeline and Frederick Arnold, Mildred and
Donald Milner and Anne Murray*

Frontispiece. City Museum and Art Gallery, Hereford. A riding habit of c. 1775 consisting of jacket and matching petticoat in pink silk and wool mixture. The jacket fastens edge to edge at the centre front with hooks and eyes. Twisted silver cord trims the collar, facings and cuffs 'à la marinière' (4983).

A Handbook of Costume

Janet Arnold

M

ISBN (paperback): 0 333 24489 3

First published 1973 by
MACMILLAN LONDON LIMITED
4 Little Essex Street London WC2R 3LF
and Basingstoke
Associated Companies in Delhi Dublin
Hong Kong Johannesburg Lagos Melbourne
New York Singapore and Tokyo

First paperback edition 1978

Filmset in Great Britain by
BAS Printers Limited, Wallop, Hampshire

Printed in Hong Kong

Contents

Preface

I have written this book because over the last ten years more people than ever before seem to have acquired an interest in costume. Successful exhibitions have been held in museums up and down the country and major museums can produce bulging files of letters requesting information on every aspect of costume history and design.

This book has been prepared as much for the general public as for students and teachers and is intended to provide a guide to the ways in which people interested in costume can obtain information for themselves.

The use of costume study extends to many fields. The art historian uses the evidence provided by changing styles of dress to date paintings more closely; archaeologists and textile conservators in museums need a knowledge of cut and construction to piece together tattered fragments and restore them to new life; the history of costume in all its aspects is essential for technical staff, as well as for amateur and professional designers, to produce good period costumes for theatre, film and television; the history of fashion and the crafts of tailoring and dressmaking provide background and inspiration for both the professional dress designer and the art college student. Costume is also an interesting aspect of social history for study in schools.

The word 'costume' covers a very wide field, from the world of fashion at one end of the scale to the clothes worn by working people at the other, with all the infinite variations between them, reflecting the social position, age and individual personality of the wearer.

Whatever the approach, we must not overlook the fact that for many people in sophisticated societies, dressing in fashion has been and still is a delightful, if not frivolous, occupation pursued with great enthusiasm in spite of satirical comment on all sides. We should gain some enjoyment from looking at fashionable dress in its own right. This is a study of another art form, whether it be the detail of an exquisitely patterned mid-eighteenth-century silk beautifully displayed in a sack dress, the convolutions of pleated trimmings applied to a bustle dress of 1875, or the shape of tiny buckled mid-eighteenth-century shoes with their own pattens, too small for most twentieth-century feet.

There are certain limitations in this book which are the inevitable result of a wide survey. Some areas have had to be treated briefly and others, for example peasant costume, almost completely ignored, as they require separate volumes to do them justice.

I would like to thank the Directors, Curators and Assistants of the museums and costume collections which I visited whilst compiling the material for this book, for all their kindness and help. I am also very grateful to the staffs of the libraries of the Victoria and Albert Museum and the British Museum, and the Westminster and Bristol Central Reference Libraries for their assistance. The chapter on conservation was written as a result of seeing the methods used by conservators in both European and American museums; I would like to thank them for allowing me to watch them at work.

During the preparation of this book I have received help and encouragement from many people. There is not enough space to mention everyone, but I would particularly like to thank Miss Judith Bolingbroke, Mrs Daphne Boothby, the late Mrs Daphne Bullard, Miss Pamela Clabburn, Mr Kenneth Cohen, Mr Charles Gibbs-Smith, Mrs Madeleine Ginsburg, Miss Zillah Halls, Miss Avril Hart, Mrs Jean Hunnisett, Miss Mary de Jong, Mr John Kerslake, Mrs Helen Larson, Mr Stuart Maxwell, Miss Ella McLeod, Miss Monica Murray, Mr Revel Oddy, Mrs Sarah Parry, Mrs Susan Ranson, Dr Ann Saunders, Miss Brenda Thomas and Miss Susan Thorn.

I owe a particular debt of gratitude to Miss Jennifer Scarce for preparing the information on the Oriental Collection at the Royal Scottish Museum, Edinburgh; to Dr Roy Strong for helpful comments on the first draft of the chapter on costume in paintings; to Miss Anne Buck for useful criticism in the early stages of the chapter on conservation and storage and for taking much time and trouble to mount the specimens of altered eighteenth-century dresses at the Gallery of English Costume, Manchester; to Mrs Karen Finch for allowing me to take photographs in her conservation workroom, for generous help and advice with the chapter on conservation and storage and the related booklist; to Miss Natalie Rothstein for her assistance in dating eighteenth-century silks and for access to her files on this subject at the Victoria and Albert Museum; to Mrs Anne Murray and Miss Santina Levey, whose interest, help and advice during the preparation of this book have been invaluable.

While writing the second half of this book I have been a Research Lecturer in the Department of Textiles at the West Surrey College of Art and Design, and I would like to thank my colleagues for all their help and encouragement. I would also like to thank the College authorities and the Surrey County Council Education Committee for a grant towards the cost of photographs.

Finally, I would like to express my appreciation to Miss Janet Macklam, Mrs Helen Whitten, Mrs Winnifred Underwood and Miss Jenny Grahame for typing the manuscript—a thankless task—and to Miss Caroline Hobhouse and Mr John Richards at Macmillan for their inexhaustible patience.

Avery Hill College of Education, London
I would also like to thank the following students in the costume course whose questions and interest prompted me to write this book: Hilary Adams, Elizabeth Bellgrove, Chris Bevin, May Brett, Sally Broomfield, Doreen Brown, Jean Campbell, Helena Ciechowska, Hilary Coote, Elizabeth Daines, Barbara Foskett, Audrey Green, Judy Hindle, May Hatton, Janet Hoffman, Sheila Kershaw, Margaret Lane, Pat Mallett, Anne Martin, Shirley Mitchell, Marilyn Mowbray, Pat Noble, Jill Pooley, Jenny Potts, Barbara Ramskill, Irene Sanson, Linda Scott, Susan Urry, Janet Ward, Kate Ward and Meryl Watkins.

PHOTOGRAPHIC ACKNOWLEDGEMENTS
Most of the photographs in this book were taken by the author, again with the unstinting help of private owners and the staff of art galleries and museums and costume collections. Each source is acknowledged beside the photograph and accession numbers have been given for many museum objects.

Plates 1, 11 and 12 are reproduced by gracious permission of Her Majesty the Queen.

Plates 143, 164, 168–173 were all taken while lecturing in I.L.E.A. colleges and are reproduced here by kind permission. Plates 126–8, 142, 176–181 are reproduced by permission of the BBC.

The following are reproduced by kind permission of their owners and from their own or museum photographs: The Duke of Bedford, the Woburn Abbey Collection, 6; The Trustees of the British Museum, 38, 50, 51, 52, 61, 62, 89; The Earl of Craven (*Photo*. Victoria & Albert

Museum, Crown Copyright), 118; Claydon House, the National Trust (*Photo*. Victoria & Albert Museum, Crown Copyright), 195; Essex County Record Office, 83; Glasgow Art Gallery & Museum, 204; The Duke of Hamilton, 26, 27; Hardwick Hall, the National Trust, 66; Kunsthistorisches Museum, Vienna, 4; City of Liverpool Museums, 213; Mrs Anne Loudon, 9; The Earl of Wemyss and March, 14; The Mauritshuis, The Hague, 3; National Army Museum, 222; National Museum of Antiquities of Scotland, 196; National Portrait Gallery, 31, 39; City of Norwich Museums, 16, 17; Nottingham Museum & Art Gallery, 231; Prado Museum, Madrid, 2; Royal Opera House, Covent Garden (*Photo*. Houston Rogers), 166; Royal Scottish Museum, Edinburgh (*Photo*. Tom Scott), 199, 200; The Royal Shakespeare Company (*Photo*. Zöe Dominic), 167; Lord Sackville, Knole (*Photo*. Courtauld Institute), 5; Sanders of Oxford, 30; Symington Museum of Period Corsetry, 227; Henry Vyner Esq. (*Photo*. Royal Academy), 7; Walker Art Gallery, Liverpool, 10, 13, 15; Victoria & Albert Museum, (*Photo*. Crown Copyright), 24.

I. Primary Sources

GENERAL INTRODUCTION TO THE MAIN VISUAL AND DOCUMENTARY SOURCES

How does one find out more about a costume in a painting or one displayed in a glass case – the way in which the material was cut, the various pieces assembled and the fastenings arranged? What kind of a person wore these clothes and on what occasion?

Certain basic principles apply to the study of any subject. The first is to ask intelligent questions, and the second to answer them by a systematic search for information, starting in the library with careful reading. With costume this then leads to a study of the wealth of primary source material to be found in museums, art galleries, country houses and churches. From earliest times men and women have been represented by artists and craftsmen in various ways, wearing ordinary dress in everyday life as well as rich and costly clothes for state occasions.

Many museums have collections of costume and 'costume accessories and often people find their interest in the subject aroused by seeing an attractive display. After looking at a costume, the first questions begin to take shape.

When was this worn?
How did it look when it was first worn?
What kind of underclothes provided the shape and support?
What kind of hairstyle would have been appropriate?
What accessories would have been worn?
What position in society did the wearer have?
What did other people wear in different classes of society at the same period?
How did the person who wore the costume feel about the style?
What comments did other people make?
After a closer inspection further questions will emerge, some of

a more technical nature. These may, in fact, be the first questions asked, depending on the approach of the enthusiast.

How did the costume look in relation to the architecture, furniture and other decorative arts of the period?

What kind of material has been used?

How has it been cut?

Where are the seam lines?

What are the pattern shapes?

How much did it cost?

The answers to all these questions can be found by studying the other primary sources, which are covered on pages 17–128 and by reading the books listed in the costume bibliography (page 217).

What are the primary sources upon which books specifically about costume are based? There are many of them: paintings, drawings, sculpture, caricatures, engravings, tapestries, fashion plates, frescoes, illuminated manuscripts, monumental effigies and brasses, mosaics, photographs, stained glass, silhouettes, embroidery and actual specimens of costume. These are all within the fields of fine and applied or decorative arts. There is also the documentary evidence which provides the background for the study of costume. The wills, inventories, letters, diaries and accounts of men and women who lived in past centuries are preserved in the archives. The literary sources, biographies, autobiographies, published letters and diaries, novels and plays, give accounts of dress in contemporary settings which are frequently entertaining in themselves, as well as providing information. (See pages 115–18.)

The most immediately useful primary sources are those with visual appeal. Many of them are described briefly on pages 17–108 with an indication of some of the pitfalls which may be encountered by the unwary. Not everyone lives within reach of the collections they need and much of the source material may have to be studied at second hand through reprints of early books, published documents and the many beautifully illustrated books on fine and applied arts. The amount of work done at first hand will depend on the determination of the individual enthusiast and the time available.

The book list which follows each section is not comprehensive, but is intended to provide visual information if the primary sources are not available locally, and to give the enthusiast a starting point for further reading.

Many art books and large comprehensive works dealing with other aspects of a period, its social and political life, as well as painting, sculpture and architecture are illustrated with a variety of the primary sources which show costume.

The costume bibliography (pages 217–32) lists books covering many aspects of the subject, based on the evidence provided by these sources.

LIST OF GENERAL BOOKS WITH USEFUL ILLUSTRATIONS

This short list provides a few examples of the many books which are illustrated with a wide variety of primary source material, showing good costume detail in many cases. They are mainly concerned with the fine arts, but other subjects – for example mythology, social history (see pages 219–220) and biographies – use the same material for illustrations.

BIOGRAPHIES

GERNSHEIM, H. and A. *Queen Victoria. A biography in word and picture.* Longmans, 1959. 400 monochrome plates.

HOLLAND, V. *Oscar Wilde, a pictorial biography.* Thames and Hudson, 1960. 128 monochrome plates.

HUISMAN, P. and DORTU, M. G. *Lautrec by Lautrec.* Translated by C. Bellow. Macmillan, 1964. Many monochrome and colour plates.

MITFORD, N. *The Sun King.* Hamish Hamilton, 1966. Many monochrome and colour plates covering *c.*1660–1715.

MYTHOLOGY

IONS, V. *Egyptian mythology.* Hamlyn, 1965. 100 monochrome and 24 colour plates. New edition 1968.

MAC CANA, P. *Celtic mythology.* Hamlyn, 1970. 100 monochrome and 24 colour plates.

PINSENT, J. *Greek mythology.* Hamlyn, 1969. 100 monochrome and 24 colour plates.

Some books are illustrated from a wide range of sources from many different periods and cultures, for example:

FRANCIS, F. (Ed.) *Treasures of the British Museum*. Thames and Hudson, 1971. 375 monochrome and 64 colour plates.

Others are illustrated from a wide range of sources relating to particular countries or cultures only. EARLY CIVILIZATIONS AND CULTURES are particularly well covered. Often more information on costume can be gained from these books than from those specifically on costume of the period.

BERRY, R. *A time of Gods*. Thames and Hudson, 1962. Monochrome plates.

BOARDMAN, J., DORIG, J., FUCHS, W. and HEIMER, M. *The Art and Architecture of Ancient Greece*. Thames and Hudson, 1967. Many monochrome and colour plates.

CHASE, G. H. *Greek and Roman antiquities*. Museum of Fine Arts, Boston, 1950. Monochrome plates.

GHIRSHMAN, R. *Iran: Parthians and Sassanians*. Translated by S. Gilbert and J. Emmons. Arts of Mankind series. Thames and Hudson, 1962. 449 monochrome and 80 colour plates. Covers 2nd century B.C. to 7th century A.D.

GHIRSHMAN, R. *Persia from the origins to Alexander the Great*. Translated by S. Gilbert and J. Emmons. Arts of mankind series. Thames and Hudson, 1964. 579 monochrome and 54 colour plates. Covers the 2nd millenium B.C. to the 5th century B.C.

MICHAELOWSKI, K. *The Art of Ancient Egypt*. Thames and Hudson, 1969. 1042 monochrome and 143 colour plates.

PALLOTTINO, M. *Art of the Etruscans*. Thames and Hudson, 1955. 123 monochrome and 3 colour plates.

POPE, A. U. *A survey of Persian art*. 6 vols. Oxford University Press, 1938–39. A standard work covering Persian art from prehistoric times onwards. Particularly useful for costume detail of pre-Achaemenid-Parthian periods.

STEVENSON SMITH, W. *The Art and Architecture of Ancient Egypt*. Pelican History of Art, 1958. Reprinted 1965.

VICTORIA AND ALBERT MUSEUM. *Early Christian and Byzantine Art*. H.M.S.O., 1955. 28 monochrome plates.

VICTORIA AND ALBERT MUSEUM. *Late Antique and Byzantine Art.* H.M.S.O., 1963. 50 monochrome plates.

ZSCHIETZSCHMANN, W. *Hellas and Rome.* Zwemmer, 1959. Monochrome plates.

LATER PERIODS are well illustrated in books ranging from general histories of art to those dealing with particular aspects of a period or country, for example:

BOLOGNA, F. *Early Italian painting: Romanesque and early Medieval art.* Van Nostrand, 1963. 100 colour plates. Wall paintings, frescoes, mosaics, manuscripts, *c.*762–1301.

CASTELFRANCHI VEGAS, L. *International Gothic Art in Italy.* Thames and Hudson, 1968. 100 colour plates of paintings, miniatures and frescoes, *c.*1416–1450.

EVANS, J. (Ed.) *The flowering of the Middle Ages.* Thames and Hudson, 1966. 439 monochrome and 192 colour plates.

HAY, D. (Ed.) *The age of the Renaissance.* Thames and Hudson, 1967. 420 monochrome and 180 colour plates.

HUSA, V., PETRÁŇ, J. and ŠUBRTOVÁ, A. *Traditional crafts and skills. Life and work in medieval and renaissance times.* Hamlyn, 1967. 358 monochrome and colour plates of material originating from the regions which today make up Czechoslovakia, from the end of the eleventh to the end of the sixteenth century.

KELDER, D. *Pageant of the Renaissance.* Praeger, Pall Mall, 1969. 80 monochrome and colour plates.

PIPER, D. *The English face.* Thames and Hudson, 1957. 145 monochrome plates of portraits from paintings, sculpture and photographs.

SAUNDERS, O. E. *A history of English art in the Middle Ages.* Clarendon Press, Oxford, 1932. 100 monochrome plates. Useful guide to the primary sources of the period.

SMITH, B. *Spain. A history in art.* Harrap, 1966. Numerous colour plates. A general survey from prehistoric times to *c.* 1900.

TIMMERS, J. J. M. *A history of Dutch life and art.* Nelson, 1959. 500 monochrome plates. A general survey from the earliest beginnings to the present day, which shows people at different periods in their ordinary occupations and costume, as well as the architectural background.

CHRONOLOGICAL GUIDE
TO THE MAIN VISUAL SOURCES

EGYPTIAN   wall paintings, sculpture
ASSYRIAN AND BABYLONIAN   sculpture
GREEK   sculpture, ceramic decorations
MINOAN   frescoes, terracotta figurines
ROMAN   sculpture, mosaics, frescoes
BYZANTINE   sculpture, mosaics, frescoes
EUROPEAN

Eleventh-century   sculpture, embroidery,
Twelfth- and thirteenth-century   sculpture, wall paintings, frescoes, stained glass, embroidery, monumental brasses, illuminated manuscripts,
Fourteenth-century   sculpture, wall paintings, frescoes, stained glass, monumental brasses, tapestries, illuminated manuscripts,
Fifteenth-century   sculpture, wall paintings, frescoes, stained glass, monumental brasses, paintings, woodcuts, drawings, ceramic decorations, tapestries, illuminated manuscripts,
Sixteenth-century   sculpture, frescoes, monumental brasses, paintings, drawings, embroideries, tapestries, miniatures, illuminated manuscripts, engravings, woodcuts,
Seventeenth-century   sculpture, paintings, drawings, miniatures, engravings, woodcuts,
Eighteenth-century   sculpture, paintings, drawings, miniatures, caricatures, silhouettes, ceramic figures and decorations, engravings, fashion plates, dolls,
Nineteenth-century   paintings, drawings, miniatures, engravings, silhouettes, caricatures, fashion plates, photographs, dolls,
Twentieth-century   photographs, films, paintings, drawings, caricatures.

I.

PAINTINGS

Paintings provide one of the major sources of information for the study of costume, particularly in periods from which few specimens of costume survive, but they should always be considered most carefully in relation to other sources whenever possible.

The textural quality of the brush strokes in a painting can blur seam lines and the grain of the fabric. Details may be obscured by layers of dirt and varnish, while restoration may have falsified the evidence. Two-dimensional evidence for a three-dimensional subject can be misleading. Elizabethan portraits, for instance, often show ruffs which appear to be tapered at the front and to disappear at the back of the neck, but this is the effect of foreshortening and perspective given by the artist. The bodice fronts with the wide French farthingales appear to be incredibly long and pointed; this again is partly an optical illusion produced by the upward tilt of the farthingale at the back, and the vertical lines of the turned-back gown fronts and long ropes of pearls.

Although generalisations can be misleading, in many cases it is true to say that the less sophisticated the painter, the more information there will be for the student of costume. As soon as a painter starts to observe the play of light on fabrics or becomes involved with new techniques of painting, the details of dress are no longer so important to him.

There are many similar points which should be noted by costume students, who should be familiar with the changing styles in painting and be able to recognise the work of different artists and schools reasonably quickly. The history of painting can be studied in the many books which are available on the subject and there is no point in repeating information which is more than adequately covered elsewhere. The purpose of this chapter is to point out some of the more obvious pitfalls and to make enthusiasts aware of the problems involved in weighing the evidence provided by paintings. The date of the picture, the subject matter, the patron, the nationality of the sitter and painter and the painting technique should all be taken into consideration. They will give rise to many questions, not all of which can be answered, but they should prevent hasty judgements being made.

From the early fifteenth century, when knowledge of oil painting techniques spread rapidly all over Europe, the Church was still the artist's major patron and the subject matter tended to be of religious inspiration. However, many of the paintings show the Virgin and Child or episodes from the lives of the saints, with all the characters wearing fifteenth-century costume. Care must be taken to distinguish between the various kinds of costume seen in these pictures. First there is contemporary dress, worn by ordinary people; second the ecclesiastical dress worn by bishops and some of the saints; third the stylised versions of medieval dress with ecclesiastical connotations for the Virgin and other saints, and finally what may probably be pageant costume worn by the Magi and similar characters. This point was discussed by Stella Mary Newton in a lecture given for the Society for Theatre Research in 1968. She noted several features of clothing which seemed to have lingered on in theatrical costume, often with a time lag of fifty years or more (see *Renaissance Theatre Costume*, by S. M. Newton). It would be interesting if documentary evidence could be found to suggest that some of these costumes were the no-longer-fashionable clothes of wealthy people with additional decorations, as well as those made specially for the purpose. The considerable number of times that an eighteenth-century dress could be re-used (see pages 131–146) makes this seem not unlikely.

In some of the large altar pieces and paintings commissioned by wealthy patrons for particular churches, their own families may be represented wearing contemporary dress. In the Portinari altar piece in the Uffizi Gallery, painted in 1473–5 by Hugo van der Goes, a Fleming, the donor, Tommaso Portinari, Italian agent at Bruges for the Medici, is portrayed with his wife, two sons and daughter. Both Maria and her daughter are dressed in the height of Franco-Flemish fashion, although the altar piece was commissioned for the Chapel of the Hospital of S. Maria Novella in Florence, of which Tommaso Portinari was patron. It is interesting

to compare the dress worn by Maria Portinari with the one shown
in her portrait by Hans Memling, painted *c*.1476, which is in the
Metropolitan Museum, New York. (Both portraits are reproduced
in *From Van Eyck to Breugel* by Max Friedlander, plates 103 and 105.)
Memling has chosen a slightly different angle for his portrait and
the material filling in the sides of the neckline shown in the altar
piece has been removed, giving an optical illusion of added width
to the neckline of what appears to be the same dress. The fur-lined
cuffs have not been turned back so far, the hennin head-dress is
plain while the one in the altar piece is decorated with little pearls,
but the neck ornament is identical.

'The French Ambassadors to London, Jean de Dinteville and
Georges de Selve, Bishop of Lavour', in the National Gallery,
London, painted by the German-Swiss artist Holbein while in
England in 1533 gives rise to several questions. Are the two men
wearing clothes made in their own country, or purchased in
England? (How is it that today one can often tell an American
before he speaks, even though dressed in clothes of English manufacture?) The Bishop of Lavour is dressed similarly to Georges
d'Armagnac, Bishop of Rodez, the French Ambassador to Venice,
as painted by Titian *c*.1540 (the portrait is owned by the Duke of
Northumberland and may be seen at Albury Park). Were the
clothes of these two clerics purchased in France? To return to the
painting in the National Gallery, how much has Holbein, himself
a foreigner, unwittingly put of his own national characteristics
onto the canvas? These points must all be considered, although it
may take a long time to reach a conclusion. Indeed, in the days
before photography, it may be difficult to reach a conclusion at all,
and even photographs can mislead. What we must do, as far as we
can, is to look at all paintings in the light of other contemporary
evidence in order to interpret the information correctly.

How far can we evaluate different contemporary versions of a
painting? Little is known about the way in which the painters
worked. It is interesting to see that in a portrait of Mary Tudor
[PLATE 1] by an unknown artist (owned by Her Majesty the Queen)
apparently after the three Antonio Mor portraits of 1554, (in the
Prado, Madrid, the Isabella Stewart Gardner Museum, Boston,
and the private collection of Earl Compton) the less skilled painter
has observed and recorded the weight of the heavy jewel pulling
the velvet down at the front neck and the creases of velvet where

the collar stands up, which are not in the Mor paintings [PLATE 2]. Concern for this type of detail and the faithfulness with which they are recorded are typical of the work of unsophisticated painters. This particular painting is by a man who had not come to terms with perspective problems, possibly working in the same studio as Mor. He attempted to copy the pose but could not manage the foreshortening, so the Queen stands against a chair back, while the Mor versions are seated. A different chair was used for his picture and a dark reddish brown velvet dress arranged for him to observe the creases of the velvet and the fur lined sleeves turned back to reveal the brocaded silk undersleeves which match the forepart. These are of a different design from those worn with the very dark rich velvet (almost black) dress depicted in the Mor paintings. After looking closely at the four pictures it becomes obvious that there are two sets of information on costume available, one from Antonio Mor's three paintings and the other from an unknown artist's portrait.

Which of several versions of a portrait is the correct one for

Left

1. Mary I. Artist unknown, c. 1554. (H.M. Queen, Royal Collection)

Right

2. Mary I. Antonio Mor, 1554. (Prado, Madrid)

costume study? The four variations of Jane Seymour's portrait
give some idea of the problem. The Holbein painting of 1536
[PLATE 4] in the Kunsthistorisches Museum, Vienna, shows the
Queen in a russet velvet gown with embroidery of gold couched
thread at the neckline and on the turned-back sleeves. The billiment
of sets of four pearls alternating with gold-mounted jewels border-
ing the front of the gable head-dress matches the jewelled band
edging the neckline. The same arrangement is used for the necklace
and girdle. The brocaded silk undersleeves match the petticoat and
the white lawn wrist ruffles are embroidered with blackwork. The
seam on the left front bodice is either top-stitched with thirteen
little stitches in gold thread or held with a row of small pins or tiny
studs. If they are pins, they are not observed in the same way as the
pin which Holbein painted in the portrait of an Englishwoman,
c.1540 (Kunsthistorisches Museum 211); it is clearly visible and
holds up the black velvet lined sleeve which is similar in shape to
that in the portrait of Jane Seymour. The decoration of gold
couched thread round the neckline continues under the arm. In a
copy made at a slightly later date, which is at Woburn Abbey
[PLATE 6], the bodice has been elongated, probably unconsciously,
to be in keeping with later styles, sometime after 1550. The version
at Knole [PLATE 5] appears at first glance to be identical with the
one in Vienna. However, after studying the picture for a few
minutes, several differences of detail become apparent. The
jewellery is quite different; the necklace is formed from one pearl
alternating with one gold bead, the head-dress is decorated with
sets of four pearls, while the neckline is bordered with one pearl
alternating with a jewel in a gold setting. The undersleeve and
forepart are completely different from those in the other painting;
it looks as if an attempt had been made to cover the brocaded silk
undersleeves with stripes of paint as a preliminary to painting the
white pleated undersleeves seen in the Mauritshuis version [PLATE 3].
The wrist ruffles are embroidered in a very different way and the
material on the left side of the bodice has been pinched up into
what appears to be a seam with twenty-five gold stitches stabbing
through four layers of material or twelve pins not very well
painted; it is unlikely that the painter would have recorded this
lumpy seam or bodice opening if he had not observed it personally.
The portrait at the Mauritshuis, The Hague, is different again from
the other versions. Holbein has observed the embroidery and

recorded the details of the pattern in a more sensitive way in this smaller picture. The neckline is decorated with two pearls alternating with a round dark red stone with a gold flower on top. The necklace is identical to the one worn in the version at Knole and the waist girdle matches it. The head-dress is bordered with three pearls alternating with one gold bead. The undersleeves are similar to those in the portrait at Knole, but made of plain white silk with deep padded pleats. The wrist ruffles are in white lawn with a blackwork border. But the most interesting variation in the treatment of the subject is the way in which the velvet of the sleeve fits neatly into the front bodice in front of the seam on the left side. Was this picture painted after the version in the Kunsthistorisches Museum? Had the neckline of the dress stretched and the front of the bodice been pulled across and the top of the sleeve moved in an inch or so to tighten it? There are certainly more wrinkles under the arm, fully observed and recorded. Was the version at Knole painted in Holbein's studio by an apprentice who worked beside Holbein while the Kunsthistorisches Museum version was being painted? He may have observed, in an unsophisticated way, the rather lumpy seam or opening; perhaps the jewellery,

undersleeves and petticoat were changed for the second portrait and he added these to his picture, since he would probably have been working more slowly.

All this can only be conjecture. It is difficult to answer all the questions which arise without a range of portraits showing similar dresses of the same period for comparison, but the costume historian must make some guesses as there are so few specimens of costume surviving from before *c.*1600. Although it would be possible to reconstruct a dress, silks and velvets are no longer hand woven from hand spun threads. The resulting irregularity gave a different texture and appearance to the surface of materials made before the industrial revolution. Modern techniques cannot produce an exact reproduction of a fabric for purposes of research, to understand exactly what the painters saw. The main point to be learned from these four portraits is that it is often possible to recognise a copy made of a painting at a later date. In this case the elongated bodice gives the clue. The painter will usually put in something of his own time; occasionally the hairstyle or the shape of the face will not suit the dress. It is then worth while carrying out further research before accepting the evidence. In some cases

Left

5. *Jane Seymour. Artist unknown, c. 1536. (Lord Sackville, Knole)*

Right

6. *Jane Seymour. Artist unknown, c. 1550. (The Duke of Bedford, Woburn Abbey Collection)*

the original painting may have been destroyed and only the copy survives. However, it is as well to remember that it may not be absolutely accurate.

Many of the ladies wearing wide French farthingales of the late sixteenth century appear to be falling forwards in the portraits, their feet in an impossible position. A good example is the Ditchley portrait of Queen Elizabeth in the National Portrait Gallery. Bearing in mind the elaborate decoration of these dresses it is likely that the lady's face was painted in a few sittings and the costume was then mounted on a stand for the painter to take his time over putting in all the details. The shoes must have been tucked underneath the hem at the front of the stand for the painter to copy, to avoid giving the effect of the dress floating in air, since the skirts in many cases seem to have cleared the ground by two or three inches. The feet would have been seen beneath the hemline when walking; the painter therefore put them in the portrait without considering if they would have been seen in that particular position. There were many perspective problems to be tackled. In the portrait of Elizabeth Brydges, later Lady Kennedy, painted in 1589 by Custodis, which is at Woburn Abbey (*The English Icon*, by Roy Strong, page 197) the lady was posed at a slight angle facing away from the viewer; the dress was added later, but was painted from the front. There is nothing wrong with the position of the ruff or the angle of the neckline. It simply means a slight visual adjustment to realise that the artist did indeed paint what he saw, but all the pieces were not there to be painted at the same time.

Although a fair number of portraits and other paintings of interest to the costume enthusiast survive from the seventeenth century, not many are available for easy reference. Many of those reproduced show the fashion for having a portrait painted *en negligée* at the end of the seventeenth and beginning of the eighteenth century. The fashionable portrait painter, like Lely, draped his sitters, particularly the ladies, in lengths of silk and satin gracefully folded about the figure and revealing glimpses of the chemise beneath. Some of these paintings do in fact show the early form of the mantua [PLATE 7], a loose gown which was popular from 1676, according to Randle Holme, writing in *The Academy of Armory and Blazon* in 1688. In some of the portraits they have simply been eased off the shoulders. Gentlemen are often seen informally posed, wearing a banyan, the loose gown from which the ladies seem to

have derived the idea of the mantua. Until the 1670s both men's and women's clothes had been made by tailors and these loose gowns are the work of early dressmakers who had little experience of fitting. It must have been a relief to wear one of them even with stays beneath, after the rigidly boned bodices of the 1660s and 70s and the contrast in style must have interested the painter, who could now arrange informal poses for his sitters. Although these portraits with loose draperies are not particularly useful for costume study they do show the hairstyles of the period. Large group pictures like 'The Tichborne Dole' by Gillis Van Tilborgh [PLATE 9], where all strata of society are depicted in great detail, are a more useful source of information.

The eighteenth century is particularly rich in paintings which show costume. There are portraits, conversation pieces and genre paintings which show clothes worn in all walks of life. 'The Rake's Progress' series by Hogarth is a good example. Perhaps the major pitfall to be avoided is the portrait in Vandyke dress, usually the artist's studio properties, if not a genuine costume stored in the sitter's attic since the seventeenth century, or a masquerade costume.

7. *Sir Robert Vyner and Lady Vyner, widow of Sir Thomas Hyde, wearing a banyan and a mantua. John Michael Wright, 1673. (Henry Vyner)*

Gainsborough's Blue Boy wears Vandyke costume. Allan Ramsay
painted eight portraits of ladies in the same Vandyke dress;
Arabella Pershall (1740), Lady Colebrook (1741), three of Jemima
Campbell, Marchioness Grey (1741), Ann, wife of John Floyer
(1743), Mrs George Hunt (1745) and Barbara St John, Countess of
Coventry (c.1740–5). The costume is reminiscent of the portraits of
Queen Henrietta Maria at Wilton House, the National Portrait
Gallery and Windsor Castle. It has been painted from eight
different angles and possibly by different hands. Perhaps the
drapery painter Van Aken, whom Ramsay used, employed an
assistant when the costume was set up in the studio. In view of the
dates it seems likely that all the pictures of the costume were
painted at the same time, the heads of the sitters being added
afterwards. The satin bodice laces down the centre front with long
waist tabs from the natural waist level and very large sleeves. This
may be a seventeenth-century bodice lengthened slightly on the
canvas to give a line more in keeping with the eighteenth century.

9. 'The Tichborne
Dole'. Gillis Van
Tilborgh, c. 1670.
(Mrs Anne Loudon)

The lace edged neckwear and the sleeve ruffles would also appear
to be of seventeenth-century origin. Another satin dress used in a
series of portraits by Ramsay would seem to have had a similar
history. The portraits are of an unknown lady (1739), Lady Hanmer
(1740), Lady Margaret Ogilvie (1743), Clementina Walkinshaw
(c.1745), Elizabeth Perkins (c.1745), the Countess of Leven (1748),
Christine Shairp (1750) and Miss Jean Ferguson (1752). The
arrangement of pearls in the hair and on the bodice and sleeves
varies slightly in each picture and the poses are all different. The
dress looks like those seen in portraits by Lely and other painters
in the 1670s and again may be an original dress rather than a
made-up studio property. Sometimes the whole family is depicted
in Vandyke costume; 'The Family of Sir William Young' by
Zoffany [PLATE 10] shows what may be family heirlooms as well as
studio properties, all worn with the hairstyles of c.1760. It is interesting to compare this group with one of c.1772–3 by the same
artist [PLATE 11] in which the sitters are wearing ordinary dress.

The paintings of the later part of the eighteenth century must also be selected carefully for costume study. The neo-classical movement which began to develop early in the eighteenth century and flourished from c.1780, was partly the result of new archaeological excavations and the published engravings of discoveries. Classical sculptures and vase decoration provided both subject matter and poses for paintings. In addition to numerous historical canvases of classical inspiration, many portraits show the use of classical rather than contemporary costume. Sir Joshua Reynolds in one of his Royal Academy *Discourses* pointed out that 'The desire for transmitting to posterity the shape of modern dress must be acknowledged to be purchased at prodigious price, even the price of everything that is valuable in art.' This outlook was shared by many painters and the costume student must therefore be careful to distinguish between the lady wearing fashionable dress of the late eighteenth century posed in a classical setting and one who is part of the scene in antique draperies. There were many painters still producing portraits of people wearing contemporary dress as well as these other paintings with their somewhat fanciful attire.

Other changes were seen in the style of painting at this time. Gainsborough, for example, was more interested in the effect produced by light on a fabric than in reproducing an exact copy of its pattern. Yet it is in the scratchy surface texture of his paintings that we can see the impression that fragile gauzes, light silks and fluttering ribbons must have given. We are fortunate that Tissot, Manet and Renoir were portraying dresses of the 1870s with a similar feeling, for this is something that a photograph cannot really catch. Although the camera records accurately what is there and the fashion plate presents an idealised version of a fashion, the painter sometimes makes us more aware of its charm as we look at it through his eyes, and makes us understand its appeal to the people who originally wore it.

Photography (see page 78), invented in the late 1840s, was to supersede painting as a source of information for costume students by 1900. The Victorian taste for historical paintings and romantic interpretations of scenes from Walter Scott's novels, Shakespeare's plays and Malory's *Morte Darthur*, costumed with loving if slightly inaccurate care, present yet another pitfall for the unwary, and should be ignored by the costume student in search of details of contemporary dress. Millais used a genuine sack dress for his

Above

*10. The family of
Sir William Young,
depicted in Vandyke
costumes which may
be family heirlooms
as well as studio
properties. Johann
Zoffany, c. 1760.
(Walker Art
Gallery, Liverpool)*

Left

*11. Queen Charlotte
with members of her
family wearing
fashionable clothes.
The child holds what
is probably a fashion
doll. (Detail.)
Johann Zoffany,
c. 1772–3. (H.M.
Queen, Royal Coll.)*

painting 'Vanessa' [PLATE 13] painted in 1868. It is interesting to
compare the hairstyle and head-dress with one of 1754 depicted by
Allan Ramsay [PLATE 14]. Nineteenth-century genre paintings are
packed with detail for the costume enthusiast. Pictures like 'A
Summer Day in Hyde Park', painted by John Ritchie in 1858 (The
London Museum), Frith's 'Derby Day' of 1857 (The Tate Gallery,
London), Ramsgate Sands in 'Life at the Seaside' of 1852–4 (H.M.
the Queen) [PLATE 12] and 'The Railway Station', 1863 (Leicester
Museum) provide a vast amount of accurately observed information on the way clothes were worn in different strata of society,
on various occasions. Items like bonnet veils and uglies (the cane-
supported additional brims for bonnets worn in the 1850s) often

seen in museum collections, which sometimes present identification problems for the beginner, can be seen in use, correctly worn.

Paintings showing actors in theatrical costume [PLATE 15] should never be used to provide information about ordinary dress. And one final word of warning which applies particularly to sixteenth, seventeenth, and eighteenth-century portraits: great care should be taken before accepting the date on the canvas as the date of the costume. The name and date were frequently added at a later period by the sitters' descendants, often incorrectly; labels too can be unreliable. Two good examples are the portraits of Elizabeth D'Oyley and Margaret Conyers at the Strangers' Hall Museum, Norwich. That of Elizabeth D'Oyley [PLATE 16] still has the

12. *Groups of people informally posed on Ramsgate Sands in 'Life at the Seaside' by W. P. Frith, 1852–4. The ladies seated on the sand at the right of the picture are wearing uglies attached to their bonnets to shade their faces from the sun. (Detail.) (H.M. Queen, Royal Collection)*

Above left

13. 'Vanessa' by
J. E. Millais, 1868.
The model is wearing
a sack dress of
c. 1770 with a
mid-nineteenth
century pose, as she
is not wearing a
corset of the correct
shape. (Walker Art
Gallery, Liverpool)

Above right

14. Lady Walpole
Wemyss. Allan
Ramsay, signed and
dated 1754. (Earl
of Wemyss and
March)

painter's inscription of the date, 1608, and sitter's age 'Ae 16' on the canvas but beneath are the words '(Isabel (?)) Pert. Coheiress of Coniers. Mother of Margaret Buxton'. The nineteenth-century label attached to the frame on arrival at the museum read 'Margaret Conyers'. The portrait of Margaret Conyers painted in *c*.1630–40 bears the inscription 'Eliz. Daughter of Edm^d Doyley. Married Robt Buxton 1608 (?).' The nineteenth-century label read 'Elizabeth D'Oyley 1608'. A mistake in identity was obviously made when the inscriptions were added to the paintings, possibly during the eighteenth century and persisted with the nineteenth-century labels.

16, 17. Elizabeth D'Oyley (left), attributed to Robert Peake, 1608, and Margaret Conyers (right), artist unknown, c. 1630–40. (City of Norwich Museums)

Left

15. David Garrick wearing theatrical costume as Richard III. William Hogarth, c. 1745. (Walker Art Gallery, Liverpool)

A SELECTION OF PAINTERS WHOSE
WORK IS USEFUL FOR COSTUME STUDY

The painters are listed chronologically according to the date when they were first known to be working or when they were born. A reasonable guide to the date from which their working life is likely to start is to add approximately twenty years to the date of birth. In some instances definite dates cannot be given because art historians have still not established them with certainty.

Painters moved from country to country, sometimes to study, sometimes following wealthy patrons; for example Holbein, a German-Swiss, spent ten years working in England, while Van Dyck, born in Antwerp, spent four years in Italy and nine years in England painting numerous portraits of fashionable people. Since it is usually costume of a particular date which is needed, it seemed more helpful to list the painters by date rather than by schools or countries. Each painter can be followed up in the many reference works on the history of painting. The student should also use the various art periodicals available. These publish articles on various painters, often with good illustrations of recently discovered works which provide valuable information on costume.

Abbreviations: A.–active D.–died

c.1370–1427	Gentile da FABRIANO
1378/9–1444	Robert CAMPIN*
c.1400–50	The Master of FLÉMALLE*
	* thought by some experts to be the same man
1395–1455/6	Antonio PISANELLO
1397–1475	Paolo UCCELLO
1399/1400–64	Rogier van der WEYDEN
1406–69	Filippo LIPPI
A. 1420–82	GIOVANNI di Paolo
c.1420–77/81	Jean FOUQUET
A. 1422/4–41	Jan van EYCK
c.1427–99	Alessio BALDOVINETTI
c.1430–1479?	ANTONELLO da Messina
1430–1516	Giovanni BELLINI
c.1433–94	Hans MEMLING
c.1435–88	Andrea del VERROCCHIO
1441–1523	Luca SIGNORELLI
1445–1510	Sandro BOTTICELLI
1445–1523	Pietro PERUGINO
1454–1513	Bernardino PINTORICCHIO
1455–96	Ercole ROBERTI
1457–1504	Filippino LIPPI
c.1460–1523/6	Vittore CARPACCIO
A. 1460–80	Joos van WASSENHOVE
1466–1530	Quentin METSYS
1467–1516	Giovanni Antonio BOLTRAFFIO
1470–1524	GIROLAMO di Benvenuto

1472–1553	Lucas CRANACH, the Elder	A. 1544	Master JOHN
c.1475–c.1534	Jan GOSSAERT, called MABUSE	A. c.1545	
		D. 1558	Gerlach FLICKE
c.1480–1556/7	Lorenzo LOTTO	1545–81	Frans POURBUS
1483–1520	RAPHAEL	A. 1547	
c.1485–1540/1	Joos Van CLEVE	D. 1619	Nicholas HILLIARD
A. 1485–1510	Giovanni di BARTOLOMMEO	1555–1641	John de CRITZ
1487/90–1576	Tiziano Vecelli TITIAN	A. 1561–1635	Marcus GHEERAERTS the Younger
c.1493–1555	Barthel BRUYN the Elder	c.1563–1639	Orazio GENTILESCHI
		1567–1641	Michiel Jansz MIEREVELDT
1494–1533	Lucas van LEYDEN	1569–1622	Frans POURBUS
1497–1543	Hans HOLBEIN the Younger	Died 1572	François CLOUET
		1573–1610	Michelangelo Merigi da CARAVAGGIO
1498–1574	Maerten Jacobsz van HEEMSKERCK	A. 1576	
		D. 1626?	Robert PEAKE the Elder
1500–71	Paris BORDONE	A. 1578/9–99	John BETTES, the Younger
1503–40	Francesco PARMIGIANINO	c.1577/8–1622	Paul van SOMER
1503–72	Agnolo BRONZINO	1577–1640	Peter Paul RUBENS
D. 1540/1	Jean CLOUET	c.1580–1657	Pieter Claes SOUTMAN
D. 1523	Gerard DAVID		
1518–94	Jacopo TINTORETTO	A. c.1580/5	
1519–75	Antonio MOR	D. 1633	William SEGAR
A. c.1531	D.	1581/5–1666	Frans HALS
before 1576	John BETTES	c.1584–1651	Cornelius de VOS
1523–84	Pieter POURBUS	1585–1634	Hendrik AVERCAMP
c.1525–78	Giovanni Battista MORONI	1588–1648	Antoine le NAIN
		A. 1589	
c.1525/30–69	Pieter BREUGHEL	D. 1593	Hieronimo CUSTODIS
1531/2–88	Alonso SANCHEZ COELLO	1590–1656	Gerard van HONTHORST
A. 1533/4–74	CORNEILLE de Lyon	c.1590 D.	
A. 1537		before 1648	Daniel MYTENS
D. 1544	William SCROTS	c.1591–1659	Wybrand de GEEST
A. 1540		1591–1656	Dirk HALS
D. 1573	Hans EWORTH	1593–1661	Cornelius JOHNSON
A. 1540?		1593–1678	Jacob JORDAENS
D. 1596	George GOWER	1596/7–1667	Thomas de KEYSER
A. 1543–68	Steven van der MEULEN	1598–1664	Francisco de ZURBARAN

1599–1641	Anthony van DYCK
1599–1660	Diego Rodriguez de Silva y VELASQUEZ
1606–69	Hermansz REMBRANDT van Rijn
A. c.1610–20	William LARKIN
1610–90	David TENIERS the Younger
1612–95	Pierre MIGNARD
1614–84	Gonzales COQUES
1617–81	Gerard TERBORCH
1618–80 A. 1625 D. 1656	Peter LELY
	Jacob van VELSEN
c.1626–79	Jan STEEN
c.1629–67	Gabriel METSU
c.1629–81	Pieter de HOOCH
1632–75	Johannes VERMEER
1634–1703	Eglon Hendric van der NEER
1646/9–1723	Godfrey KNELLER
1656–1746	Nicolas de LARGILLIÈRE
1656/9–1743	Michael DAHL
1679–1752	Jean François de TROY
1679–1772	Marcellus LAROON
1684–1721	Antoine WATTEAU
1685–1766	Jean Marc NATTIER
1697–1764	William HOGARTH
1690–1743	Nicolas LANCRET
1692–1780	Joseph HIGHMORE
1697–1768	Antonio CANALETTO
1699–1779	Jean Baptiste CHARDIN
1702–85	Pietro LONGHI
1703–70	François BOUCHER
1708–87	Pompeo BATONI
1711–87	Arthur DEVIS
1713–84	Allan RAMSAY
1714–89	Claude Joseph VERNET

1718–93	Alexandre ROSLIN
1723–92	Joshua REYNOLDS
1724–1806	George STUBBS
1727–75	François Hubert DROUAIS
1727–88	Thomas GAINSBOROUGH
1728–79	Anton Raffael MENGS
1733?–1810	Johann ZOFFANY
1737–1815	John Singleton COPLEY
1746–1828	Francisco de GOYA y Lucientes
A. 1750–65	Joseph BLACKBURN
1755–1842	Louise Elizabeth VIGÉE-LEBRUN
1756–1823	Henry RAEBURN
1758–1810	John HOPPNER
1763–1804	George MORLAND
1780–1867	Jean Auguste Dominique INGRES
1758–1823	Pierre Paul PRUD'HON
1770–1837	Baron François GÉRARD
1789–1863	Horace VERNET
1819–1909	William Powell FRITH
1834–1917	Edgar DEGAS
1836–1902	James TISSOT
1840–1926	Claude MONET
1841–1919	Pierre Auguste RENOIR
1845–1931	Giovanni BOLDINI
1856–1925	John Singer SARGENT

BOOKS WITH USEFUL ILLUSTRATIONS

There are thousands of books on all aspects of painting, many illustrated with good reproductions showing details of costume. These illustrations are often of better quality than those in books on costume. The books listed give some idea of the types available.

The Penguin Dictionary of Art and Artists by Peter and Linda Murray is a helpful guide to the painters. The comprehensive reference books *Allgemeines Lexikon der Bildenden Künstler* by Thieme-Becker (text in German), *Dictionnaire des Peintres, Sculpteurs, Dessinateurs et Graveurs* by E. Bénézit (text in French) and Bryan's *Dictionary of Painters and Engravers* are available in most large reference libraries. *The Dictionary of National Biography* will help when tracing the dates of portraits of well known people to obtain precise dates for costume.

CATALOGUES of exhibitions and permanent collections are often illustrated with reproductions showing good costume detail, for example:

BODLEIAN LIBRARY, Oxford. *Portraits of the 16th and early 17th centuries.* Bodleian picture book series, no. 6. Introduction by J. N. L. Myers. O.U.P., 1952. 23 monochrome plates of dated portraits, 1523–1644.

GOWING, L. *Hogarth.* Tate Gallery, 1971. Catalogue for the exhibition with monochrome and colour plates.

HASWELL MILLER, A. E. and DAWNAY, N. P. *Military drawings and paintings in the Royal collection.* Phaidon, 1967. First volume is a general introduction with 470 plates. Catalogue to follow in 2 volumes.

KERSLAKE, J. *Early Georgian portraits in the National Portrait Gallery,* 1714–60. H.M.S.O., 1973. 800 monochrome and some colour plates.

MILLAR, O. *Pictures in the Royal Collection. Tudor, Stuart and Early Georgian Pictures.* Phaidon, 1963. 226 monochrome and colour plates.

MILLAR, O. *The age of Charles I. Painting in England 1620–1649.* Tate Gallery, 1972. Catalogue for the exhibition with 258 monochrome and a few colour plates.

PIPER, D. *Catalogue of seventeenth century portraits in the collection of the National Portrait Gallery,* Cambridge, 1963. 33 pages of monochrome plates.

STRONG, R. *Tudor and Jacobean portraits.* 2 vols., vol. 1 text, vol. 2 plates.

H.M.S.O., 1970. 400 pages of monochrome and 8 colour plates. This catalogue deals with all the portraits in the National Portrait Gallery down to the end of the reign of James I in 1625, with other extant portraits of the sitters.

STRONG, R. *Hans Eworth, a Tudor artist and his circle*. The Museums and City Art Gallery, Leicester, 1965. An exhibition catalogue with 32 monochrome plates of pictures covering the period 1549–1657, which show English costume.

PAINTERS: Books dealing with the life and work of individual artists may include paintings of people in countries he visited as well as those in his own country. The work of portrait painters is particularly useful. See list of painters on pp 34–6.

ANTAL, F. *Hogarth and his place in European art*. Routledge and Kegan Paul, 1962. 152 monochrome plates of paintings, drawings and engravings.

CARDONA, E. *Boldini nel suo tempo*. Daria Guarnati, Milan, 1951. 42 monochrome plates of portraits dating from *c.*1880 to *c.*1920. Text in Italian.

DAVIES, M. *Rogier Van Der Weyden*. Phaidon, 1972. 186 monochrome and 14 colour plates.

GARLICK, K. *Sir Thomas Lawrence*. Routledge and Kegan Paul, 1954. 119 monochrome plates.

GOLDSCHEIDER, L. *Jan Vermeer*. The paintings, complete edition. Phaidon Press, 1958. 83 monochrome and 34 colour plates.

LAUTS, J. *Carpaccio: paintings and drawings*. Phaidon, 1962. 203 monochrome and 17 colour plates of all surviving works.

LAVALLEYE, J. *Pieter Breughel the Elder and Lucas van Leyden*. Thames and Hudson, 1967. 491 monochrome plates.

LUNDBERG, G. W. *Roslin*. 2 vols. Allhems Förlag, 1962. Over 200 monochrome and colour plates of portraits 1743–93. Text in Swedish with French résumé.

MILLAR, O. *Zoffany and his Tribuna*. Paul Mellon Foundation for British Art. Routledge and Kegan Paul, 1966. 36 monochrome plates.

NICOLSON, B. *Joseph Wright of Derby*. Paul Mellon Foundation for British Art. 2 vols. Routledge and Kegan Paul, 1968. Includes a selection of portraits which are useful for costume detail.

ORMOND, R. *John Singer Sargent*. Phaidon, 1970. 168 monochrome and 32 colour plates.

PACHT, O. *The Master of Mary of Burgundy*. Faber and Faber, 1948. 48 monochrome plates many showing details of costume of *c*.1475–1485.

PIGNATT, T. *Longhi. Prints and drawings complete edition*, translated by Pamela Waley, Phaidon, 1969. 550 monochrome and 24 colour plates.

POULSEN, E. *Jens Juel*. Gyldendal, 1961. 102 monochrome plates mainly of portraits *c*.1765–1800. Text in Danish.

PROWN, J. D. *John Singleton Copley in America 1738–1774*. Harvard University Press, 1966. 334 monochrome plates of portraits.

RAINES, R. *Marcellus Laroon*. Routledge and Kegan Paul, 1967. 146 monochrome plates of paintings and drawings, from the first half of the eighteenth century.

ROBERTS, K. *Breugel*. Phaidon, 1971. 48 colour plates.

RUHMER, E. *Lucas Cranach 1472–1553*. Translated by J. Spencer. Phaidon Press, 1963. 48 colour plates.

SALAS, X. de. *Velasquez*. Phaidon, 1962. 48 colour plates.

SLIVE, S. *Frans Hals*. 2 vols. Phaidon, 1970. Over 500 monochrome and colour plates.

UEBERWASSER, W. *Rogier van der Weyden*. Batsford, 1947. 7 colour plates.

WATERHOUSE, E. *Gainsborough*. Edward Hulton, 1958. 292 pages of monochrome plates.

WEBSTER, M. *Francis Wheatley*. Routledge and Kegan Paul 1970. Plates of drawings, paintings and engravings.

WILDENSTEIN, G. *Ingres*. Phaidon, 1954. 120 full page plates in monochrome and colour. 200 reproductions in catalogue raisonné.

WILDENSTEIN, G. *Chardin*. Cassirer, 1969. Catalogue raisonné. Many colour plates giving good costume detail *c*.1730–1775.

SCHOOLS OF PAINTING: Many books on various schools of painting, the development of painting at specific periods in different countries and the history of painting in a particular country are illustrated with good reproductions which give useful costume detail, for example:

BENESCH, O. *German painting: Dürer to Holbein.* Skira, 1964. 91 colour plates giving good details of textiles and costume.

BERENSON, B. *Italian pictures of the Renaissance: Florentine School.* 2 vols. Phaidon, 1963. 590 monochrome plates in vol. I and 888 in vol. II. 1 colour plate in each.

CAMPBELL, W. P. *101 American primitive water colours and pastels from the collection of Edgar William and Bernice Chrysler Garbisch.* National Gallery of Art, Washington, 1966. Includes many monochrome and colour plates of American naive portraits, c.1770–1845.

DE VRIES, A. B. *Het Noord-Nederlandsch portret in de tweede helft van de 16e eeuw.* Amsterdam, 1934. 63 plates from 16th-century Netherlandish portraits.

EDWARDS, R. *Early conversation pictures from the Middle Ages to about 1730.* Country Life, 1954. 95 monochrome and 1 colour plate showing domestic life in paintings by various artists, in the Netherlands, Germany, Italy, France and England.

FRIEDLANDER, M. J. *From Van Eyck to Breugel.* Edited and annotated by F. Grossman. Phaidon, 1956. 293 monochrome and 9 colour plates.

GIBSON, R. and ROBERTS, K. *British portrait painters.* Phaidon, 1971. 48 colour plates.

MAAS, J. *Victorian Painters.* Barrie and Rockliff, 1969. Many monochrome and colour plates of paintings where the difference between fashionable dress, working clothes and studio properties can be seen clearly.

MAIURI, A. *Roman Painting*, translated Stuart Gilbert. Skira, 1953. 84 colour plates

MARTIN, G. *Flemish painting.* Art of the Western World series. Hamlyn, 1964. 24 colour plates, many showing details of costume from the mid-fifteenth to the mid-seventeenth centuries.

PAVIERE, H. S. *The Devis family of painters.* F. Lewis, 1950. 52 monochrome and a few colour plates mainly of portraits.

PRAZ, M. *Conversation pieces. A survey of the informal group portrait in Europe and America.* Methuen, 1971. 349 monochrome and 31 colour plates.

PUYVELDE, VAN L. *Flemish painting from the Van Eycks to Metsys.* Weidenfeld and Nicolson, 1970. 174 monochrome and 40 colour plates.

REYNOLDS, G. *Painters of the Victorian scene.* Batsford, 1953. Paintings in which artists dealt with the day-to-day scene showing people in ordinary dress.

REYNOLDS, G. *Victorian painting*. Studio Vista, 1966. Historical painting and anecdotal illustration of literature, as well as living people in their contemporary setting.

SITWELL, S. *Conversation pieces. A survey of English domestic portraits and their painters, c.1665–1880*. Batsford, 1936. 130 monochrome and 6 colour plates. A guide to the artists of the period who are useful for costume reference.

SLIVE, S. *Dutch painting: fifteenth through seventeenth centuries*. Thames and Hudson, 1953. 16 colour plates.

STRONG, R. *Portraits of Queen Elizabeth I*. Oxford, 1963. 20 pages monochrome and 3 colour plates.

STRONG, R. *The English Icon: Elizabethan and Jacobean portraiture*. Routledge and Kegan Paul, 1969. Over 360 monochrome and 14 colour plates.

WHINNEY, M. *Early Flemish painting*. Faber and Faber, 1968. 96 monochrome and 4 colour plates.

WILLIAMSON, G. C. *English conversation pictures*. Batsford, 1931. Monochrome plates.

Some books trace the development of a particular theme through the history of painting, for example musical instruments, weapons or dancing. Often they show costumed figures in movement. A few trace the development of dress, for example:

BELVES, P. and MATHEY, F. *Beaux costumes à travers l'histoire de la peinture*. Gautier-Langereau, Paris, 1969. Numerous colour plates of costume in paintings through the ages. Text in French.

2.

SCULPTURE

Sculpture is the most widespread of all the arts and examples survive from earliest times; it can broadly be defined as the art of representing observed or imagined objects in solid materials and in three dimensions by modelling or carving.

From the point of view of the costume historian it is the record of an observed object, the clothed human figure, which is of interest. Sculptures in stone which have endured the ravages of time are often the only sources of information still in existence for early periods from which few or no examples of textiles have been preserved.

Although paintings and other two-dimensional sources can give a great deal of information about costume there are often occasions when it would be useful to see the back and side views as well as the front. The few specimens of costume which have survived prior to the eighteenth century answer many questions but it is extremely helpful to have other three-dimensional evidence and the detail recorded by sculptors and wood and ivory carvers [PLATE 19] can be most useful. Statuary is completely three-dimensional and although in many museums pieces are positioned so that they cannot be viewed from every angle the detail is perfect all round.

In relief sculpture the figures project from the background; high relief figures stand out and in some parts may be detached from the ground. In low relief work [PLATE 20] the image projects very little and in some ancient Egyptian and Assyrian examples the figures are almost engravings rather than reliefs, but still provide much information. Vast slabs of low relief sculptures which decorated walls of Assyrian palaces show the costume of kings, queens, priests, attendants and warriors hunting [PLATE 18] and feasting, in battle scenes and in processions recording a victory. Many examples may be seen in the British Museum.

Sculptures of interest as a source for costume study can be broadly divided into four groups: pieces used for decoration as part of an architectural setting, portrait studies, commemorative works, and pieces associated in some way with religion, either pagan or Christian.

Examples surviving from Ancient Egypt range in size from small carved wooden figures found in tombs to immense commemorative statues of Pharaohs and officials of rank. There are a number of figures with stiff frontal poses from the archaic period

18. This limestone relief of an Assyrian lion hunt from the North Palace of Ashurbanipal at Nineveh shows the king wearing laced boots and a robe of patterned cloth hitched above the waist with a belt. c. 648–30 B.C. (British Museum 124875–82)

of Greek sculpture from 625–480 B.C. During the second half of the sixth century B.C. Greek sculptors treated drapery in a formal way, using straight lines for folds with zig-zag edges which were apparently never disturbed by movement. This is a sculptors' convention and it should be compared with material draped in the same way on a figure to understand the costume properly. By the early fifth century B.C. more naturalistic treatment is seen and this

Above

*19. Portrait of an unknown man
carved in pearwood on a miniature
scale. The hair, beard and shirt are
closely observed. Friedrich Hagenauer,
German, 1534(?). Victoria & Albert
Museum A. 509–1910.*

Right

*20. An Assyrian attendant wearing a
long garment with a tasselled fringe
at the hemline and what appears to be
a long fringe hanging from the top
edge, with a sword passing beneath it.
The curled hair, headband, ear-ring
and bracelets at wrist and upper arm
are clearly defined. Limestone relief
from the Palace of Sargon II at
Khorsabad, c. 710 B.C. (British
Museum 118823)*

develops [PLATE 21] until later it is possible to observe an Ionic chiton slipping off the shoulder and the movement of the figure beneath the draperies, as in the relief of Nike untying her sandal dating from 410–409 B.C., from the Acropolis Museum, Athens. The Romans continued this naturalistic approach to sculpture and there are many portrait busts showing hairstyles and full-length figures wearing togas.

Medieval sculpture was subordinated to religious architecture. The twelfth-century monastic church of La Madeleine at Vezelay in France has a portal which is a good example of the Romanesque style; Christ, the central figure, is wearing the stylised Byzantine draperies, from which ecclesiastical vestments used today have descended, surrounded by smaller figures of saints and apostles and bordered by a frieze of people on an even smaller scale wearing ordinary twelfth-century dress. There are hundreds of figures forming part of the architectural decoration of the Gothic cathedral of Chartres dating from the twelfth and thirteenth centuries. The clothes depicted on the earlier sculptures are still very stylised, with long straight folds. The later ones are more naturalistic and in one of the best examples, a group of shepherds, it is possible to see the

21. High relief sculpture showing the movement of the fabric used for the chiton on the left hanging open at one side below the waist. The obvious strain on the fabric suggests that the chiton on the right is joined at the side and offers a clue to the width of the loom used. Part of the frieze of Herakles and the Greeks fighting the Amazons, from the Temple of Apollo at Bassae. C. 400 B.C. (British Museum)

22. Elizabeth Suckling's skirt has a pinned flounce over a small padded hip roll. Her daughter has a pleated flounce at the top of the skirt. (Tomb of Robert Suckling, d. 1589, and his first wife Elizabeth, erected 1611 in St Andrew's Church, Norwich)

23. A marble portrait bust dated 1578 of Cassandra Sirigatti, by Ridolfo Sirigatti. The veil is held to the bodice with visible pins. The chemise with a frill at the edge of the collar is turned back beneath the bodice of patterned cut velvet; the pile is a different height from the ground weave. (Victoria & Albert Museum A. 13–1961)

creases in the hoods, sleeves and stockings. All over Europe, inside churches, abbeys and cathedrals, there are altar pieces, screens, portrait corbels and tombs dating from the medieval period to the seventeenth century, showing figures wearing contemporary dress. Their greatest usefulness to the costume student ends with the swirling draperies of the Baroque style. Examples of these stone sculptures and wood carvings may also be seen in museums; the Victoria and Albert Museum has a particularly good selection.

Effigies on tombs represent kings, queens, nobles, knights, ladies, ecclesiastics, merchants and children dressed in contemporary clothes. In very rare cases they may be in representations of earlier dress. Full-size recumbent effigies appear in Europe towards the end of the eleventh century and there are many more from the twelfth century onwards. German examples include a bronze grave slab of Rudolph Von Schwaben, at Merseberg Cathedral, dating

5. *Matthew Boulton still wears a hairstyle with a queue, fashionable in his younger days. Wax portrait bust by Peter Rouw, signed and dated 1814. (Victoria & Albert Museum, 1085–1871)*

Right
24. *A superb example of the rippling curls in a long full-bottomed wig fashionable in the late seventeenth century. Marble portrait bust of Charles II by Honoré Pellé, signed and dated 1684. (Victoria & Albert Museum 239–1881)*

from 1080 and the effigy of Wittkind, Duke of Saxony at Bielefeld, also of the late eleventh century. In England there are many examples of mail-clad knights dating from the twelfth and thirteenth centuries which may be seen at Ely, Salisbury and Wells cathedrals and in many others as well. Although the stone is now plain, evidence shows that from the thirteenth century effigies in England were painted. Many Elizabethan and Jacobean tombs have been restored to their original colour in recent years. They show the nobility as well as merchants and citizens kneeling with their wives and children [PLATE 22]; the detail has usually been observed with infinite care and this is an extremely useful source for a period when the little costume which has survived is in a very fragile

state. During the seventeenth and eighteenth centuries there are
many examples of the enthusiasm for the revival of antique styles
and the costume student should not use these representations of
Roman armour, togas and Greek draperies as a primary source of
information for these periods. Care should be taken at all periods
to check the date of the costume depicted. Although the date of
death is given, some tombs were commissioned several years
previously; in other cases the memorial might have been erected
much later, by members of the family.

Funeral effigies, which may be seen on display in Westminster
Abbey, have in some cases been re-dressed at a later date, so care
must be taken to check the evidence carefully. Portrait busts of all
periods [PLATES 23, 24] are very useful for information on wig and
hair styles; some of the wax portraits of the eighteenth century are
very finely detailed [PLATE 25]. Many portrait busts may be seen in
museums and country houses all over Europe as well as in England.
The cast court at the Victoria and Albert Museum has plaster casts
of many of the types of sculpture mentioned on permanent display.

One of the most important points which should be made about
the use of sculpture as a source for costume study in early periods

is that the sculptor's style will often change the character of a costume. A simple garment like a chiton or a cloak can vary widely in appearance when depicted by different craftsmen; the differences will be particularly noticeable when compared with the two-dimensional evidence of the same period given, for example, by a vase painting, a fresco or an illuminated manuscript.

BOOKS WITH USEFUL ILLUSTRATIONS

Books on sculpture of many different countries and periods provide illustrations of three-dimensional sources for costume study. Often in early periods little other evidence survives. In later periods it is useful to be able to compare the contemporary three-dimensional information with that seen in paintings and surviving costume.

GUIDE BOOKS providing information on sources to visit are often illustrated, for example:

BAKER, M. *Discovering Statues 1. Southern England (excluding London)*. Shire Publications, 1968. 12 pages of monochrome plates. Useful guide.

BENNETT, J. D. *Discovering Statues 2. Central and Northern England*. Shire Publications, 1968. 8 pages of monochrome plates. Useful guide.

BAKER, M. *Discovering London. Statues and Monuments*. Shire Publications, 1968. 33 monochrome plates. Useful guide.

The illustrations in the following examples of books on sculpture range from small carvings to very large reliefs. Costume details may be seen in many of them. The majority of the books listed deal with early civilisations and cultures.

BARNETT, R. D. *Assyrian palace reliefs and their influence on the sculptures of Babylonia and Persia*. Batchworth, 1959. 173 monochrome and a few colour plates.

BECATTI, G. *Colonna di Marco Aurelio*. Editoriale Domus, Milano, 1957. 73 monochrome plates showing costume in the time of Marcus Aurelius, A.D. 161–180, from the column in Rome.

FREEDEN, M. Von. *Gothic sculpture: the intimate carvings*. Oldbourne Press, 1962. 32 monochrome plates of thirteenth, fourteenth and fifteenth century carvings.

GAYA NUNO, J. A. *Escultura Ibérica*. Impresso en España por S.A.I.L. Madrid, 1964. Monochrome plates of early Spanish sculpture. Text in Spanish.

GIULIANO, A. *Arco di Constantino*. Institute Editoriale Domus, Milano, 1955. 60 monochrome plates of details of the sculpture on the arch of Constantine in Rome, *c.* A.D. 312–315.

MALRAUX, A. *Le musée imaginaire de la sculpture*. La Galérie de la Pléiade, 1952. Many monochrome plates. Particularly useful for hairstyles and head-dresses of the ancient Egyptians, Greeks and Romans.

MALRAUX, A. *Des bas-reliefs aux grottes sacrées*. La Galérie de la Pléiade, 1954. Many monochrome plates. Useful for Assyrian, Babylonian and ancient Egyptian costumes.

MOLESWORTH, H. D. *Sculpture in England: Medieval*. The British Council, Longman, 1951. 56 monochrome plates.

ROUBIER, J. and DESCHAMPS, P. *Chartres*. Challamel, 1950. 60 monochrome plates.

SALVINI, R. *Medieval sculpture*. Vol. 2 in the series *A History of Western Sculpture* edited by J. Pope-Hennessy. Michael Joseph, 1969. 360 monochrome plates.

STONE, L. *Sculpture in Britain in the Middle Ages*. Penguin Books, 1955. 192 monochrome plates.

WHINNEY, M. *Sculpture in Britain 1530–1830*. Pelican History of Art. Penguin Books, 1964. 192 monochrome plates.

PORTRAIT SCULPTURE: The illustrations give useful details of hairstyles and jewellery, for example:

GOLDSCHEIDER, L. *Roman portraits*. Phaidon Press, Allen and Unwin, 1940. 120 monochrome plates. Good for hairstyles.

HEINTZE, H. Von. *Römische Porträt-Plastik aus sieben Jahrhunderten*. Hans E. Gunter Verlag, Stuttgart, 1961. 48 monochrome plates showing costumes and hairstyles of the Romans. Text in German.

REILLY, D. R. *Portrait waxes*. Batsford, 1953. 59 monochrome plates.

RICHTER, G. M. A. *The Portraits of the Greeks*, 3 vols. Phaidon, 1965. 2,100 monochrome plates from sculpture and coins. Particularly useful for hairstyles.

INDIVIDUAL SCULPTORS: Books on the work of one man will often give details and different views of a piece of sculpture, for example:

ESDAILE, K. A. *The life and works of Louis François Roubiliac.* O.U.P., 1928. 48 monochrome plates, mainly useful for hairstyles.

PANSTWOWY INSTYTUT WYDAWNICZY: *Wit Stwosz: Oltarz Krakowski,* Introduction by Tadeusz Dobrowolski and Jozef Dutkiewicz. 1951. 141 monochrome and 20 colour plates of a painted wood altar piece carved by Wit Stwosz in the late fifteenth century at Cracow.

TOMB SCULPTURE AND FUNERAL EFFIGIES

CROSSLEY, F. H. *English church monuments. A.D. 1150–1550.* Batsford, 1921. Monochrome plates.

ESDAILE, K. A. *English monumental sculpture since the Renaissance.* SPCK. 1927. 33 monochrome plates. Mentions many tombs with useful costume detail.

ESDAILE, K. A. *English church monuments 1510–1840.* Batsford, 1946. 149 monochrome and 1 colour plate. Useful guide to monuments with figures in costume.

GARDNER, A. *Alabaster tombs of the pre-reformation period in England.* Cambridge University Press, 1940. 305 monochrome plates are usefully listed under ladies' head dresses, heads and collars etc. Small photographs but very useful for details of costume and armour.

GARDNER, A. *English medieval sculpture.* Cambridge University Press. 2nd edition enlarged, 1951. 683 monochrome plates. Invaluable reference and source book for medieval costume, head-dresses, hairstyles, etc.

OBERHAMMER, V. *Die Bronzestatuen am Grabmal Maximilians I.* Tyrolia Verlag, Innsbruck, 1955. 112 monochrome plates of the bronze figures on the tomb of Maximilian I at the Hofkirche, Innsbruck.

PANOFSKY, E. *Tomb sculpture.* Thames and Hudson, 1964. 446 monochrome plates showing tombs from Egyptian to Renaissance.

ST. JOHN HOPE, W. H. 'On the funeral effigies of the Kings and Queens of England', in *Archaeologia*, Vol. LX, 1907 pp. 517–70.

TANNER, L. E. and NEVINSON, J. L. 'On some later funeral effigies', in *Archaeologia* Vol. LXXV, 1936, pp 169–202. 21 monochrome plates showing details of wigs and costumes worn by the effigies.

3

GRAPHIC ARTS:
DRAWINGS, ENGRAVINGS, ETC.

The graphic arts of drawing and engraving provide much source material for the costume student. A pen, chalk or pencil sketch [PLATE 31] will give an impression of movement that is often lacking in a painting, while a careful drawing in a medium like silverpoint can convey a great deal of information. An artist may carry out drawings simply out of interest in the way the fabric hangs in a particular dress; the observant eye of Pintoricchio recorded the charm of a pageant dress as well as a dead man's body wearing a shirt and hose with points. Drawings may be preparatory sketches for paintings, in which case it is useful to compare them with the finished work. Water-colour drawings with very delicate and fine treatment [PLATE 32] give detailed information; painstaking amateur efforts [PLATE 30] often provide more than those of the professional, as any Victorian album will show.

Some of the books prepared for large stores and Couture Houses like *Lucile* are still in existence, containing charming little water-colour drawings of each model [PLATE 35], occasionally with samples of fabric attached to the page. Drawings of a similar type were prepared for fashion plates by artists like Jules David, Anaïs Toudouze and Héloïse Leloir. The engravings from them were reproduced in many fashion magazines during the nineteenth century. Drawings to record the latest fashions often have greater clarity of line than a photograph and many may be found in newspapers and fashion magazines, of which *Vogue* and *Harper's Bazaar* are the best known, throughout the twentieth century. There are many artists whose work is worthy of study, Erté, Gruau, Francis Marshall, John Ward and Bouché among them.

Woodcuts [PLATE 28], produced by cutting away the background of a block to leave lines standing up to print black shapes on a

28. A German woodcut of an old woman spinning, with spectacles tied to her head-dress. The bold lines show sleeve seams and the small frills at the chemise necklines of the girl and the old woman. c. 1550. (Victoria & Albert Museum, 11705)

29. This fine woodcut of Karl Meig (d. 1572) shows the shoulder seam and cartridge pleats at the front of a gown. It is probably from Contrafacturbuch, (Strasbourg, 1587) with 300 portraits by Tobias Stimmer. (Victoria & Albert Museum 29130–1)

white background, were used for book illustrations after the mid-fifteenth century; the early results are rather crude, but the basic shape of the costume is outlined and folds of fabric are shown, with occasional details of pleats and lacing. The subject matter is often of considerable interest to the costume historian; many of the illustrations show occupational dress of people in various trades. Later woodcuts of the sixteenth century like those of Burgkmair are incredibly fine [PLATE 29]. Woodcuts originated in Germany in the early fifteenth century and were very popular there and in the Netherlands from c.1460 onwards and from c.1470 in Italy. The source of any woodcut detached from a book should be checked to find out which country's costume is depicted.

Line engraving, which seems to have evolved in goldsmiths' workshops in the Rhine basin between c.1410 and 1430, gradually gained in popularity as a means of reproducing pictures cheaply and easily. Dürer produced very fine work in this medium.

31. *A lively chalk drawing gives
an impression of movement to a
dress. Sarah Siddons by
J. Downman, signed and dated
1787. (National Portrait Gallery)*

32. *A delicate wash
drawing of court
dress dated July 1796.
(London Museum)*

30. *A pencil and watercolour drawing of nineteen English girls, 'Fraulein, the German governess', 'Miss Andrew, the English governess' and 'Aunt Mary'. The names are inscribed beneath with the note 'This picture is not nearly finished. The faces are not meant to be like the girls only the height and dress are correct. November 1864.' (Sanders of Oxford)*

33. *A detail of a wedding scene from a fan leaf, painted in body colour. c. 1660–70. (British Museum, Schreiber Collection, Book 4, p. 57, no. 362)*

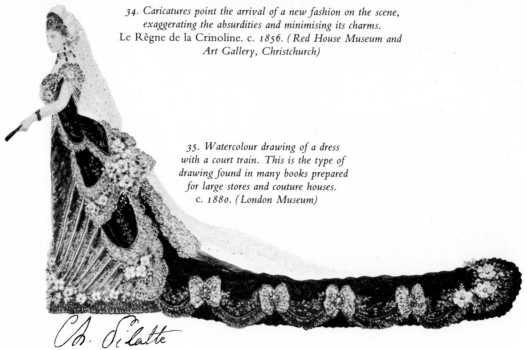

34. *Caricatures point the arrival of a new fashion on the scene, exaggerating the absurdities and minimising its charms.*
Le Règne de la Crinoline. c. 1856. *(Red House Museum and Art Gallery, Christchurch)*

35. *Watercolour drawing of a dress with a court train. This is the type of drawing found in many books prepared for large stores and couture houses. c. 1880. (London Museum)*

Etching is the process of biting lines or areas on a copper plate with acid. The difference from a line engraving can be seen in the lines, which diminish fairly abruptly; in an engraving they increase and grow finer gradually. Wenceslaus Hollar produced some superb studies of dress in this medium in the early seventeenth century.

Prints of architecture, fêtes, and gardens became very popular from the second half of the seventeenth century. Many little figures may be seen in the foreground of these engravings and very often the costume can be dated accurately from the evidence of important events depicted in them. In many cases the print is dated and the name of the engraver and publisher is usually given beneath.

Engravings continued to be used as a method of cheap reproduction of works of art into the twentieth century. Where possible they should be compared with the original painting, as the en-

36. A fashion plate showing seaside promenade dresses in their appropriate setting. English-woman's Domestic Magazine, c. *1879. (Author's collection)*

graving has already moved one stage away from the first statement made by the artist and may have been slightly altered in the process. There is a difference between an original engraving, the independent work of art created by the engraver, and a reproductive engraving which is a copy of a painting, drawing or sculpture by another artist. Fashion plates [PLATE 36] have already been mentioned; the charming hand-coloured engravings which started at the end of the eighteenth century continued throughout the nineteenth century until they were superseded by photographs. Many bound volumes of magazines containing these plates still exist but many more have been broken up and the plates sold separately. Collections of them are to be found in many libraries and museums but they are often undated and the information about the fabric used has been destroyed. The name of the journal is usually printed beneath the picture and it is sometimes possible to track down a bound volume to trace the exact date. It is important to remember that although the engravings are of real dresses and the name of the dressmaker is often given, the artist has exaggerated the line just as the fashion artist or fashion photographer does today, to present the fashionable ideal which all women could modify and adapt to suit themselves.

Caricatures [PLATE 34], both drawings and engravings, provide an immense field for costume study; the eighteenth century is particularly rich in satirical comment and many caricatures are directly concerned with dress. Many of the thousands of political satires are also extremely useful for costume detail. From 1840 onwards, *Punch* provides an easily available unbroken series of humorous comment. Information taken from caricatures should be compared with other contemporary sources as it is always exaggerated. Nevertheless it will point the arrival of a new fashion on the scene very effectively; other sources will prove whether it lasted.

The field of book illustration [PLATE 37] has already been mentioned. Perhaps the main warning here is to avoid using twentieth-century reprints of eighteenth and nineteenth-century novels with modern illustrations. However carefully the illustrator has carried out his research the pictures cannot be considered as primary sources for costume study.

A SELECTION OF ENGRAVERS, ILLUSTRATORS AND CARICATURISTS WHOSE WORK IS USEFUL FOR COSTUME STUDY

Most art galleries and museums will have a few examples of the work of many of these artists and there are large collections in the Departments of Prints and Drawings at the British Museum, the Victoria and Albert Museum, the Metropolitan Museum, New York, and the Bibliothèque Nationale, Paris. (See also list of painters, page 34, for drawings).

1471–1528	Albrecht DURER	c.1636–1718	Nicolas BONNART
1473–1531	Hans BURGKMAIR	1642–1711	Henri BONNART
c.1485–1527/8	Urs GRAF	1645–1708	Romeyne de
c.1500–1559	Christopher WEIDITZ		HOOGHE
1539–1591	Jost AMMAN	1652 died	
1540–1587?	Abraham de BRUYN	after 1729	Robert BONNART
1592–1635	Jacques CALLOT	1654–1726	Jean-Baptiste
1602–1676	Abraham BOSSE		BONNART
1607–1677	Wenceslaus HOLLAR	1656–1708	Antoine TROUVAIN

1673–1733	Bernard PICART	1736–1807	Augustin de SAINT-AUBIN
1678–1726	Jean Baptiste Henri BONNART	1741–1814	Jean Michel MOREAU called MOREAU LE JEUNE
working at the end of the seventeenth century	Nicholas ARNOULT	1746–1816	Claude Louis DESRAIS
working at the end of the seventeenth century	Jean Dieu de SAINT-JEAN	c.1756–1810/11	Isaac CRUIKSHANK
		1756–1827	Thomas ROWLANDSON
		1757–1815	James GILLRAY
1688–1754	Charles Nicholas COCHIN	1761–1837	Nicholas HEIDELOFF
		1792–1878	George CRUIKSHANK
c.1689–1762	Nicholas BONNART	1808–1879	GAVARNI
1697–1764	William HOGARTH	1804–1866	Honoré DAUMIER
1699–1773	Hubert GRAVELOT	1817–1864	John LEECH
1726–1801	Daniel CHODOWIECKI	1834–1896	George DU MAURIER
		1867–1944	Charles Dana GIBSON

BOOKS WITH USEFUL ILLUSTRATIONS

There are many books on drawing, engraving, fashion plates and caricatures. Those listed provide a selection of the type of book available. Although the books of drawings may not be concerned primarily with portrait studies, they often include many illustrations which show costume.

CATALOGUES of temporary exhibitions and permanent collections are often well illustrated, for example:

ADHEMAR, J. *Les Clouet et la Cour des Rois de France*. Bibliothèque Nationale, Paris, 1970. 39 monochrome plates. Catalogue of an exhibition of drawings.

FOGG ART MUSEUM, HARVARD UNIVERSITY. *Ingres centennial exhibition catalogue, 1867–1967*. 1967. 116 monochrome plates of drawings, watercolours and oil sketches from American collections.

SANDERS OF OXFORD. *Costume in print and drawing. Fashion and caricature*. 1972. 20 monochrome plates. A useful catalogue of an exhibition of fashion plates and caricatures, compiled by Christopher Lennox-Boyd.

ILLUSTRATORS: Some books and periodicals with useful illustrations are available in their original editions in specialised libraries.
There are also many books on individual illustrators and their work. In
some cases they may be biographies, in others selections of the artist's
work, these three for example on George du Maurier.

DU MAURIER, G. *Society pictures drawn by George du Maurier selected from
    'Punch'*. Bradbury, Agnew, 1891. 256 pages of drawings.

ORMOND, L. *George du Maurier*. Routledge and Kegan Paul, 1969. 18
    monochrome plates with 142 drawings in the text.

WHITELEY, D. P. *George du Maurier*. London: Art and Technics, 1948.
    Over 50 plates of du Maurier's drawings.

Illustrators often convey a sense of period style and give the characteristic
poses rather than elaborate details of costume, for example:

DOWNEY, F. *Portrait of an era – as drawn by C. D. Gibson*. Charles Scribner's
    Sons, 1936. Numerous reproductions of Gibson's drawings. Par-
    ticularly useful for fashionable society women of the 1890s and
    1900s.

DRAWINGS by painters, particularly studies for portraits, are often
very useful for showing costume with more movement than is usually
seen in paintings.

MÜNZ, L. *Breugel. The drawings*. Phaidon, 1961. 205 monochrome plates,
    many showing details of costume worn by peasants and burghers.

OPPÉ, A. P. (Ed.) *The drawings of William Hogarth*. Phaidon, 1948. 91
    monochrome plates.

OPPÉ, A. P. *The drawings of Paul and Thomas Sandby at Windsor Castle*.
    Phaidon, 1948. Over 150 monochrome and colour plates.

PARKER, K. T. *The drawings of Hans Holbein at Windsor Castle*. Phaidon,
    1945. 84 monochrome plates of portrait drawings useful for hairstyles,
    head-dresses and hats.

VAYER, L. (Ed.) *Master Drawings from the Budapest Museum of Fine Arts*.
    Thames and Hudson, 1957. Includes drawings by Leonardo, Raphael,
    Dürer, Rembrandt and Breughel.

WILLIAMSON, G. C. *John Downman, R.A. Connoisseur* extra number. 1907.
    Monochrome plates of portrait drawings.

CARICATURES illustrate many books on social history (pp 219–20) as well as the type of books listed here.

BEERBOHM, M. *Max's nineties drawings, 1892–9*. Introduction by Osbert Lancaster. Rupert Hart-Davis, 1958.

GEORGE, M. D. *Hogarth to Cruikshank: social change in graphic satire*. Allen Lane, The Penguin Press, 1967. 201 monochrome and 16 colour plates.

HILL, D. *Fashionable contrasts. Caricatures by James Gillray*. Phaidon, 1966. 101 monochrome plates of caricatures of fashion.

KRUMBHAAR, E. B. *Isaac Cruikshank*. University of Pennsylvania Press, 1966. 130 monochrome plates. A catalogue raisonné with a sketch of his life and work.

PASTON, G. *Social caricature in the eighteenth century*. Methuen, 1905. Plates of contemporary drawings and paintings showing English life.

WARK, R. *Isaac Cruikshank's drawings for drolls*. Huntington Library, San Marino, California, 1968. 114 plates of satirical drawings showing costume.

WENDEL, F. *Die Mode in der Karikatur*. Paul Aretz Verlag, Dresden, 1928. 364 monochrome and 16 colour plates of contemporary drawings and paintings covering from the fifteenth century to 1928. Text in German.

ENGRAVINGS, ETCHINGS AND WOODCUTS illustrate books on the techniques used to carry them out as well as books on the artists' work. There are also reprints of early books, many in paperback editions.

AMMAN, J. *Eygentliche Beschreibung aller Stände auss Erden*. Verlag Müller and Kiepenheuer, Hanan/Main, 1966. Facsimile of work published in 1568 with 114 plates of engravings of craftsmen of all trades.

AMMAN, J. *Gynaeceum; or the theatre of women, wherein may be seen the female costumes of all the principal nations, tribes and peoples of Europe, of whatsoever rank, order, estate, condition, profession or age*. Edited by Alfred Aspland. The Holbein Society, 1872. Facsimile of work published in 1586 with 122 plates of engravings.

BURGKMAIR, H. *The triumph of Maximilian I*. Translation of descriptive text, introduction and notes by Stanley Appelbaum. Dover Publications Inc., New York, 1964. 137 woodcuts by Hans Burgkmair and others. This edition is based on the longer edition published by Holzhausen in 1883–4. The first edition appeared in 1526. An important source for costume, armour, heraldry etc. of the period 1512–19.

BURKE, J. and CALDWELL, C. *Hogarth, the complete engravings*. Thames and Hudson, 1968. 267 monochrome plates. Covers the first half of the eighteenth century.

DIEDERICHS, E. *Deutsches Leben der Vergangenheit in Bildern: ein Atlas mit 1760 Nachbildungen alter Kupfer – und Holzschnitte aus dem 15ten–18ten Jahrhundert.* 2 vols. Jena, 1908. Vol. I. Fifteenth century–seventeenth century. Vol. II. Seventeenth century–eighteenth century. 1760 plates of prints and engravings. A useful source book for all kinds of German costume from the fifteenth to the eighteenth century.

HIRTH, G. *Les grands illustrateurs, trois siècles de vie social, 1500–1800.* French edition. 6 vols. G. Hirth, Leipzig, Munich, 1881–90. Numerous plates of famous engravings.

KNAPPE, K. A. *Dürer: the complete engravings, etchings and woodcuts.* Thames and Hudson, 1965. Monochrome plates.

VRIES, L. de and LAVER, J. *Victorian advertisements.* John Murray, 1968. A selection of engravings many showing costume and accessories.

WEIGEL, H. *Habitus Praecipuorum populorum . . . Tractenbuch.* A facsimile reprint of the original book of 1577. Walter Uhl. Unterschneidheim, 1969. 220 woodcuts of dresses of the peoples of the world.

FASHION PLATES are illustrated in many books on costume as well as those listed below, which are specifically on the subject.

CORNU, P. (Ed.) *Galerie des modes et costumes Francais. 1778–87.* Facsimile reproduction of the original edition. 13 vols. Librairie Centrale des Beaux Arts, 1910. Thirteen volumes of colour plates with explanatory text.

HOLLAND, V. *Hand-coloured fashion plates, 1770–1899.* Batsford, 1955. 129 monochrome and 5 colour plates of fashion plates. Contains lists of French, English and German periodicals.

MOORE, D. L. *Fashion through fashion plates 1770–1970.* Ward, Lock, 1971. 53 pages of monochrome and 64 of colour plates.

NEVINSON, J. L. *Origins and early history of the fashion plate.* United States National Museum Bulletin 250. Contributions from the Museum of History and Technology paper 60, pages 65–92. Smithsonian Institution Press, Washington, 1967. 34 monochrome plates.

SPENCER, C. *Erté.* Studio Vista, 1970. 183 monochrome and colour plates of theatrical costume and fashion illustrations for *Harper's Bazaar*.

4

MANUSCRIPT ILLUMINATIONS
AND PORTRAIT MINIATURES

Books containing richly coloured illuminations [PLATE 38] provide
one of the main sources for European costume study from the end
of the tenth century until the sixteenth century, when they were
superseded by printed books. The subject matter of an illumination
may vary from a scene in the life of Christ to a hunt with nobles
dressed in the latest fashions. The manuscript may be a copy of the
Gospels, a Book of Hours or a psalter but the figures in the illuminations, or forming part of the highly decorated capital letters, will
be wearing contemporary dress. The central characters – Christ, the
Virgin and the saints – are usually treated in a more conservative
way and often wear garments with ecclesiastical connotations.

The early illuminated manuscripts are decorated with pure
ornament, but from the beginning of the ninth century the first
pictures of people appear. The drawings have a linear quality
which shows costume detail clearly. The large bibles and service
books which they illustrated were commissioned for cathedrals
and abbeys but from the late twelfth century onwards there was
an increasing demand for personal prayer books from both the
nobility and wealthy churchmen. These psalters were usually
preceded by a calendar which showed people in contemporary
dress carrying out the labours of the months and the Hours of the
Virgin might be added. Books of Hours gradually became more in
demand than psalters and by the end of the fourteenth and beginning of the fifteenth century were produced for many people, not
only for the nobility and clergy. The most famous of all the Books
of Hours is the *Très Riches Heures de Jean Duc de Berry* painted in
c.1415, which has been reproduced many times.

Many versions of the romances with useful illustrations survive,
for example the *Roman de la Rose* and the tales of King Arthur and

the Knights of the Round Table. Many books were also written on hunting and jousting; probably one of the best known is the *Traité de la Forme et Devis d'un Tournoi* by René, Duc d'Anjou.

Some of the little pictures are directly concerned with dress; for example, an illumination dating from the mid-fourteenth century in *Tacuinum Sanitatis* (Bibliothèque Nationale Nouv. Acq. lat. 1673) by the Master of Lancelot, shows a tailor's shop with a lady having her sleeves fitted. Although illuminated manuscripts provide an excellent source of information, one point should be noted; the pictures were intended to decorate the page and the craftsman was restricted in his colour range partly by the pigments

38. Ecclesiastical dress, fashionable men's clothes with wide padded shoulders (mahoîtres) and shoes with side lacing and long pointed toes are depicted in minute detail in this manuscript illumination of John I of Portugal entertaining John of Gaunt. From a late fifteenth-century manuscript of the Chronique d'Angleterre *by Jean de Wavrin. (British Museum Royal MS. 14 E. iv, f. 244b)*

available and partly by his consideration for the finished effect of the page. Anyone using this source for information on medieval costume should also make a study of natural dyestuffs and mordants with the resulting colours on wool, linen and silk.

In the second half of the sixteenth and early seventeenth centuries *alba amicorum* provide a source of charming little illustrations; travellers would collect autographs and pictures painted by their friends, by professionals and by themselves in books, as a memento of a journey through a foreign country. The idea seems to have originated in Germany and most of these little books were kept by

39. Dominique Serres in a deep red cloth or velvet coat, with gold buttons and a palest aquamarine silk waistcoat. Portrait miniature by P. Jean 1788. (National Portrait Gallery)

students. The pictures are very small but show a great amount of detail.

In contrast to the microcosm of the manuscript illuminations the portrait miniature [PLATE 39] gives a wealth of detail about the clothes and hairstyle or wig worn by one person. Some of the most beautiful of these little portraits were executed in the sixteenth and seventeenth centuries, but the fashion for miniatures, contained in lockets or brooches or framed to hang on a wall, continued well into the nineteenth century when it was superseded by the photograph. Portrait miniatures were most popular in the eighteenth century, and many museums contain a few examples. The National Portrait Gallery and the Victoria and Albert Museum, among others, also have sixteenth and seventeenth-century miniatures in their collections.

A SELECTION OF MINIATURE PAINTERS WHOSE WORK IS USEFUL FOR COSTUME STUDY

1497/8–1543	Hans HOLBEIN	active	
1483/4–1561	Simon BENNINCK	1667–1708	Nicholas DIXON
1547–1619	Nicholas HILLIARD	?–1724	Lawrence CROSSE
?–1617	Isaac OLIVER	1682–1740	Bernard LENS
1594?–1647	Peter OLIVER	1742?–1821	Richard COSWAY
1593?–1661/2	Cornelius JOHNSON	1742–1810	Richard CROSSE
1609–1672	Samuel COOPER	1742/3–1811	John SMART
?–1665	John HOSKINS	1750–1829	George ENGLEHEART
1635–1688	Thomas FLATMAN	1769–1810	William WOOD

BOOKS WITH USEFUL ILLUSTRATIONS

Manuscript illuminations and portrait miniatures reproduce very well, as normally they have to be reduced in size very little, if at all. They have usually been protected from light and the colours have not faded.

ANCONA, P. D.' and AESCHLIMANN, E. *The art of illumination*. Phaidon, 1969. 121 monochrome and 24 colour plates of European illuminated manuscripts from the sixth to the sixteenth century.

COULTON, G. G. *The chronicler of European chivalry*. Studio, special winter number, 1930. 75 monochrome and 8 colour plates showing French and English court life in the 15th century.

GRAY, B. *Iran: Persian miniatures – Imperial library*. Introduction by André Godard. New York Graphic Society with UNESCO, 1956. 32 colour plates.

LOGNON, J. and CAZELLES, R. *Les très riches heures du Duc de Berry*. Translated from the French by Victoria Benedict. Thames and Hudson, 1969. 139 facsimile colour plates.

LOOMIS, R. S. with LOOMIS, L. H. *Arthurian legends in mediaeval art*. O.U.P., 1938. 420 monochrome and a few colour plates from English, French, German, Italian and Netherlandish illuminated manuscripts of the 12th–14th centuries.

MARTIN, K. *Minnesinger*. Translated by E. Bestaux. Arts et Métiers Graphiques, 1956. 12 colour plates from an early 14th century illuminated manuscript showing details of costume of all classes.

METROPOLITAN MUSEUM OF ART: *Forty paintings from an early 14th century manuscript of the Apocalypse of St John the Apostle (c.1320)*. Calendar, 1970. 40 colour plates.

MITCHELL, S. *Medieval manuscript painting*. The Contact history of art, Weidenfeld and Nicolson, 1964. 112 monochrome and 64 colour plates.

NICKSON, M. A. E. *Early autograph albums in the British Museum*. British Museum, 1970. 16 monochrome and 4 colour plates. Useful booklet with lists of the autograph albums in the Department of Manuscripts.

PIRANI, E. *Gothic illuminated manuscripts*. Hamlyn, 1970. 69 colour plates, showing details of costume of all classes.

SMITAL, O. and WINKLER, E. (Ed.) *René Duc d'Anjou. Livre du Cuer d'Amours Espris*. 3 vols. Edition de L'Imprimerie de l'Etat Autrichien, 1927. Vol. 2 contains 23 monochrome plates. Vol. 3 has 18 facsimile reproductions of the ms. All the costumes date from c.1460–70

SUMBERG, S. L. *The Nuremberg Shembart Carnival*. Columbia University Press, 1941. 60 plates of a manuscript in the Nuremberg Stadtbibliothek.

TREVE, W. and others (Eds.) *Das Hausbuch der Mendelschen Zwölfbruderstiftung zu Nürnburg*. Bruckmann, München, 1965. 275 pages of monochrome and colour plates showing costume from the housebook of the Mendel Institution at Nuremburg c.1426–1541.

UNTERKIRCHER, F. *European illuminated manuscripts in the Austrian National Library*. Translated by J. M. Brownjohn. Thames and Hudson, 1967. 60 colour plates.

WALDBURG-WOLFEGG, J. G. *Das mittelalterliche Hausbuch. Betrachtungen vor einer Bilderhandschrift*. Prestel Verlag, Munich, 1957. 48 reproductions from a German manuscript c.1480. See also facsimile reproduction edited by H. Bossert and W. F. Storck for larger plates.

WALTHER, R. *Der Hausbuch der familie Melem ein trachtenbuch des Frankfurter Patriziats aus dem 16 Jahrhundert*. Verlag für Wissenschaftliche Literateur-Frankfurt-am-Main, 1968.

WEIDITZ, C. *Das Trachtenbuch des Christoph Weiditz von seinen Reisen nach Spanien (1529) und den Niederlanden (1531–2)*. Introduction and text by Dr Theodor Hampe. Walter de Gruyter, Berlin–Leipzig, 1927. A pictorial record of a journey in Spain in 1529 and the Netherlands in 1531–2, with 154 reproductions of the artist's drawings. Text in German, English and Spanish.

PORTRAIT MINIATURES

AUERBACH, E. *Nicholas Hilliard*. Routledge and Kegan Paul, 1961. 252 monochrome and 7 colour plates.

FOSKETT, D. *British portrait miniatures*. Methuen, 1963. 191 monochrome and 14 colour plates.

FOSKETT, D. *A dictionary of British miniature painters*. 2 vols. Faber, 1972. 1,067 monochrome and colour plates.

REYNOLDS, G. *Nicholas Hilliard and Isaac Oliver*. H.M.S.O., 1971. 205 monochrome and 4 colour plates.

VICTORIA AND ALBERT MUSEUM. *Portrait miniatures*. Small picture book, no. 11. H.M.S.O., 1948. 48 plates of miniatures, c.1540–1825.

WILLIAMSON, G. C. *Richard Cosway R. A. and his wife and pupils, miniaturists of the eighteenth century*. George Bell and Sons, 1897. Monochrome plates.

5.

WALL PAINTINGS, FRESCOES, MOSAICS AND STAINED GLASS

These sources are grouped together as they are all used for architectural decoration and in most cases are to be found in the building where they were first placed.

Both wall paintings and frescoes provide an extremely useful source for costume study, but while all frescoes are wall paintings, all wall paintings are not necessarily frescoes. Frescoes are painted on freshly applied lime plaster walls with colours which dry and set with the plaster, becoming a permanent part of the wall. In a dry climate, protected from the elements, they will last for a very long time. Wall paintings are carried out on the surface of the wall and can be wiped off with water, so they are much less likely to survive.

Wall paintings were used throughout the long history of Egyptian civilisation [PLATE 40]. They decorate the interiors of tombs and are still brilliant in colour because they were protected from sun and rain. There are hunting scenes, banquets and processions, showing all ranks of society from priests to slaves, with many clear details of clothing.

Fragments of true frescoes dating from 1500 B.C. may be seen in Crete and there are some Etruscan ones at Tarquinia. None have survived from Ancient Greece but whole walls of Roman fresco paintings have been preserved at Pompeii and Herculaneum dating from before A.D. 79. There are other later fragments which show Byzantine costume and there is a particularly fine series of biblical scenes, angels and prophets completely covering the nave, side aisles and porch of the Basilica of S. Angelo in Formis, near Capua in Campania (c.1058–87) with interesting costume detail.

European artists worked a great deal in fresco from the thirteenth century to the sixteenth, particularly in Italy, and examples survive in almost perfect condition in many chapels, churches, cathedrals and palaces. Among particularly well-known ones with extremely fine costume detail are the 'Life of Christ and the Virgin' series by Giotto [PLATE 41], in the Arena chapel at Padua (c.1305–6), 'The Procession of the Magi' by Benozzo Gozzoli in the Riccardi-Medici Palace, Florence (c.1460), 'The Legend of the True Cross' by Piero della Francesca in the Church of S. Francesco, Arezzo (c.1452–66), the series depicting scenes from the life of Pope Andreas Piccolomini by Pintoricchio in the Library of Siena Cathedral (c.1495–1510), the frescoes of the Camera degli Sposi by Mantegna in the Castello, Mantua (finished in 1474) and the frescoes by Domenico Ghirlandaio in the Basilica of S. Maria Novella, Florence (c.1490).

40. Although the figures are stylised and seen from one angle, there is a great deal of information to be gained about dress from this wall painting of ladies at a banquet. On the head of each one is a cone-shaped lump of perfumed fat which would gradually melt and run down over the wig. From the Tomb of Nebamun, Thebes, c. 1400 B.C. (British Museum 37986)

In England wall paintings were carried out in many churches from the twelfth to the fifteenth century and the people depicted in biblical stories are all wearing contemporary dress. Unfortunately, the damp English climate is not good for the preservation of wall paintings and during the sixteenth and seventeenth centuries reformers covered them with lime wash. Many more paintings were destroyed in the nineteenth century when the plaster was

stripped from the walls to reveal the stonework. Surviving paintings are not in very good condition and it is often difficult to make out the details in a church where the light is dim and the picture high on the wall. It is advisable to take binoculars or opera glasses to study them.

Mosaics were used as decorative surfaces in both domestic and ecclesiastical architectural settings. Patterns and pictures were made by setting small pieces of stone, mineral, glass or tile into floors, walls and ceilings. Many of these pictures used costumed figures for decoration. In the second and early third century A.D. a great amount of mosaic work was used all over the Roman Empire. Christian wall mosaics in early Byzantine style date from the sixth century A.D. and good examples may be seen in Ravenna [PLATE 43], particularly in the Basilicas of S. Apollinare Nuovo and S. Vitale. Mosaic pictures provide a useful source for costume in periods where there is not very much material. However, it should be noted that most Christian mosaics have been restored at different times and so their present appearance may not be exactly as the original. Mosaic is a fairly coarse medium and the details are therefore outlined somewhat crudely.

Far left
41. Frescoes provide clear costume detail on a large scale. The baby is supported by a sling round the mother's neck in this detail of the Virgin and Child from the frescoes painted by Giotto in 1306 in the Arena Chapel, Padua.

Centre left
42. Although the glass is broken into small areas by the leading, costume detail can be seen in this stained glass window, formerly in the Chapel of the Holy Blood, Bruges. It shows Mary, Duchess of Burgundy (1457–82) daughter of Charles the Bold and Isabel of Bourbon, who married Maximilian in 1477. c. 1485 (Victoria & Albert Museum c. 439–1918)

Right
43. The broken surface of a mosaic gives information for a period when not a great deal of material survives. This detail of the apse mosaic in S. Vitale, Ravenna, shows a purple and white patterned chlamys (semi-circular cloak) with a deeper tablion (the oblong embroidered panel). c. A.D. 520–35

Stained glass windows [PLATE 42] are an important element in church decoration from the beginning of the twelfth century onwards. During the Middle Ages they played an important part in glorifying the Church and its saints and telling the scripture stories; there are many figures depicted in contemporary dress from the twelfth to the fifteenth century. The early glass is simple in design and the costume detail boldly outlined, but by the late fourteenth and early fifteenth century the designers were more interested in trying to obtain portrait realism and the decline set in. The windows of Chartres Cathedral (1200–36) are the best known, but there are many others in Europe, mainly in cathedrals and churches, although some have been moved to museums.

.Binoculars or opera glasses are again a help in seeing details, as the windows are too far away for close study; it is often easier to see them in coloured reproductions. As craftsmen were limited in their colour range, the glass is predominantly blue, red and purple, with yellow as a later addition; information on colour in medieval costume gained from this source should therefore always be compared with a study of the colours produced by natural dyestuffs and mordants on wool, linen and silk.

BOOKS WITH USEFUL ILLUSTRATIONS

This selection indicates the kind of books available. Illustrations of
the sources listed in this section will also be found in books in the
categories on pages 13–15.

FRESCOES AND WALL PAINTINGS

BRION, M. *Pompeii and Herculaneum.* Elek Books, 1960. 132 monochrome
and 50 colour plates.

CECCHI, E. *Giotto.* Oldbourne Press, 1960. 37 monochrome, 60 colour
plates. Details of the frescoes at Padua, Assisi and Florence showing
costume of the late thirteenth and early fourteenth century.

DESROCHES-NOBLECOURT, C. *Egyptian wall paintings from tombs and temples.*
Fontana UNESCO Art Book, 1964. Colour plates.

LONGHI, R. *Piero della Francesca.* Batsford, 1949. 14 colour plates.

ROUSE, E. C. *Discovering wall paintings.* Shire Publications, 1968. 16 pages
of monochrome plates. A pocket guide to medieval and post-Refor-
mation wall paintings in England, with county lists.

STUBBLEBINE, J. H. *Giotto: The Arena Chapel frescoes.* Thames and Hudson,
1969. 129 monochrome plates.

UEBERWASSER, W. *Giotto, Frescoes.* Batsford, 1951. 17 colour plates.

STAINED GLASS

AUBERT, M. and COULTON, G. G. *Stained glass of the twelfth and thirteenth
centuries from French cathedrals.* Batsford, 1951. 19 colour plates.

STETTLER, M. *Swiss stained glass of the fourteenth century from the church of
Koenigsfelden.* Batsford, 1949. 16 colour plates.

MOSAICS

L'ORANGE, H. P. and NORDHAGEN, P. J. *Mosaics from antiquity to the early
middle ages.* Methuen, 1966. 98 monochrome plates.

VOLBACH, W. F. and HUCH, R. *Early Christian mosaics from the fourth to
the seventh centuries.* Batsford, 1947. 14 colour plates.

6

MONUMENTAL BRASSES

Monumental brasses provide an extremely useful source for costume detail. English churches are particularly well endowed in spite of the destruction at the time of the dissolution of the monasteries and again during the Civil War and the Commonwealth. A large collection of over 2,200 brass rubbings is kept in the Department of Prints and Drawings at the Victoria and Albert Museum. It is unnecessary for anyone studying costume to take rubbings and because of the present state of many brasses, from which much of the detail has already been obliterated, it is undesirable. Careful drawings can be made either from the brasses or from existing rubbings, many of which have been reproduced, or a photograph can be taken for study purposes.

Many fine brasses may be seen in Germany and the Low Countries. In England the majority are in Kent, Essex, Norfolk, Suffolk and the Home Counties; there are fewer in the North and West of the country. Brasses show details of academic, ecclesiastical, military and legal costume as well as fashionable dress. The earliest brass still surviving in England is that of Sir John D'Aubernon, dating from 1277, at Stoke D'Abernon, although brasses are known to have been made early in the thirteenth century. The fourteenth century is the best period for engraving and the details of costume are clearer. By the middle of the fifteenth century the fashion for commemorative brasses had spread from knights and their ladies and ecclesiastics to wealthy merchants and their wives and by the end of the century to all ranks. As more brasses were made so the standard of engraving began to decline and the introduction of shading to give a three-dimensional effect in the sixteenth century can be misleading, as it sometimes looks like fur.

Little is known about the way in which the craftsmen worked,

or how much guidance was given for preparing the engraving. The will of Thomas Denny, 'son and heir of Edmund Denny, late one of the Barons of the Exchequer', 10 May 1527, gives instructions for making a memorial brass: 'a picture of me to be made kneeling and holding up my hands, ingraven and gilted with my armes another side', but does not describe the clothes. The engravers obviously had considerable problems when trying to represent fur, cut velvet or any other textured material, but the rubbings provide good linear details showing folds in the fabric, seams, belts, buttons, hairstyles and head-dresses on black figures [PLATE 44].

Costume on brasses should always be compared with costume from contemporary sources of the same period as the inscription. They may be considerably out of date for several reasons. The first is that the brass may be a 'palimpsest by appropriation', a technical term meaning that a fresh inscription has been added to an old design. The costume may be up to a hundred years out of date. In a few examples a 'converted' brass has the design of the costume altered to suit the fashions of a later date. In others, where the costume is only a few years out of date, it may simply be a provincial time lag. The enthusiast should be wary of immediately accepting the date on the brass as the correct date for the fashion.

BOOKS WITH USEFUL ILLUSTRATIONS

ASHMOLEAN MUSEUM. *Notes on brass rubbings, with a list of some of the brasses in the Oxford region and a summary of the remaining figure brasses in the British Isles.* Revised by H. W. Catling, 1969.

BOUTELL, C. *The monumental brasses of England.* 1849. 71 plates of wood engravings from brass rubbings, giving costume details.

CLAYTON, M. *Catalogue of rubbings of brasses and incised slabs, classified and arranged in chronological order.* Victoria and Albert Museum, 1929. Reprinted 1970. 72 monochrome plates.

HAINES, H. *A manual of monumental brasses.* First published 1861. Introduction, biographical note and bibliography by Richard J. Busby. Adams and Dart, 1970. 200 plates of wood engravings of brass rubbings.

MANN, SIR J. *Monumental brasses.* Penguin books, 1957. 32 monochrome plates, redrawn from brass rubbings.

MONUMENTAL BRASS SOCIETY (formerly Cambridge University Association of Brass Collectors, founded 1887). *Portfolios of loose plates of reproductions of brass rubbings.*

MONUMENTAL BRASS SOCIETY. *Transactions.* Society publications, 1894–1914, 1935 to date. For previous volumes see Cambridge University Association of Brass Collectors, Transactions.

STEPHENSON, M. *A list of monumental brasses in the British Isles.* Republished by the Monumental Brass Society. Headley Bros, 1964.

7

SILHOUETTES, DAGUER-ROTYPES, PHOTOGRAPHS AND FILMS

Silhouettes, the little shadow portraits which were very popular between c.1770 and c.1860 [PLATE 45] are the forerunners of the photograph. They were known as 'shades' or 'profiles in miniature' and were either cut in paper or painted on plaster, glass or card. The word 'silhouette' was given to this form of portraiture in the nineteenth century from the name of Etienne Silhouette, whose hobby was cutting profiles from black paper, although the art had been perfected long before. Silhouettes provided the equivalent of snapshots; quick and accurate likenesses could be produced easily and cheaply. As a source of information about costume they have the advantage of forcing the observer to study the outline of the costumed figure; they give a very clear impression of the fashionable stance and of the proportions of hairstyles in relation to dress. The detail in a dress can be distracting and can obscure the general line; the eye is caught by the fabric design, the trimmings, the shape of a sleeve and the lace at the neckline, and finds difficulty in eliminating this mass of information to see the shape of the costume. There is a large collection of silhouettes at the Victoria and Albert Museum and a small group at the National Portrait Gallery, and there are many other examples displayed in museums all over the country.

Early attempts at photography were made by Joseph Niepce, Jacques Daguerre and William Talbot. Talbot's calotype process was used by David Octavius Hill when commissioned to paint a group of the Church of Scotland ministers who in 1843 resigned their benefices and formed the Free Church of Scotland. There were over four hundred figures to be painted and Hill turned to photography as a quick and easy method of recording the faces, rather than making drawings. Working with Robert Adamson, an Edinburgh photographer, he made hundreds of portraits of people in all walks of life, which are still spontaneous in spite of long exposures of one minute in bright sunlight. This long exposure accounts for the slight blurring of detail in early photographs. Both calotypes and daguerrotypes provide a wealth of detailed and accurate information on costume; tightly fitting bodices, creased beneath the arms with the strain on the silk, small waists produced by the optical illusion of converging darts and full pleated skirts, as well as boned corsets beneath.

By the late 1840s photography was a thriving business in

45. A group of silhouettes cut from black paper by August Edouart. From left to right, 'Miss Jane Anderson of County Perth 6th July, Miss Esther Ainslie 12 Dublin St. 26th January, Miss Helen Anderson 5 Manor Place, Mrs Arkley, 4 Saxe Coburgh Place and Charles Atheron Esq.' c. 1830 (National Portrait Gallery)

America. Frederick Scott Archer's faster wet collodion process introduced in 1851 enabled *carte de visite* portraits to be taken in a few seconds, and it is after this date that photographers proliferated in England. Thousands of *cartes de visite* [PLATE 46] survive, many of them still in albums, with names and dates beside them. Stereographic photographs consist of paired images, giving a three-dimensional effect when viewed properly, making a room of crinolined ladies seem even more crushed than in an ordinary photograph. Patent viewers and stereographic photographs are preserved in many museums.

As techniques and equipment improved, so did the photographs. Colour techniques were invented at the turn of the century. The Lumière Autochrome process introduced in 1907 was the first one to be commercially successful; the Autochrome portrait by Alfred

46. A Carte de visite *taken as a souvenir for a friend in a realistic setting. These photographs show the reality of middle-class costume in contrast to the fashion plate. c. 1885. (Author's collection)*

47. Photographs of fashionable clothes in exaggerated poses can be misleading. Those for couture house guard-books or, as here, for design patents, are more truthful, although still usually attractively posed. Black wool jacket with paillettes by Schiaparelli, February 1938. (Victoria & Albert Museum)

Stieglitz (*Encyclopaedia Britannica*, Plate 1, facing page 974, Vol. 17, 1970) shows a lady wearing a Fortuny pleated dress with a knitted jacket over it, as an example of this early colour photography.

Many different photographic subjects are of use to the costume historian and particularly to the theatre and film designer; in the records of the Crimean and American Civil War battlefields photography is first used for reporting. There are pictures of family groups and portraits taken as keepsakes, and topographical photographs which include figures, often in occupational and working dress. At the end of the nineteenth century fashion photographs first appeared showing actresses wearing exquisite toilettes [PLATES 48, 49] on and off stage.

Although most photographs, particularly those which are straight reporting, do not lie, beware of the carefully posed studio photograph with properties. H. R. Robinson used dressed-up

models to play 'country girls'; unsightly creases in fashion photographs were frequently painted out and skirts were pinned back to give a good line when the pose was set. Some of the truest photographs of fashionable dress [PLATE 47] are those taken for the guard books of couture dress houses, as these were used simply as records and not to sell the dresses. Some of those from the House of Vionnet are at the Centre de Documentation du Costume, Paris.

Newsreels provide the most accurate evidence of costume we have because they record a whole range of people at a given time and show how clothes looked on moving subjects. The costumes for many feature films were and are usually specially designed and should be regarded with as much caution as a fashion photograph. However, when a star acts the part of a fashionable woman, a leading designer may be employed. Bonnie Cashin, for instance, designed Gene Tierney's wardrobe in the 1944 Preminger thriller

48, 49. Many photographs of actresses dressed in the latest fashions were reproduced for their admirers in the early twentieth century. Miss Kate Cutler (c. 1900–3) (left) is swathed in furs, while Miss Mabel Love (c. 1902–5) (right) stands poised with a parasol and swirling skirts. (Author's collection)

Laura: The costumes in historical romances should never be used as accurate evidence.

The National Film Archive has underlined the problem of making this material available to the public. Before 1951 films were made on nitrate-based stock; old films gradually decompose and eventually become a fire risk. Many of the 18,000 films in the archive are being copied on to safety stock but more money is urgently needed. A catalogue has recently been issued detailing the three thousand viewable copies of films available to the public.

Most local museums have small collections of photographs of various types and there are often exhibitions of specialist themes, for example *David Octavius Hill and Robert Adamson* mounted by the Scottish Arts Council in 1970 and *From Today Painting is Dead*, an exhibition on the beginnings of photography at the Victoria and Albert Museum in 1972. The student should start with this material and the books listed below before approaching the larger photographic collections. The National Photographic Record, a directory of British photographic collections, will be published in 1975. It will expand the research on the project already done by the Royal Photographic Society.

BOOKS WITH USEFUL ILLUSTRATIONS

A few of the books listed were printed early in the present century and are only obtainable in specialised libraries. They have been included to give an indication of the type of publication which can provide much useful material. In addition to the other books, of which the majority are recent works and easily available, many biographies and autobiographies are illustrated with photographs, as well as books on social history.

PHOTOGRAPHS

GERNSHEIM, H. and GERNSHEIM, A. *Roger Fenton, photographer of the Crimean war.* Secker and Warburg, 1954. 85 monochrome plates.

GERNSHEIM, H. and GERNSHEIM, A. *Historic events 1839–1939.* Longmans, 1960. Numerous monochrome plates.

HUBMANN, F. *The Habsburg Empire: the World of the Austro-Hungarian Monarchy in original photographs 1840–1916.* Routledge and Kegan Paul, 1972. Photographs of people at work, on holiday and at state ceremonials.

LARTIGUE, J. H. *Diary of a century*. Weidenfeld and Nicolson, 1970. Photographs showing people in all strata of society, mainly in France. Early action shots of fashionable dress before World War I.

MACKENZIE, D. (Ed.) *The Debutante and Court Illustrated. Season 1925.* John Horn, 1925. Annual photographic record of the Season's presentations at their Majesties' Court. First issue.

MEREDITH, R. *Mr. Lincoln's camera man, Matthew B. Brady.* Charles Scribner's Sons, New York, 1946. Many photographs from the time of the American Civil War to 1893. Particularly useful for all types of men's clothes.

MINTO, C. S. *Victorian and Edwardian Scotland from old photographs.* Batsford, 1970. 205 monochrome plates many showing occupational and working dress.

SCHWARZ, H. *David Octavius Hill, master of photography.* George Harrap, 1932. 80 monochrome plates.

STONE, B. *Sir Benjamin Stone's pictures. Records of national life and history.* 2 vols. Cassell and Co., c.1903. Sir Benjamin Stone's photographs of parliamentary scenes and portraits, festivals, ceremonies and customs. Shows occupational costume.

WINTER, G. *A country camera 1844–1914.* David and Charles, 1971. 159 monochrome plates.

WINTER, G. *Past positive. London's social history recorded in photographs.* Chatto and Windus, 1971. 155 monochrome plates, c.1860–1910. Particularly useful for occupational and working dress.

SILHOUETTES

HICKMAN, P. *Two centuries of silhouettes. Celebrities in profile.* A. and C. Black, 1971. 88 pages of plates.

JACKSON, F. N. *Ancestors in silhouette.* John Lane, 1921. Over 200 monochrome plates.

WOODIWISS, J. *British silhouettes.* Country Life, 1965. 67 monochrome and 1 colour plate.

8.

CERAMICS, GLASS, COINS, MEDALS
AND OTHER OBJECTS WHICH USE
COSTUMED FIGURES FOR DECORATION

Many of the objects in this section are fairly small and the student may have to search more for material than with any other source. Quite often the discoveries are accidental.

The field of ceramics offers more information than is at first apparent. The word 'ceramics' covers pottery in its widest sense, all objects made from clay and hardened by fire. Many ceramic statuettes were made for religious purposes and buried with the dead. Tanagra figures in unglazed earthenware are examples of this custom. During the eighteenth century small porcelain figures, many in contemporary dress as well as costumes of the Commedia dell'Arte, were made for table decorations; before this period they had been modelled by confectioners who worked in sugar. Glazed tiles were often decorated with people wearing every-day clothing or uniform as are the guards of King Darius depicted in the Palace at Susa, in Iran, which date from the fifth century B.C. Sixteenth-century German tiles and eighteenth-century Dutch and English tiles [PLATE 53] with useful details are to be found in many museum collections.

Perhaps the most useful of all the items for costume study in the field of ceramics are the Attic black figure and red figure pots, from which we derive much of our knowledge of Greek costume. During the archaic period from c.600–480 B.C. Athens slowly became the centre of pottery manufacture. Potters discovered how to mix red ochre with clay to produce a warm orange tan colour and then decorated the pots by painting a shiny black pigment over the top. The details of features and drapery were given by incised lines and occasionally the use of white and purple. It was a difficult medium to handle; Exekias was one of the finest craftsmen to perfect the technique and he managed to achieve very finely engraved draperies. The work of some of the other potters is extremely stiff and stylised; although decorative and a useful source of inspiration for stage designers the information should be used with care by the costume historian. The figures appear to be clothed in narrow strips of cloth without folds in many cases, probably because it was too difficult to superimpose lines on top of a patterned background [PLATES 50, 51]. They should be compared with pieces of sculpture and knowledge of contemporary weaving techniques and loom widths. This will make it clear that although some of the chitons may have been narrower than others none of

50. On this vase the decoration on the chitons is given by excising lines on a shiny black pigment, a difficult technique to perfect. This artist obviously had difficulty in presenting both decoration and fold lines at the same time. A black figured Athenian Hydria from Vulci. c. 530–20 B.C. (British Museum Vase B 333)

them are tightly fitting, darted and seamed dresses as they appear to be. From c.530 B.C. the red figure technique was adopted by the best artists who were quickly followed by less skilled craftsmen. With this method the background was painted black, leaving the terracotta surface for painting pictures with far more detail. It allowed greater freedom of expression and a more naturalistic treatment of the human figure with the flowing lines of draped material [PLATE 52].

51, 52. The incised lines indicating folds are freely drawn on the black figured Athenian Hydria of c. 542–10 B.C. from Vulci (right) giving a more accurate impression of the draperies than in Plate 50, but the artist has put less decoration on the chitons. A different technique used on the Attic red figured vase of c. 490–80 B.C. (below) allows a freer style and the decoration on the himation does not interfere with the lines of the folds (Vases B336 and E140 British Museum).

Costumed figures, some in masque costume, were frequently used for decoration on Italian majolica or tin enamel ware [PLATE 55], the distinctive pottery of the Renaissance period; it was flamboyant, brilliantly coloured in characteristically bright greens, yellows and blues. Tableware was often decorated with engravings

during the 1770s and 1780s. Cups, saucers and dishes survive with little scenes incorporating figures in contemporary dress [PLATE 54]. Porcelain portrait medallions of the same period are also useful.

Pottery figures have already been mentioned. English Staffordshire pottery figures of the 1740s, porcelain figures modelled by J. J. Kaendler of Meissen during the same period and Nymphenburg figures of the mid-eighteenth century are of particular interest. They give a three-dimensional view of mid-eighteenth century hooped skirts, sack dresses and the jutting angle of the corseted body. It is interesting that many of the ladies are wearing 'undress', informal styles which include riding habits and jackets, seen less frequently in paintings. They are most useful for showing how surviving specimens were worn. For example one piece of Meissen modelled by J. J. Kaendler in c.1741 (V. & A. c. 115 – 1932) shows a lady informally posed wearing a jacket very similar to one at Snowshill Manor. A plain white porcelain Nymphenburg group of 1759 (V. & A. c. 21 – 1946) gives a clear picture of the line of the corset beneath the tightly buttoned riding habit jacket with its turned down collar. Both lady and gentleman are in riding dress. Some of the figures have been modelled from engravings; two

54. Some designs are very intricate and provide greater detail. A dish decorated with a copperplate engraving by Hancock, Worcester, c. 1765. (Victoria & Albert Museum Sch. I/649)

Below opposite

53. A lively drawing of a pet-en-l'air seen from the back, giving a feeling of movement. English tile, Bristol, c. 1760. (Victoria & Albert Museum Sch. II/18)

Above right

55. *A finely detailed portrait showing an embroidered shirt, with a frill at the neckline, which is undone at the front. Tin glazed earthenware dish, painted by Nicolo Peligario, Castel Durante. c. 1530. (Victoria & Albert Museum 8930–1863)*

Above left

56. *Occasionally dishes are dated, as in this tin glazed earthenware dish of 1639, Italian, Monte Lupo. (Victoria & Albert Museum 6668–1860)*

57. *A slashed cap and a fur collar on the gown is seen in this carved pearwood draughtsman decorated with a coloured gesso portrait head. German, circle of Friedrich Hagenauer c. 1530–40 (Victoria & Albert Museum Salting Bequest A. 521–1910)*

58, 59. A gallant and his lady taking snuff are both dressed in riding habits and give a three-dimensional view of the costume. Porcelain figures modelled by J. J. Kändler, Meissen, c. 1740. (Cecil Higgins Museum, Bedford c. 857)

very well-known examples dating from *c.*1750 are Kitty Clive (Derby) in the character of 'The Fine Lady' in *Lethe* based on an engraving by Charles Mosley, and Henry Woodward (Bow) in the character of 'The Fine Gentleman' in the same play, from an engraving by James McArdell. These figures may be seen with the engravings in the Cecil Higgins Museum, Bedford and in the Victoria and Albert Museum.

It is interesting to compare Staffordshire portrait figures of the nineteenth century with the contemporary engravings from which many of them were derived. The details are a little clumsy on most of them and there are many other more useful sources for the period. However some were inspired by a fashion, for example the Bloomer costume of 1851 and others show theatrical costume of which few examples survive.

Glass objects are not so often found with decorations for use as a source of information. There are examples of Italian enamelled glass of the late sixteenth century, German enamelled glass of the late seventeenth century, many of the pieces dated, glass engraved in Holland in the mid-seventeenth century, also dated in some cases, and in the 1760s.

Coins, medals and seals [PLATES 60, 61, 62], although the designs are on an extremely small scale, provide useful profiles and front views with hairstyles, head-dresses, hats and neckwear in minute detail. They are particularly useful for periods when little else survives and the profiles are invaluable for periods when our knowledge of costume is mainly derived from portraits painted from the full front view. Some of the early Greek coins dating from *c.*460 B.C. onwards show heads with details of beards and hairstyles. During the fourth and fifth centuries B.C., coin artists began to attempt showing the head in a frontal pose as they experimented with designs in depth. A useful development in Greek coins was the replacement of the head of a god or goddess with a portrait from life.

Domestic objects incorporating costumed figures as part of a decorative surface include pastry cutters, butter pats, warming pans and knife handles among many other items. Quite often the details are clear although the object may be small; a good example is a carved ivory knife handle of *c.*1660 in the Victoria and Albert Museum [PLATE 64]. Playing cards and chessmen frequently use figures in contemporary dress, but the costume should be compared

60. *Although on a very small scale, this cylinder seal shows costume detail. Old Babylonian cylinder seal c. 1900–1600 B.C. (British Museum 89432)*

62. *Medals can be a useful source of information for head dresses and hairstyles, as they often provide side views. A silver gilt medal of Mary I, by Jacopo da Trezzo, 1555. (British Museum CM 14)*

61. *Back views of hats, hairstyles and cloaks may be seen quite clearly on the reverse side of 'The Great Seal of England, 1651'. The scene shows the House of Commons in session, with the Speaker in the chair, a Member addressing the House and two Clerks at the table. (British Museum Seal XXXIV 17)*

Above

63. Seventeenth- and eighteenth-century fans frequently used figures in fashionable dress for decoration. Detail from a fan of c. 1785. (Royal Scottish Museum, Edinburgh 1945–4539)

Right

64. This tiny carved ivory knife-handle gives three-dimensional information about dress and hair style. The silver ferrule is engraved 'Anne D'Oyley', c. 1660. (Victoria & Albert Museum 522–1893)

Far right

65. A room companion, the wooden shape carved in outline and then painted, c. 1610–20. (St John's House, Warwick)

with other sources as sometimes there are fanciful additions or earlier styles have been used. Seventeenth - and eighteenth-century room companions [PLATE 65] are an unexpected life-size source of information and a reminder that the techniques involved in the production of the decoration may place the object under one of the other primary source headings, in this case painting. In some cases a costume accessory may be decorated with figures in fashionable dress: seventeenth- and eighteenth-century fans provide many good examples [PLATE 63].

BOOKS WITH USEFUL ILLUSTRATIONS

This selection indicates the kind of books available. Illustrations of the sources listed in this section will also be found in books in the

CERAMICS

ARIAS, P. E., HIRMER, M. and SHEFTON, B. *A History of Greek Vase Painting*. Thames and Hudson, 1962. 240 pages of monochrome and 211 pages of colour plates.

CHARLESTON, R. J. (Ed.) *World Ceramics*. Hamlyn, 1968. 1019 monochrome and colour plates.

FRIIS JOHANSEN, J. *The Iliad in early Greek art*. Munksgaard, 1967. Monochrome plates of vase paintings.

GORDON PUGH, P. D. *Staffordshire portrait figures and allied subjects of the Victorian era*. Barrie and Jenkins, 1970. 900 monochrome and 37 colour plates.

HAGGAR, R. G. *The concise encyclopedia of continental pottery and porcelain*. André Deutsch, 1960. 160 pages of monochrome and 24 colour plates.

HALL, J. *Staffordshire portrait figures*. Letts, 1972. 61 colour plates.

LANE, A. *English porcelain figures of the eighteenth century*. Faber, 1961. 96 monochrome and 4 colour plates.

PAULS-EISENBEISS, E. *German porcelain of the 18th century*, translated by Diana Imber. 2 vols. Barrie and Jenkins, 1972. 176 monochrome and 91 colour plates in vol. 1 and 84 monochrome and 39 colour plates in vol. 2.

RICHTER, G. M. A. *Red figured Athenian vases in the Metropolitan Museum, New York.* 2 vols. O.U.P. 1936. One vol. of monochrome plates of vases, one vol. of descriptive text.

COINS AND MEDALS

BRITISH MUSEUM. *Guide to the exhibition of historical medals in the British Museum.* 1924. 120 monochrome plates.

JENKINS, K. *Coins of Greek Sicily.* The British Museum, 1966. 16 monochrome and one colour plate of coins, many with details of hairstyles, *c.*550–400 B.C.

WEISS, R. *Pisanello's medallion of the Emperor John VIII Palaeologus.* The British Museum, 1966. 16 monochrome and 1 colour plate.

GLASS

WEISS, G. *The book of glass,* translated by Janet Seligman. Barrie and Jenkins, 1971. Over 500 plates, many in colour.

WILKINSON, R. *The hallmarks of antique glass.* Richard Madley, 1968. Monochrome plates. A few examples of costume used for glass decoration.

9

DOLLS

Almost all the museums with costume collections mentioned in this book have a selection of dolls and dolls' clothes; some of them are very large indeed, and many of the items are of very high quality.

The first and most obvious type of doll for costume study would be the fashion doll, elaborately coiffured and dressed to carry the news of the changing styles. There are records of them in contemporary accounts but, surprisingly, very few authenticated ones have survived [PLATES 68, 69]. However, it is possible that the exquisitely detailed dolls seen in many portraits of children from the late sixteenth to the end of the eighteenth century, which are usually of a slightly earlier date than the painting, may be fashion dolls. A good example is shown in the portrait of a little girl with the inscription *Arabella Cometissa Lennox Aetae Sue 23 menses A DNI 1577* at Hardwick Hall [PLATE 66]. The doll is like a miniature adult and may well have been a doll used to exchange fashion news and afterwards given to the child as a toy. Spangles are stitched to the hem of the doll's gown matching those on the child's wrist ruffles, but the rest of it is perfectly in proportion and dates from *c.*1567–75. The few surviving specimens which would appear to be fashion dolls all date from the eighteenth century, and there do not seem to be any from earlier periods. One doll surviving from *c.*1590 still dressed in its original clothes is preserved in the Livrustkammaren, Stockholm, but this seems more likely to have been a child's toy.

Hand-painted paper dolls like cut-out fashion plates with wardrobes of clothes are preserved in many museums. They date from the early 1800s to the end of the nineteenth century and represent both men, women and children [PLATE 67]. Twentieth-century paper dolls are more usually of children.

66. *The doll in this portrait of Arabella Stuart, 1577, may have been made to convey fashion news and then handed down as a toy. (Hardwick Hall, National Trust)*

Below

67. *'The Protean Figure and Metamorphic Costumes', a cut-out paper doll 8½" high with 12 complete outfits, including a mourning suit, Turkish costume and a monk's habit. A walking-dress is shown here with a dark blue coat, yellow striped waistcoat, pale grey breeches and a top hat. English, 1811. (Victoria & Albert Museum E. 2645–1953)*

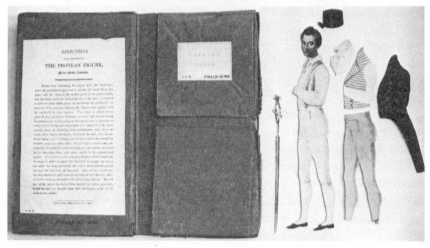

68, 69. A rare
example of a court
dress and train,
c. 1770–5, made to
fit a fashion doll,
perfect in every
detail. It is now
mounted on a padded
stand as the original
doll has not been
preserved. The dress
is very similar in
style to a court dress
which dates from
1766 in the
Livrustkammaren,
Stockholm, made for
the Danish Princess
Sophia Magdalena.
(Museum of
Costume, Bath)

Left

70. *A wax doll wearing an afternoon dress in ivory net trimmed with lace and a lace hat with a wired brim decorated with pink velvet flowers, made by Kate Reily Ltd, Dover St, London. The hat is labelled inside the crown.* C. 1905–7. *(Victoria & Albert Museum* T. 23–1943*)*

Below

71. *Few examples survive of the princess line dresses of 1867. This doll, which is a child's toy, shows the style perfectly in miniature. (Gallery of English Costume, Manchester 1940. 569)*

No. 120.

Length of Doll,.................... 14 inches.
Material, 22 inches wide, for the Costume, 1 yard.
Material, 22 inches wide, for the Blouse,... ¾ yard.
Ribbon, for a Sash,........................ 1 yard.
Embroidery Silk, 3 skeins; Buttons,...... 3.

PRICE, 10d.

LADY DOLLS' COSTUME AND BLOUSE.
(ISSUED DECEMBER, 1888.)

☞ The costume in this Set is differently pictured at Figure No. 306 A in the DELINEATOR for December, 1888. ☜

These patterns consist of twelve pieces: Seven Pieces for the Costume: Front, Surplice Front, Back, Surplice Back, Sleeve, Skirt, and Belt; and Five Pieces for the Blouse: Front, Back, Sleeve, Collar, and Wristband. Fold the goods *lengthwise* through the middle, placing the selvedges together. Lay all the patterns on the goods, placing the edge of the skirt and blouse back *having a double perforation,* and either end of the collar and belt, on the fold, and the *front edge* of the blouse front and surplice front, the *back edge* of the surplice back, and the *front edge of the extended portion* of the remaining front, on the *selvedges,* and the wristband, and the *line of perforations near the center of each remaining portion, lengthwise.* Pin them all smoothly, mark all the notches and perforations, cut the parts out, and take off the patterns. Take up the dart in each front, placing *corresponding perforations together.* Turn under each front, surplice front, blouse front and surplice back at the notches, for hems. Shirr each surplice front and surplice back along the outlet line of perforations at the shoulder edge from the fold to the notch, along the lower edge between the fold of the hem and the notch, at the cross-line of perforations, and once midway between the lower two shirrings. Join the back edges of the backs below the notches. Arrange the surplice fronts on the fronts, with the corresponding notches, hems and edges even; also arrange the surplice backs on the backs, with the corresponding notches and edges even, and the hems meeting at the center seam; draw the shirrings as closely as necessary, and tack them to position. Gather the blouse front and blouse back along the neck edge between the notches, and at the cross-lines of perforations. Baste the seams of the waist and blouse separately according to the notches and perforations, basting them along the lines of perforations. Try the waist and blouse on; and if they be too large or too small, take in or let out the seams at the perforated edges. Sew the collar to the neck of the blouse. Shirr the costume (larger) sleeve along the upper edge between the double notches, along the lower edge between the single notches, at the cross-line of perforations, and twice between the lower two shirrings, making the shirrings in the group at equal distances apart. Gather the lower edge of the blouse sleeve between the notches, and close the seam of each sleeve according to the notches; then, holding each sleeve toward you, sew the top to its respective arm's-eye, with the single notch at the shoulder seam, and the seam at the front. Join the ends of the wristband, and sew its perforated edge to the lower edge of the blouse sleeve, with the seams together. Turn under the lower edge of the skirt as shown by the notches in the ends of the pattern, for a hem. Finish a placket opening at the center of the back of the skirt. Gather the top of the skirt, and sew on the belt. Close the blouse with button-holes and buttons, and the waist with hooks and loops. Fasten a belt of the blouse material about the waist of the blouse. Bind the lower edges of the waist sleeves with silk. Decorate the lower edges of the blouse and wristband, the upper edge of the collar, and all the edges of the blouse belt, with fancy stitching. Tie a ribbon sash about the waist of the costume. Allowance for ¼-inch seams is made in the patterns.   (II.)

Address : THE BUTTERICK PUBLISHING CO. [Limited],
171 to 175 Regent St., London, W.; or 7, 9 and 11 West Thirteenth St., N. Y.

IMPORTED FROM THE UNITED STATES.

Front View.
LADY DOLLS' BLOUSE.

Front View.
LADY DOLLS' COSTUME.

Back View.
LADY DOLLS' COSTUME.

Back View.
LADY DOLLS' BLOUSE.

Ordinary dolls are depicted as well as fashion dolls in paintings of children. Good examples may be seen in 'A Children's Party' painted by Hogarth in 1730 (see cat. 32, L. Gowing, *Hogarth*, Tate Gallery, 1971) and a family group in pastels of *c.*1735–40 by C. Troost (acc. no. 609 at the Mauritshuis, The Hague). Many of these dolls still survive from the eighteenth century and there are many beautifully dressed ones from the whole of the nineteenth century, the numbers increasing from *c.* 1850, some dressed by couturiers in the latest fashions [PLATE 70].

When particularly good costume detail is noted the doll should be examined closely and dated from the evidence of the body construction, head, wig, type of eyes and arms and legs. Each

72, 73. *The envelope of a Butterick Pattern with pictures and instructions for making a lady doll's costume and blouse. The pattern pieces are cut in white tissue paper. December 1888. (Butterick Pattern Company Archives)*

74. *A page of
designs for dolls'
clothes patterns from
Butterick's* The
Delineator,
*December 1894.
(Source unknown)*

period has its own characteristics and, in the nineteenth and
twentieth centuries, trademarks and patent marks as well. The doll
may be dressed as an adult, as a child, or as a baby. The enthusiast
should be very careful in assessing the evidence. Some of the clothes,
or all of them, may be of a later date than the doll, dressed by a new
owner as commercial patterns with full instructions were available
for dolls' clothes from the 1870s onwards [PLATES 72, 73, 74]; sometimes it may have been completely re-dressed in clothes made from
the correct period fabrics by the owner of an antique shop.

It should also be remembered that these small garments, however accurate in detail they may be, cannot be scaled up accurately
to full size; the fastenings are usually out of proportion as they have
to be large enough to be handled by children. The doll with
unaltered clothes can provide a great deal of information for the
costume enthusiast [PLATE 71] but only after comparison with
other contemporary sources.

BOOKS WITH USEFUL ILLUSTRATIONS

BIRMINGHAM CITY MUSEUM AND ART GALLERY
    Dolls. Series A. Set of annotated photographs 1–6, *c.*1835–1875.
    Dolls. Series B. Set of annotated photographs 7–12, *c.*1855–*c.*1914.

BLUMSTEIN, M. (GINSBURG, M.) *Dolls.* Victoria and Albert Museum small
    picture book. H.M.S.O., 1959, second edition 1968.

BOEHN, M. Von, *Dolls.* Translated by Josephine Nicholl. Dover Publi-
    cations, Inc., New York, 1972. 277 monochrome plates.

CENTRAAL MUSEUM, UTRECHT: *Poppenhuis.* November 1963. Mono-
    chrome plates of dolls and dolls' houses.

COLEMAN, D. S., E. A., and E. J. *The collector's encyclopedia of dolls.* Robert
    Hale, 1970. 1725 monochrome plates. Useful guide to dating dolls.

GRÖBER, K. *Die Puppenstadt der Fürstin Augusta Dorothea von Schwarzburg-
    Arnstadt.* Verlag-Karl Robert Langewiesche Königstein im Taunus.
    30 monochrome and colour plates.

HILLIER, M. *Dolls and Dollmakers.* Weidenfeld and Nicolson, 1968. 264
    monochrome and colour plates.

LEESBERG-TERWINDT, J. H. M. *Poppenhuizen.* Rijksmuseum Amsterdam,
    1955. 33 monochrome plates. With English text.

NYLEN, A. M. 'Dräktdocka fran Karl IX's tid', in *Livrustkammaren,
    Journal of the Royal Armoury.* Vol. XI. I. Stockholm, 1967. 15 mono-
    chrome and one colour plate. Doll from Charles IX period, *c.*1590.

SOER, I. J. 'De Kostums int het 17de eeuwse poppenhuis'. Article in
    Jaarboek oud Utrecht 1971. 26 monochrome plates. Text in Dutch.

STANILAND, K. *Costume in miniature.* Gallery of English Costume picture
    book. Corporation of Manchester, 1970. A picture book of dolls and
    their clothes.

TAPESTRIES, EMBROIDERY, PRINTED AND WOVEN TEXTILES

Costume enthusiasts often think of textiles simply as the materials from which clothes were made, but they can also be a source for costume study. Textiles were frequently decorated with people wearing contemporary dress, either as part of the woven fabric or applied afterwards in the form of needlework or printing.

Tapestries provide the most useful source in the field of textiles. During the fourteenth and fifteenth centuries they were hung over the stone walls of large living rooms in castles and palaces for decoration and warmth. Later, from the sixteenth to the eighteenth century, they were used in country houses as well. Some tapestries remain in the architectural settings for which they were originally intended, while others are now exhibited in museums all over Europe and in America.

The subject matter of these hangings can be a useful source for costume detail. Designs of fourteenth and fifteenth-century tapestries were inspired by religious themes and by the tales of courtly love which may be found in illuminated manuscripts and are recorded in the songs of the period. The character of the king, prince or duke who commissioned the tapestries might be compared with the hero of a romance or with a hero of mythology or the antique world, Hercules, Alexander or Caesar. Stories of the Knights of the Round Table, the Crusades, hunting scenes, allegories on life, the deadly sins, and representations of the virtues and vices were also used. They often included characters attired in what is probably pageant costume during the later fifteenth and early sixteenth century. Many of these themes continued to be popular during the sixteenth century with the addition of others depicting the deeds of ancestors of many Spanish, Swedish, Danish and Portuguese noble houses, During the seventeenth century

allegorical, classical, mythological and pastoral themes continued in popularity but the figures are usually dressed in swirling baroque draperies and are no longer of use as a source for information on contemporary dress. The scenes illustrating contemporary events are more helpful. Tapestries cease to be of use as a source for costume detail during the eighteenth century when the pastoral themes gradually took precedence over all others.

In the early middle ages tapestry warps were coarse and the designs very bold, with few details. From the fifteenth century the texture of the weave grew progressively finer as the designs needed different effects. Seventeenth and eighteenth-century taste demanded an exact copy of the painter's cartoon rather than the weaver's interpretation of it. The most informative tapestries for costume study are those carried out from the early fifteenth to the sixteenth century where the designs are still linear in quality and the weaver has put in all the buttons, seams and patterned fabrics [PLATES 75, 76].

Among the earliest surviving tapestries with costume detail are the set depicting the Nine Heroes, woven in *c.*1385, which are exhibited in the Cloisters Museum, a branch of the Metropolitan

75, 76. Both the diamond pattern in the beige undergown worn by the miller's wife (left), and the pin in her veil have faded. The shadowy line above the edge of the skirt may indicate hemline stitching. Detail from 'Falconry' one of the Franco-Flemish Devonshire hunting Tapestries c. 1425–50. Bodice seams are clearly defined (right) in the Flemish tapestry 'The Triumph of Chastity over Love' c. 1500–10. (T202–1957 and 440–1883, Victoria & Albert Museum)

Museum, New York. Among the many others of interest are 'The
Story of St Piat and St Eleuthere' (1402) at Tournai Cathedral; the
Devonshire Hunting Tapestries from Chatsworth (c.1420–30) at the
Victoria and Albert Museum; 'The Presentation of the Roses'
(1440–50) at the Metropolitan Museum, New York; 'The Caval-
cade of Falconry' (1440–50) and 'The Dance of the Wild Men and
Women' (c.1460–70), both at the Church of Notre Dame de
Nantilly, Saumur; 'The Hunt of the Unicorn' (c.1490–5) at the
Cloisters, New York; the Noble Pastoral series (c.1500) at the
Musée du Louvre, Paris; 'The Story of St Stephen' (c.1500–02),
'The Vintage' (c.1500–10) and the series of Courtly Life (c.1500–10),
all at the Musée de Cluny, Paris, and 'The Story of St Gervais and
St Protais' (c.1505–9) at Le Mans Cathedral.

The dates of costumes seen in tapestries should be carefully
checked as the work may have taken several years to complete, or
an old cartoon used, and they may be out of fashion compared
with the date of purchase which has sometimes been recorded. A
tapestry will show the characteristic dress styles of the country in
which it was designed and woven and, as already mentioned, some
of the characters may be wearing pageant costume. There are close
resemblances between some of the tapestry designs. For example
a nobleman and his halberdier wear clothes almost identical in cut

79. An embroidered valance from Switzerland, dated 1598, of the wise and foolish virgins, all wearing contemporary dress. (Victoria & Albert Museum 211–1898)

in two tapestries depicting the departure for the hunt; one is at the Musée de Cluny, Paris, and the other at the Art Institute, Chicago (see R. Weigert, *French Tapestry*, plates 25 and 26). The colours and design of the fabrics differ but the figures in both tapestries were obviously worked from the same original drawing, the weaver probably providing the variations. It would be interesting to know if the designs of the material for the nobleman's gown were both taken from life, or if one of them is from the weaver's imagination.

When using tapestries as a source for costume study it is important to remember that many of them have undergone a considerable amount of restoration through the centuries. All the evidence should be compared carefully with other sources for the same period. The colours may have faded beyond all recognition and the tapestry may be so dirty that what colour there is cannot be seen clearly. This is unfortunate, as the wool for the weft was dyed with natural dyestuffs and offers evidence of colour for

80. An English embroidered valance of c. 1585–95 depicting fashionable dress; the lady carries a large muff. (Victoria & Albert Museum T. 134–1913)

Right

81. A fragment of green Italian cut velvet with a design of gentlemen wearing doublets and trunk-hose. c. 1600. (Victoria & Albert Museum T. 255–1920)

medieval costume when very few fragments of garments survive. However, close examination of the threads at the back of a tapestry will usually produce some traces of the original colour.

The figures used in designs for both secular and domestic embroidery also provide a source for costume detail. Embroidered fragments incorporating costumed figures have survived from the pre-Inca period in Peru. *Opus Anglicanum*, the English church embroidery of the thirteenth and fourteenth centuries, used many figures of saints and characters from the bible stories and although in some cases the figures are very small, the technique of depicting fine detail with split stitch presents a very clear picture. Altar frontals and copes made abroad as well as in England during this period should also be studied. Examples are preserved in churches and museums all over Europe. Embroidered domestic hangings and pictures frequently use figures in contemporary dress as part of the design. The Bayeux Tapestry, which is in fact not a tapestry but a needlework picture, designed and executed by English needlewomen in *c*.1080, illustrates a theme which was Norman in interpretation, possibly commissioned by Odo, Bishop of Bayeux, William the Conqueror's half-brother.

So much embroidery is seen covering costume in Elizabethan paintings that one tends to forget that there are other pieces of domestic embroidery which may provide useful information. The valances which surrounded the edges of four-poster beds were often of canvas stitch embroidery depicting hunting scenes, processions and bible stories, with figures in contemporary dress [PLATES 79, 80]. Many portions of them have survived, as they were not subjected to the continuous handling and folding of the rest of the bed hangings. Cushion covers and table carpets with similar designs have also been preserved. During the seventeenth century stumpwork embroidery designs [PLATE 77] frequently incorporated figures wearing contemporary dress for small pictures and for decorating caskets and mirrors. These little figures, padded to stand away from the background, often provide helpful costume detail, although the designs were very similar and were used over a number of years.

In designs for woven and printed textiles for both clothing and furnishings, costumed figures are used less than for embroidery. However, there are fragments of silk and cut velvets [PLATE 81] dating from the late sixteenth and early seventeenth centuries in which they may be seen as part of a woven design, although the details are not very clear. They tend to be used more to date the material than as a source of information. The tapestry of Sion, a North Italian linen wall-hanging dating from the late fourteenth century, printed with figures, is in the collection at the Historical Museum, Basle. A few fragments of block printing on linen, which show figures in black, have been preserved from the mid-sixteenth century and are of German origin. It is in the mid-eighteenth century, after Oberkampf started a factory at Jouy in 1759, that figure subjects became popular for printed textile designs and the vogue continued until the end of the century [PLATE 78]. Examples of embroidered, printed and woven textiles which are of use as a source for costume study may be seen in the Victoria and Albert Museum and in museums all over Europe and in America.

BOOKS WITH USEFUL ILLUSTRATIONS

See also books listed on page 232.

DENNY, N. and SANKEY, J. F. *The Bayeux tapestry.* Collins, 1966. 57 pages of colour plates.

GIBBS-SMITH, C. *The Bayeux Tapestry.* Phaidon, 1973. 41 monochrome and 4 colour plates.

RORIMER, J. *The Unicorn tapestries at the Cloisters.* Metropolitan Museum of Art, 1962. 34 monochrome plates.

SVENSMA, W. S. *Tapestries.* Translated by Alexis Brown. Merlin Press, 16 pages of monochrome and 16 pages of colour plates.

STENTON, SIR F. M. *The Bayeux tapestry.* Phaidon, 1957. 150 monochrome and 13 colour plates. Article by J. L. Nevinson on the costume and one by Sir James Mann on the armour.

VIALE, M. *Tapestries.* Hamlyn, 1966. 70 colour plates.

WEIGERT, R. A. *French tapestry.* Translated by Donald and Monique King. Faber and Faber, 1962. 64 monochrome and 4 colour plates.

WINGFIELD-DIGBY, G. assisted by HEFFORD, W. *The Devonshire hunting tapestries.* H.M.S.O., 1972. 4 pull-out plates showing the whole tapestries, 22 monochrome and 20 colour plates and 42 reproductions in the text.

ARCHIVE MATERIAL, LITERARY SOURCES, PERIODICALS AND NEWSPAPERS

Any enthusiast intending to use archives should first read the paragraph at the front of the *Guide to the Contents of the Public Record Office* by M. S. Guiseppi. 'Serious students are always welcome in the Search Rooms and are encouraged to make full use of the facilities for research available. In their own interests, however, students are urged not to embark on the examination of original records before they have exhausted the information relevant to their enquiries which is available in printed sources.' Students are warned that they may have to sift through a great many documents before finding any relevant material. Some, but not all, County Records Offices will have indexed references.

Not only should they follow this advice but they should also take a course in reading and interpreting documentary material written before 1800 at a University Department of Extra-Mural Studies. Although it is perfectly possible for students to acquire a degree of skill by their own study, it is usually quicker to take a course covering court and secretary hand and the abbreviations used. For material earlier than the sixteenth century, it is also necessary to understand Latin, the language used by clerks and scribes.

The records which are relevant to the costume student are the inventories, wills, household accounts, royal wardrobe accounts, customs records, diaries, letters, bills, business account books, indentures and sumptuary laws which give valuable background material for existing costumes and provide much helpful evidence for periods when little else exists. Inventories provide names of garments and quantities of clothing used in households ranging from Court and landed gentry to merchants and small householders. Wills may provide a great deal of information, particularly in the sixteenth and seventeenth centuries, giving detailed descriptions of clothing. Even if the wills do not prove useful for costume study the published list of occupations of the testators may be illuminating. *Wills at Chelmsford 1400–1619* by F. G. Emmison, published by the British Record Society in 1958, lists the following, all associated with textiles and clothing: clothiers, clothmakers, clothworkers, cordwainers, drapers, frieze tawers, fullers, fustian weavers, glovers, haberdashers, hat makers, a jerkin maker, a lace weaver, linen drapers, mercers, patten makers, shoemakers, starch makers, weavers and woollen drapers, with the dates of all the wills. Information in household accounts may range from the briefest of entries in a sprawling hand to detailed descriptions of clothing written out most carefully among all the other items. The Royal Wardrobe Accounts dating from the Middle Ages kept in the Public Record Office provide details of the type of clothing to be supplied, any special orders, the material to be used, the yardage and the cost of labour. Customs records give the quantities of different types of clothing and textiles imported and mark changes in fashion.

Diaries written by people who were extremely interested in their clothes provide a wealth of background information on the choice of a dress or suit; Pepys's diary is one of the best known but there are many others which have been published. As they are subject to editing, the editors' footnotes should be read carefully, as in some cases the references to clothing may be cut. For example, a page and a half of the original is omitted from Boswell's *Journal in Holland* before he comments on 2 November 1763 'But after all these profound reasonings on breeches, I should like to know what is the best material to make them of. I am now wearing a kind of black stuff made I think at Utrecht. It is composed of linen and silk, but it is extremely thin and does not wear well.' For full details one must return to the original manuscript.

Letters are often an even better source of information than diaries. Sometimes little sketches will be included, or little scraps of material pinned to a page [PLATE 82]. For example, Christine Williamson writing to her brother Edmund in 1764 gives details for his wife of how to trim a sack dress and petticoat, with a sketch of the flounce. The letter is preserved in the Bedford County Archives. Jane Austen's letters to her sister Cassandra give a wealth of minute detail about purchases of bonnets, material for new dresses and alterations carried out. In May 1801 a tiny sketch gives the shape of the back bodice of a round gown.

Bills and business accounts give dated evidence of the prices paid for all kinds of clothing. Birmingham City Museum and Art Gallery is fortunate in possessing a suit in rich tan cut velvet ordered by Lord Riverstone in 1763 with the tailor's bill for £27 10s 3d; the Essex Institute, Salem, have two dresses labelled *Jenny, Paris* and with them the headed bills, giving the model names *Hirondelle* and *Sappho* as well as the prices.

Early apprenticeship indentures [PLATE 83] give conditions of work and details of training for apprentices to tailors, seamstresses, weavers and many other trades allied to the clothing industry. Later ones are more stereotyped and less useful. Sumptuary laws governing dress exist from the Middle Ages to the Board of Trade Regulations about utility clothing in the 1939–45 war. They were originally designed to prevent people spending an extravagant amount on dress beyond their means, and as an effort to keep a visible distinction between the different ranks of society. It is difficult to know how far they were ever successful. Judging from contemporary accounts of extravagance in dress the results do not seem to have been very long-lasting. At times they were intended to prevent hardship in certain trades, and during the 1939–45 war to ensure that everyone was adequately clothed. Even if they were not always strictly adhered to, they provide information about materials and the latest fashions.

The County Records Offices house large quantities of local material; the Essex County Records Office is a good example of one which is well catalogued with publications to help the student, and there are many others.

The Royal Commission on Historical Manuscripts does not maintain records but has issued over two hundred printed volumes of reports upon privately owned records and *Record Repositories in Great Britain* (H.M.S.O. 1971), a guide for students who wish to know where record material is available in this country, which gives addresses of County Records Offices and libraries with archive material. The National Register of Archives is housed in the Commission's offices. It records the location, content and availability of all collections of documents in England and Wales regardless of size, other than those of the central government

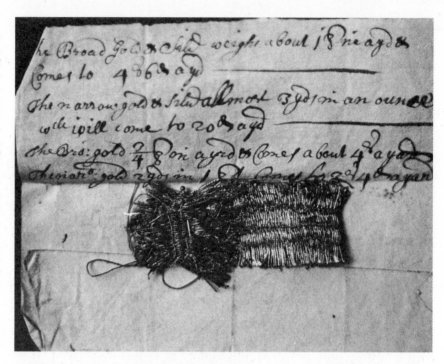

which are in the Public Records Office, where the Royal Wardrobe
Accounts are kept. The information leaflet for readers points out
that they will save themselves a good deal of time and trouble if
they have familiarised themselves with the printed sources for their
subject and have a clear idea of the type of material they can
reasonably expect to find. Many manuscripts may be printed
already with the full text, or as a calendar or perhaps as an index,
and H.M.S.O. publishes guides to these publications.

Another source of documentary evidence particularly useful for
dating garments from the mid-nineteenth century onwards are
the patent specifications housed in the Patent Office Library. The
volumes of *Abridgements of Specifications for Wearing Apparel*
(H.M.S.O.) give a guide to some of the inventions which may be
studied in depth; among many other items they include inflatable
crinolines, apparatus for taking the measurements of coats, plaited
straw and braided wire bustles, waterproof garments, umbrellas,
riding habits, corsets, suspenders, sewing machines and gloves.

The latest vagaries of fashion have always provided an entertaining topic for moralists and satirists. References to clothing also
appear as part of descriptive accounts in novels. The student should

take care not to use references in historical novels, but those setting the scene in contemporary life provide reasonably accurate information, although it should always be compared with other primary sources. Novels of no great literary merit of the late nineteenth and early twentieth century often include much interesting costume detail. An extract from *An Unknown Lover* by Mrs George de Horne Vaizey written in 1912 gives a good example: 'Katrine entered to behold a Romney picture in grey chiffon piroietting before the glass, a ridiculous buckram bandeau pressed turban-like on her head, to which she was endeavouring to anchor a vast hat, encircled by sweeping white feathers. The feathers swept, they did not soar . . . a distinction between beauty and fashion.' And later, 'I've got to balance this tent upon my head and nothing short of clamps will do it. And there's one hairpin, a fiendish anarchist of a hairpin, simply sticking into my scalp. Which would you rather do – keep the car waiting while I take it down and do it again, or have me scratching at my head all afternoon . . . Put your fingers in Katrine! Prod about! Can you feel it? Not that one, no! For the land's sake don't scatter my curls on the floor . . . now for the skewers . . . deadly aren't they? But I have screws for the ends.' These descriptions, allied to the fashion

83. An indenture made on 25 September 1597 between the Lady Catherine Peeter and a London widow, Josint Graunger, for an apprentice, Margarett Davys, to be taught 'all manner of Cutt-woorke Bonelaces Needlewoorke edginge And allso all manner of nettwookes and nettwoorke edginges with Florisshinges and all manner of Black-woorkes And also to woorke with goulde and silke and all manner of playne-woorkes . . . (Essex County Records Office D/DP Z26)

plates and photographs of the period, help us to understand so much more about the hats and their wearers. Many of these novels are to be found in serial form in women's magazines.

Printed diaries, letters, memoirs, autobiographies, poems and plays are a never-ending source of information. It is a good idea to keep a card index and record interesting items for future reference with date, page number, title, author and publisher.

Periodical publications and newspapers provide written evidence as well as visual material. Magazines like *Punch*, which was first published in 1840, record changes of fashion and the social conditions of the people who made and wore them. Fashion journals give descriptions of the fabric used for the dresses in their fashion plates and often the name of the dressmaker as well, from the end of the eighteenth and throughout the nineteenth century. Newspapers provide satirical comment from the eighteenth century as well as fashion reports in the nineteenth century. Since the Second World War fashion reports have been given more and more space, in addition to drawings and photographs, and offer an extremely useful source of information. Bound copies of local newspapers are kept in many reference libraries and there is a store of London newspapers before 1800 in the British Museum Reading Room; those printed after that date are kept at Colindale with the National Collection of Newspapers.

It is important to remember that newspapers and fashion magazines will record the most sensational – and therefore newsworthy – clothes. Hemlines will be up or down overnight; the information must be compared carefully with all the other sources to get a balanced view.

The costume enthusiast will also discover that the change of nomenclature used at different periods to describe similar garments can be misleading. When is a 'coat' a petticoat and when is it a coat? When is a 'frock' a man's informal coat and when is it a dress? These details require careful study.

USEFUL ADDRESSES

National Register of Archives, Quality House, Quality Court, Chancery Lane, London W.C.2.

Patent Office Library, Southampton Buildings, Chancery Lane,
  London W.C.2.
Public Record Office, Chancery Lane, London W.C.2.
Royal Commission on Historical Manuscripts, Quality House,
  Quality Court, Chancery Lane, London W.C.2.

ORIGINAL TEXTS REPRINTED

These are examples of books which provide many quotations from
original manuscripts, early printed books, old newspapers and
journals with useful references to costume, not easily available to
students. In some cases the texts are complete. Scholarly societies
(for example, the Early English Text Society) from the nineteenth
century onwards have printed these texts, in some cases in facsimile.
Women's magazines 1693–1968 by C. L. White (Michael Joseph,
1970) and *Women in print* by A. Adburgham (George Allen and
Unwin, 1972) contain useful lists of periodicals, some of which are
available in provincial reference libraries as well as in London.

ANON. *Sir Gawain and the Green Knight.* Written *c.*1350. Translated with
  an introduction by Brian Stone. Penguin Books, 1959.

CHAUCER, G. *The Canterbury tales.* Written *c.*1387. Translated into modern
  English by Nevill Coghill. Penguin Books, 1951.

CORYATE *Crudities hastily gobbled up in five months travells in France, Savoy,
  Italy etc.* Written before 1607. James MacLehose, 1905.

TOUR-LANDRY, G. DE LA. *The book of the knight of la Tour-Landry, compiled
  for the instruction of his daughters.* Translated from the original French
  (of 1371–2) in the reign of Henry VI and edited from the MS. in the
  B.M. (Harl 1764) and Caxton's print A.D. 1484. Introduction and
  notes by T. Wright. Early English Text Society, 1906.

GODDARD, E. R. *Women's costume in French texts of the eleventh and twelfth
  centuries.* Johns Hopkins Press, 1927. 12 monochrome plates.

PHILLIPS, M. and TOMKINSON, W. S. *English women in life and letters.*
  O.U.P., 1926. Many extracts concerning dress, both wearing and
  their manufacture.

PICCOLOMINI, A. *Raffaella or rather a dialogue of the fair perfectioning of
  Ladies, 1538.* Translated by J. L. Nevinson. The Costume Society:
  Extra Series no. 1, Robert MacLehose, Glasgow, 1968.

SANLIENS, C. de. *The Elizabethan home discovered in two dialogues by Claudius Hollyband and Peter Erondell*. Edited by M. St. Clare Byrne. Methuen, 1949.

SPECTATOR 1711–14, by Addison, Steele and others. The original edition as published daily. Text edited and annotated by G. Gregory Smith. 8 vols. Dent, 1897.

STUBBES, P. *Anatomy of abuses in England in 1583*. Edited by F. J. Furnivall for New Shakespeare Society, 1882.

WEAVER, J. *Epigrams in the oldest cut and newest fashion, 1599*. R. B. McKerrow, 1922.

WILLAN, T. S. *A Tudor book of rates*. Manchester University Press, 1962. The contents of the entire book of 1582, including many items of clothing, are listed.

Some of these books reproduce the original illustrations with the text, for example:

ARMY AND NAVY CO-OPERATIVE SOCIETY. *Yesterday's shopping. The Army and Navy Stores Catalogue 1907*. Introduction by Alison Adburgham. David and Charles, 1969. Over 150 pages of illustrations of clothing for men, women and children, with prices.

CAULFEILD, S. F. A. and SAWARD, B. C. *The dictionary of needlework. An encyclopedia of artistic, plain and fancy needlework*. Hamlyn, 1972. Facsimile of the 1882 edition with over 800 engravings.

THE LADY'S REALM. Introduction by Lady Georgina Coleridge. Arrow Books, 1972. A selection from the monthly issues: November 1904 to April 1905, with the original illustrations.

BIOGRAPHIES, AUTOBIOGRAPHIES, MEMOIRS, LETTERS AND DIARIES

This short list includes biographies, autobiographies and memoirs, which are useful for costume references (in some cases for illustrations as well) and a few of the published collections of letters, diaries and journals which are available in many editions. In some there are a large number of direct references to dress; in others there may be only a few, but there may be details about dressmakers and tailors, new fabrics and trimmings which are also of interest. There are thousands of similar books available but this selection will provide a starting point.

BERESFORD, J. (Ed.) *The diary of a country parson, the Reverend James Woodforde*, 5 vols. The Clarendon Press, 1968. Written between 1758 and 1802.

BUXTON, E. E. (Arranged by E. Creighton) *Family sketchbook*. Geoffrey Bles, 1964. Covers the period *c.*1864–6.

CHAPMAN, R. W. *Jane Austen's letters to her sister Cassandra and others*. Oxford University Press, 1932, second edition 1952. Written between 1796 and 1817.

DELANY, M. (Mrs). *The autobiography and correspondence of Mary Granville, Mrs Delany, with interesting reminiscences of King George III and Queen Charlotte*. Edited by the Right Honourable Lady Lanover. Richard Bentley, 1861.

FIENNES, C. *Through England on a side saddle in the time of William and Mary*. Leadenhall Press, 1888. Written between *c.*1685 and 1703.

GREIG, J. (Ed.) *The diaries of a Duchess*. Hodder and Stoughton, 1926. Extracts from the diaries of the first Duchess of Northumberland (1716–1776).

HAM, E. *Elizabeth Ham, by herself. 1783–1820*. Introduced and edited by Eric Gillett. Faber and Faber, 1945.

HERBERT, A. *The diary of the Lady Anne Clifford*, with an introductory note by V. Sackville-West. William Heinemann, 1923. Written between *c.*1603 and 1619.

HOWE, B. *Arbiter of elegance*. Harvill Press, 1967. 11 monochrome plates. Biography of Mrs Haweiss, the author of *The Art of Dress* published in 1879. Covers the period *c.*1858–98.

JEBB, Caroline, Lady. *With dearest love to all. The life and letters of Lady Jebb*. Edited by M. R. Bobbitt. Faber and Faber, 1960. 27 monochrome plates. Covers the period from the early 1860s to the mid 1920s.

KEPPEL, S. *Edwardian daughter*. Hamish Hamilton, 1958. Arrow paperback edition, 1961. Covers the period *c.*1900–1920.

LENNOX, Lady Sarah. *The life and letters of Lady Sarah Lennox 1745–1826*. Edited by the Countess of Ilchester and Lord Stavordale. 2 vols. John Murray, 1901.

PAPENDIEK, C. L. H., Mrs, *Court and private life in the time of Queen Charlotte: being the journals of Mrs Papendiek, Assistant Keeper of the Wardrobe and Reader to Her Majesty*. Edited by her granddaughter

Mrs V. D. Broughton. 2 vols. Bentley and Son, 1887. Covers the period c.1770–92.

PASTON, *The Paston Letters (1422–1509)*. Edited with an introduction by John Warrington. 2 vols. Everyman's Library, no 752, 753. Dent, London; E. P. Dutton, New York, 1956.

PEPYS, S. *The diary of Samuel Pepys*. A new and complete transcription edited by Robert Latham and William Matthews. Bell, 1970–. The diary covers the years 1660–1669.

PUREFOY, E. and H. *Purefoy Letters 1735–1753. Letters written by Elizabeth and Henry Purefoy*. Edited by G. Eland. 2 vols. Sidgwick and Jackson, 1931.

RAVERAT, G. *Period piece. A Cambridge childhood*. Faber and Faber, 1952. Covers the period c.1890–1905.

SAINT-SIMON, Louis de Rouvroy, duc de. *Historical memoirs of the duc de Saint-Simon* edited and translated by Lucy Norton. Hamish Hamilton. Vol. 1. 1691–1709. 1966. Vol. 2. 1710–1715. 1968. Vol. 3. 1715–1723. 1972.

SHORE, W. T. *D'Orsay, or the Complete Dandy*. John Long, 1911. Useful details of dress in text, covering c.1815–52.

SIBBALD, S. *The memoirs of Susan Sibbald 1783–1812*. Edited by Francis Pagett Hett. John Lane, 1926.

TROUBRIDGE, L. *Life amongst the Troubridges*. Edited by Jacqueline Hope-Nicolson. John Murray, 1966. Covers the period 1873–1884.

WILLIAMS, H. *It was such fun*. Hutchinson, 1935. 34 monochrome plates many showing fancy dress. Memoirs, including a description of the Jubilee Year Devonshire House ball in 1897.

PATTERNS AND TECHNICAL WORKS ON TAILORING AND DRESSMAKING

One of the easiest ways of dating a costume is to study the information on cut and construction which it provides. Although comparison with dated weavers' samples in museum collections can sometimes provide a very close date for the fabric from which it is made, a dress may have been altered several times and it is the shape of the pattern pieces and the dressmaking methods which will enable the enthusiast to arrive at the correct date (see pages 129–46).

Tailoring and dressmaking are highly skilled crafts and the cutting of the garment is the most important part of the work. Incorrectly cut garments will never hang properly and dissatisfied customers soon turn elsewhere. A pattern which was well cut by an experienced person was – and is – a valuable and carefully guarded asset to a business. The master tailor would in some cases give copies of patterns to his apprentices if this was stipulated in the indenture, but only on condition of complete secrecy. This tradition of secrecy has survived to the present day. In a wholesale couture dress house in 1954 I personally recall an elderly tailoress who always drew her suit patterns on to the cloth with chalk, politely refusing to have cardboard patterns made, obviously because she wished to keep them secret. It was also the practice to destroy the pattern when a model dress had been taken out of production, at the end of a season. This explains why so few professional patterns survive. There are, however, many diagrams in technical works on tailoring and dressmaking, as well as commercial paper patterns from the mid-nineteenth century onwards, which were used by home dressmakers. It is important to remember that these commercial patterns do not show the intricate cut of a couture dress until the 1950s. Vogue Couturier patterns of the mid 1930s were certainly more complicated than any other styles but it was not, apparently, until 1948 that contracts were signed with couture houses and Vogue Paris Original patterns were created from original designs, with increasingly detailed dressmaking instructions. The early paper patterns are very basic indeed and would have been fairly easy to make up.

The earliest technical works are the Spanish tailors' books, *Libro de Geometria Practica y Traça* by Juaan de Alcega, and *Geometria y Traça* by La Rocha Burguen, printed in Madrid in 1589 and 1618. These contain diagrams of women's bodices, sleeves and farthingales and men's breeches, doublets, capes and various ecclesiastical garments. The pattern pieces are arranged on various widths of velvet, silk and wool to enable the tailor to cut economically; they are not drawn to scale. *Le Tailleur Sincere* by le Sieur Benist Boullay, printed in Paris in 1671, also gives layout diagrams, the patterns varying in size, with very simple instructions. *The Academy of Armory and Blazon* by Randle Holme, printed in 1688, gives information on 'the instruments used in all Trades and Sciences, together with their terms of Art', providing much useful information on the materials and techniques used for dressmaking and tailoring, but without diagrams.

Descriptions des Arts et Métiers Faites ou Approuvées Par Messieurs de l'Académie Royale des Sciences by François Alexandre Garsault was printed in Paris in 1769. It contains 'Le Tailleur d'Habits d'Hommes', 'Les Culottes de Peau'; 'Le Tailleur de Corps de Femmes et Enfants'; 'L'Art de la Couturière et la Marchande de Modes', and is the first serious work on dressmaking and tailoring which gives detailed accounts of construction methods as well as clear diagrams. Garsault's text is used again in Diderot's *Encyclopédie* of 1771, but some details of construction have been brought up to date. *The Taylor's Complete Guide, or a Comprehensive Analysis of Beauty and Elegance in Dress . . . The Whole Concentrated and Devised by a Society of Adepts in the Profession* of 1796 is the earliest known book on tailoring printed in England. It explains how to draw the coat onto the cloth using measurements and following the diagrams. Instruments are given for measuring and cutting out a lady's riding habit and there is also a section on alterations.

The first folding full-size paper patterns are given in *The Lady's Economical Assistant* of 1808, and are for children's clothes. Users are advised to trace the patterns on to thin paper and then to cut the pieces out accurately to avoid damaging the patterns in the plates, advice which still holds good today. Existing commercial paper patterns are usually in a very fragile condition. They should be placed on a clean sheet of card on a flat surfaced table, smoothed gently to remove creases and covered with a sheet of thin acetate film. Tracing paper can then be put over the acetate and the pattern traced without doing any damage. Direct tracing on to a pattern can score and dent the paper badly.

There were shops in London which sold tailors' patterns from the beginning of the nineteenth century and there were advertisements in journals like *Townsend's Monthly Selection of Parisian Costumes* in the mid 1820s for paper patterns which were sold to professional rather than home dressmakers. One in *The World of Fashion*, October 1836, describes '. . . every new style of dress, exquisitely formed in the exact models and colours in which they are worn, consisting of full length and small size French paper. Millinery and dresses of every description, sleeves, trimmings, etc., etc., – sold at 10s per set (comprising four articles).' In the 1870s paper patterns are advertised as half- or full-size paper models made up accompanying the flat pattern, although the flat pattern could be purchased singly. The *Ladies Treasury* in June 1880 comments, 'In every case where these prices are mentioned it is to be understood that for 1s 1d a plain single pattern is sent; for 2s 1d a pattern is made up but untrimmed and an extra plain pattern is sent by which to cut'.

The early patterns of 1836 may have been the made-up variety rather than flat patterns. None for adults seem to have survived but there are three for children at the Worcester County Museum, dating from the 1870s, made in bright blue tissue paper [PLATE 85]. Tissue paper is fragile and once out of date scraps of paper like this might have been used for lighting fires.

From *c.*1840 home dressmaking rapidly gained in popularity and there are many helpful little books with diagrams of patterns and information on dressmaking processes. Both French and English fashion magazines provided printed paper sheets of full size bodice and sleeve patterns, one of the earliest I have seen being from *Le Petit Courrier des Dames*, September 1844. These early printed patterns showed just one garment, with an illustration, the pieces overlapping each other. By the 1850s there might be two designs and by the 1870s three or more with fashion engravings and crochet patterns on the reverse side. As the century progressed the sheets of paper on which these patterns were printed became larger and much

84. A printed folding paper pattern from The Milliner and Dressmaker, including a walking dress for a young girl, a dress for the seaside and a child's jacket. c. 1878–9 *(The London Museum)*

Below

85. A flat white tissue paper pattern for a boy's Norfolk suit. A demonstration version made up in blue tissue paper with black paper trimmings is included. c. 1870–5 *(Worcestershire County Museum 1965–2145)*

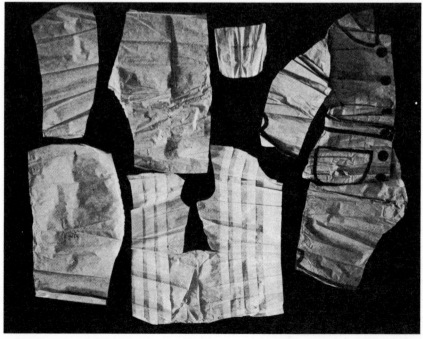

86, 87. *A white tissue paper pattern marked with perforations and notches, for a boy's parole suit 'breast measurement 25 in., usual size for 4 years of age', packed in an envelope printed 'Mme Demorest, Maison de Patrons, Haute Nouveauté, Paris and New York'. A detail of the envelope* (left) *shows the instructions printed in French, Spanish, Italian, German and Dutch as well as English. c. 1890 (Worcestershire County Museum 1968–492)*

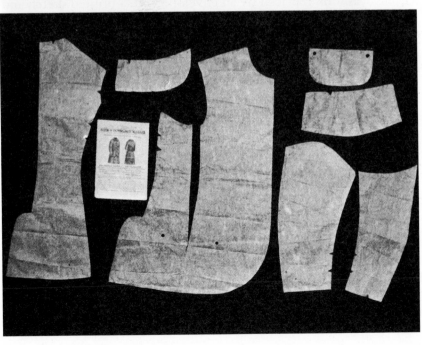

thinner paper was used [PLATE 84]. By the late 1890s ten or more designs would be superimposed on each other (a method still used in German magazines today) and the effect was extremely complicated. Some of the surviving sheets have been used as tissue paper to wrap other objects. When found they should be smoothed out carefully, using a very cool iron, and encased between two thin sheets of acetate film. They can then be rolled up to avoid further creasing when in store, if there is insufficient shelf space to store them flat. Under no circumstances should adhesive tape be used to repair them.

The commercial pattern companies were founded in America, where the sewing machine had been invented. The Butterick paper pattern service was started in 1863 by Ebenezer Butterick of Sterling, Massachusetts, and was followed in 1870 by McCall's Pattern Company. By 1876 Butterick had branches in London, Paris, Berlin and Vienna. Vogue was founded in 1905 and Simplicity followed in 1927.

The early patterns were cut in plain white tissue paper with notches and perforations, and then wrapped in a piece of paper with a picture of the garment and a few instructions for assembling it. This was soon replaced by an envelope with a printed sketch and more instructions, sometimes in five languages [PLATES 86, 87]. The first Butterick instruction sheet for each pattern was introduced in c.1919 and was called the 'Deltor'. It was the prototype for the extremely detailed layout sheets which are provided today, with 'lays' for different sizes and widths of fabrics and illustrations with instructions to show how the garment should be assembled and finished.

The first printed paper pattern was produced by McCall's in 1920. This was far easier to use than the plain tissue paper pattern and eventually Butterick began printing patterns in 1950 in America and in 1961 in Britain. Vogue, now part of the Butterick company, also print their patterns today.

Scientific methods of constructing patterns by the use of body measurements and mathematical calculations were first introduced for men's clothing. An advertisement for *Le Somatometre* of 1839 shows a framework to be fitted over the body to obtain exact measurements for the tailor. From the 1870s onwards scientific systems were devised in increasing numbers for women's pattern making as well. They were based on the natural proportions of the

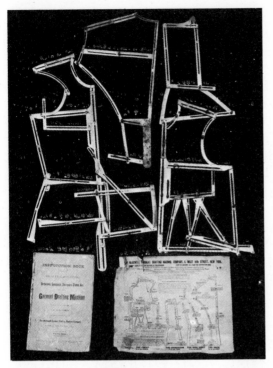

88. Metal frame, diagram and instructions for drafting and cutting patterns, patented in 1891 by the McDowell Garment Drafting Machine Company. (Author's coll.)

Below

89. The 'Ladies Own Charts, the Anglo-Parisian system of Dress Cutting', patented by S. A. Cooke. These cardboard charts were used in the same way as French curves, with an instruction book. c. 1891 (British Museum)

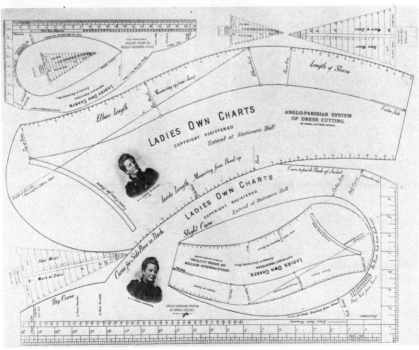

body and mathematical calculations, using a shaped piece of cardboard rather like a set of French curves [PLATE 89] or a complicated metal framework [PLATE 88] with a book of instructions. Several of these systems have been preserved, although not always complete with their instruction booklets. Paper patterns have no market value but they provide very useful information and should be preserved carefully. The Gallery of English Costume, Manchester, has a small collection, there are some at the Victoria and Albert Museum and a few of them can be seen on display at Bethnal Green Museum. Others are preserved in Worcester County Museum, Worthing Museum and other provincial museums.

If put on display, they are best flattened onto a felt surface, held at the corners with small strips of acetate to avoid pinholes and then covered with heavy perspex or glass. They should never be pinned or stapled as the fragile paper will eventually disintegrate.

TECHNICAL WORKS ON PATTERN CUTTING, TAILORING AND DRESSMAKING

These are a few examples of the many books on the subject which may be found in one or more of the following libraries and museums – the British Museum Reading Room, the Centre de Documentation du Costume, Paris, the Costume Institute of the Metropolitan Museum, New York, the Gallery of English Costume, Manchester, the Lipperheide Kostümbibliothek, Berlin, the London Museum and the Victoria and Albert Museum Library. A few are available in some public reference libraries. See also *Technical Works* pages 231–232. Most of the books listed include quotations and diagrams from these sources. There is a list of technical works on dressmaking and pattern cutting published between 1860 and 1940 on page 88, J. Arnold *Patterns of Fashion II*, 1972.

Information on terminology may be found in books of this type. In some cases they also give diagrams of patterns and descriptions of techniques.

BOOK OF TRADES, Part III 1804.

DIDEROT, D. and D'ALEMBERT, J. LE R. *Encyclopédie.* 1751–72.

GARSAULT, F. A. de. *Descriptions des Arts et Métiers faites ou approuvées par Messieurs de l'Académie Royale des Sciences.* 1769.

GENERAL DESCRIPTION OF ALL TRADES digested in alphabetical order 1747.

HOLME, R. *The Academy of Armory and Blazon.* 1688.

MURPHY, W. S. *Modern drapery and allied trades (wholesale and retail)* 4 vols. Gresham Publishing Co. 34 Southampton Street, Strand, London, 1914.

PERKINS, E. E. *A treatise on haberdashery and hosiery.* 1834 and 1853.

Early tailoring books show the shape of patterns, although not to scale, drawn out on varying widths of cloth.

ALCEGA, J. de. *Libro de Geometria y Traça.* 1589. [A xerox copy of this work is available in the Victoria and Albert Museum Library].

LA ROCHA BURGUEN, F. de. *Geometria y Traça.* 1618. [A xerox copy of this work is available in the Victoria and Albert Museum Library].

From the end of the eighteenth century there are many books on tailoring which give diagrams showing pattern construction based on scientific systems of measurement.

COUTS, J. *A practical guide for the tailor's cutting room.* A treatise on measuring and cutting clothing in all styles and for every period of life from childhood to old age. Blackie, c.1845.

LADIES' TAILOR. *The ladies' tailor.* John Williamson, c.1901.

THE TAYLOR'S COMPLETE GUIDE, or a comprehensive analysis of beauty and elegance in dress. The whole concerted and devised by a society of adepts in the profession. 1796.

VINCENT, W. D. F. *The pocket edition of the cutter's practical guide.* John Williamson, c.1905. Later edition, c.1909.

WALKER, G. *The tailor's masterpiece.* 1838.

WYATT, J. *The tailor's friendly instructor.* 1822.

Books on dressmaking and dress pattern cutting increase in number during the nineteenth and twentieth centuries. Guides to dressing economically often give instructions to the home dressmaker with diagrams of patterns.

BRAY, N. *Dress pattern designing.* Crosby Lockwood, 1961.

BRAY, N. *More dress pattern designing.* Crosby Lockwood, 1964.

BRAY, N. *Dress fitting.* Crosby Lockwood, 1970.

CAULFEILD, S. F. A. and SAWARD, B. C. *The dictionary of needlework, An encyclopedia of artistic, plain and fancy needlework.* 1882.

CORY, Mrs. *The art of dressmaking containing plain directions in simple language from the fitting of the pattern to the finish of the dress.* 1849.

ENGELMANN, G. *The American garment cutter for women.* American Fashion Company, 1904.

HANDBOOK. *Handbook of plain and fancy needlework.* 1882.

HOWELL, M. J. *The handbook of dressmaking.* 1845.

HOW TO DRESS. *How to dress neatly and prettily on ten pounds a year by one who has done it for ten years.* E. W. Allen, *c.*1880.

THE LADIES' *hand-book of plain needlework.* 1842.

THE LADIES' *hand-book of millinery, dressmaking and tatting.* 1843.

A LADY. *The Lady's economical assistant or the art of cutting out and making wearing apparel.* 1808.

A LADY. *The workwoman's guide.* 1838.

A LADY (COOK, M. W.) *How to dress on £15 a year as a lady.* 1873.

MYRA, *Dressmaking lessons.* Four parts. Myra, 1888.

WELDON AND CO. *Weldon's home dressmaker for striped materials,* 1888.

WELDON AND CO. *Weldon's easier dressmaking.* 1935.

WHITELEY, T. *The complete dressmaker for the million.* Manchester, 1875.

WOMAN'S INSTITUTE OF DOMESTIC ARTS AND SCIENCES. *First steps in dressmaking.* Scranton Pa. 1928.

WOMAN'S INSTITUTE OF DOMESTIC ARTS AND SCIENCES. *Harmony in dress.* International Educational Publishing Co. Scranton, Pa. 1924.

There are many scientific systems of dress pattern cutting still in existence, for example:

AMERICAN SCIENTIFIC SYSTEM. *American scientific system of dress-cutting.* London, 1883.

BOEHMER, M. *French scientific dressmaking with map of chart specially adapted for self instruction.* Glasgow, 1887.

FURNISS, C. *The 'Burton-on-Trent Excelsior'. An improved system of cutting ladies' and children's clothing by measurment.* 1889.

LADIES' OWN CHART. *Diagram for dress cutting.* 1889.

II. Dating Costume from Construction techniques

Giving an accurate date to a dress or suit or even fragments of a garment may present considerable problems to the beginner. It cannot be done without a reasonably good knowledge of the history of costume acquired by the study of the primary source material (pages 17–128) and by looking at costumes displayed in museums.

There are many factors to be taken into consideration; the fabric, the embroidery, the details of stitching and trimming, the cut and construction methods used and the shape of the dress in wear. The last two provide the safest way of dating a specimen, as it is dangerous to assume that the date of the fabric is also the date when the dress was made. It might well have been when the original dress was first made, but the fabric may have undergone a considerable number of transformations, the final dress being produced as much as two hundred years later. Sometimes the dress has simply been altered; seams may have been restitched, taken in or let out, but the holes made by the needle remain. Often there are numerous lines from several alterations and one has to decide which was the original position of a seam line. The study of the pattern shapes and dressmaking methods of each period will enable the enthusiast to arrive at the correct date. Where should one look for this information? Many patterns and technical works on tailoring and dressmaking are still in existence (see pages 126–8). Patterns may be taken from existing costumes which have not been altered and are in good condition. This should only be done by people who have had considerable pattern-cutting, dressmaking and tailoring experience; the amount of time and work involved are wasted unless full technical notes are made and this is impossible for the novice. A knowledge of weaving techniques and of the structure of fibres will also help to provide complete information about the specimen. It is essential to have dry hands and to handle the material most carefully, as damage can be done by heavily perspiring hands and rough or insensitive treatment. It is important to remember that it may take twenty hours to take a pattern and make detailed notes about a complicated, fragile specimen.

There are two methods of taking patterns. One is to lay white cotton mull (a loosely-woven lightweight material) over the garment, matching the grain lines with the original fabric and to pin the cotton into shape at each dart and seam, gently smoothing the surface until it has taken the same shape as the material beneath. The cotton is then lifted away, marked with a pencil on all darts and seams and then unpinned, providing a full-scale pattern. The best method is to measure each piece of the garment by the straight grain with a tape measure, using an occasional fine silk or entomologist's pin to mark the points on the fabric. These do no damage if eased between the threads and are soon removed. Ordinary dressmaker's pins should never be used as they can mark finely woven materials. The measurements are plotted on graph paper (a scale of $\frac{1}{8}$ inch = 1 inch is easiest) until the shape of the garment emerges in a series of little dots which are then joined together. This pattern can then be enlarged to full scale, drawing directly onto cotton. This is by far the most accurate way of taking a pattern and it is also much easier to make detailed observations of lining and construction. With the first method, if the cotton mull slips at all, the final result will be on the wrong grain and the fabric will not hang properly. Ideally the novice should take several patterns from old and expendable garments for practice, then from a new and expensive dress belonging to a friend. The care which will be taken to avoid marking the fabric is good practice for handling an eighteenth-century dress. When the pattern is drawn out to scale, detailed notes should be made of the type of stitching used, trimmings, etc. It should then be enlarged to full size, cut out in plain white cotton, tacked together and compared with the original. A critical eye is needed at this point to see if any damage has been done to the original dress and if the copy is an accurate one. The short-sighted person is at a considerable advantage when doing this type of work, as it is possible to see the grain of fabric very clearly. For a long-sighted person it may be almost impossible.

Under no circumstances whatsoever should any garment be unpicked. This is quite unnecessary and could destroy valuable evidence.

Alterations to men's clothes seldom extended to more than sewing up or adding a buttonhole, letting out a side seam, or adjusting the position of buttons or trimmings. There are a few examples of banyans and dressing gowns made up from eighteenth-century silks previously used for women's sack dresses; in the City of Nottingham Museum and Art Gallery there is a dressing gown of c.1830 made from saffron-yellow brocaded silk of c.1750–60. A black patterned cut and uncut velvet doublet and trunk-hose apparently of c.1600 [PLATE 90] in the London Museum turns out, on a closer examination of construction techniques, to have been partly cut and sewn in the late nineteenth century. The front and back of the doublet are in one kind of cut velvet and were probably originally a jerkin of c.1600. A peascod belly has been added, protruding through the fronts left open at the bottom, and the doublet fastens at two side openings with hooks and eyes [PLATE 91]. The sleeves, and the breeches which look like canions, are made of

90, 91. A velvet doublet and trunk hose, some pieces dating from c. 1600 and others from the mid-seventeenth century, assembled in the nineteenth century perhaps as a painter's studio property. The detail (right) shows the alterations made to what was originally a jerkin. Side openings were made after the front had been closed to accommodate a peascod belly. (London Museum Joicey Coll. A. 12514)

cut velvet of a different pattern which probably dates from the mid-seventeenth century. It is likely that the pieces of fabric were found together and the decision to construct the suit made by a painter of historic scenes for use as a studio property. There are few examples of this type of alteration to men's costume, but many women's dresses have been completely remade from early fabric at a later date.

The study of eighteenth-century silks and the way in which they were made, altered, unpicked and remade at different periods gives some idea of the problem involved when dating a dress. The Gallery of English Costume at Manchester has a useful collection of specimens which provides much evidence about the way in which eighteenth- and nineteenth-century dressmakers altered dresses; to understand their work and the type of alterations made, one needs a knowledge of perfect specimens and their pattern shapes, with the stitching characteristic of the different periods.

Why have so many dresses surviving from the eighteenth century been altered? Many people reading these words will have taken up and let down hems in the 1960s to keep in step with fashion. Eighteenth-century silks were as expensive as they were beautiful, and it is understandable that people faced with similar changes in fashion would not wish to waste them. Quite often the gap in time between the dates when they were used is long enough for the fabric design to have become fashionable again.

Although at first sight there were only two basic dress styles in the eighteenth century, the sack and the robe *en fourreau* with its tightly fitting bodice, there were an infinite number of variations. A sack of 1720 is quite different from one of 1775. There were fashions in the arrangement of skirt pleating, the fullness at the sides, the shaping of the bodice, all of which can be seen in paintings and surviving unaltered dresses. The sack dress used lengths of material with very little cutting, running from shoulder to hem at the back. Straight lengths of material were used for the petticoat. Altogether about twenty yards of silk, nineteen inches wide, were needed for a typical sack dress with matching petticoat. With changing fashion the dress might have a minor alteration made, by unpicking and restitching the pleats, which grew narrower as the century progressed. Or the whole dress might be carefully unpicked, pressed and recut as a gown with a close-fitting bodice, either at the time or several years later.

What kind of a dress would result from the remodelling of an unpicked sack? In most cases a perfectly wearable one, though the fabric might be a little out of date. Sometimes the weight of the silk was not suitable for the later style. Natalie Rothstein was able to date the woven silk of one particular dress [PLATE 92] precisely to a design of 16 June 1743 by Anna Maria Garthwaite, which is in the Victoria and Albert Museum. The dress was completely remade in c.1780, and there are joins running across the shoulders where there was insufficient material. The design has been matched most carefully, even though its size created considerable problems. In fact, if we are to be critical, the large design must have looked much more attractive in its original form as a sack. The long pleat lines at the back would have displayed the big repeat to advantage, whereas the tiny pleats at the waist, characteristic of the 1780s, are rather too small for silk of this weight, and they tend to break slightly; a finer silk is needed.

The flat pattern shape of the sack can be seen clearly in the diagram given by François Garsault in *L'Art du Tailleur* printed in 1769 [PLATE 93]. The sleeve shape with its two flounces is shown made up at 6 in the diagram. The figure 1 indicates the back of the gown and 3 shows it pleated up, 2 indicates the front of the gown and 4 shows it pleated into position. The little wedge shape at the side of the back panel would have been cut out and joined on at the side of the skirt to make a gore.

The specimen of a perfect unaltered sack dress [PLATE 94] shows how this pattern would have looked when made up. There are bands of pleated trimming and deep flounces on the petticoat, all of which were cut on the straight grain and would have taken several yards more material.

The dress which is illustrated in Plate 95 is a classic example of how an unpicked sack could be remodelled. The final gown of c.1780–5 is seen in pieces. The crease marks and the shapes of the fragments show that this was originally a sack dress with matching petticoat. The silk dates from c.1760 although the construction of the bodice, lined with white linen, is of the mid 1780s [PLATE 97]. Each piece was mounted on a linen lining, and all the raw edges turned in towards each other and slipstitched. The whole bodice was then assembled by overhanding, or with tiny stab stitches. This is the typical method of construction for a fitted bodice of the 1780s. There was very little piecing done on the bodice except

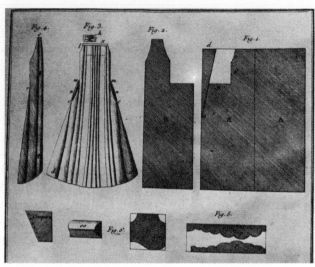

Above left

92. A robe en fourreau remodelled in c. 1780 from unpicked silk dating from 1743, originally a sack dress. (Gallery of English Costume, Manchester 1947.827)

Above right

93. Diagram of a sack dress pattern, from L'Art du Tailleur by François Garsault, 1769. (Victoria & Albert Museum)

under the arms. The two fronts were cut from quite large pieces of material [PLATE 96] which seemed puzzling as the silk is often joined (albeit unobtrusively) in several places in alterations of this type. The raw edges where the skirt would have been joined to the waistline and the strings for looping it up as a polonaise can still be seen, although the silk is rather stiff and would not have draped very well for this style. Across the back the line of stitching which marks the position of the skirt in its last alteration in c.1793–5 can be seen. The skirt has been detached from the bodice but crease marks remain to show the way in which it had been pleated in the mid 1780s and in c.1793–5. The creases which show the original sack pleating are still there as well, although very faint. The fabric has been pieced together most carefully so that the side front skirts as well as the full pleated back could be used. These pieces of material were originally parts of the flounces which had trimmed the petticoat. The joins can be seen very clearly from the wrong side, with the decorative pinked edges of the flounces, although the pattern of the fabric makes them almost invisible from the right side. At first glance the original petticoat of the sack dress has not been altered at all, except that the decorative flounces have been removed, leaving faint traces of stitching on the inside and a slightly deeper shade of pink across the front breadth where they had originally been placed. The petticoat waist was pleated up and stitched to tapes which tied at the sides. However the puzzle of the source of the large pieces of material which had been used for the

Far Left

94. The back of an
unaltered sack gown,
showing the long
pleats. c. 1770–5.
(Snowshill Manor,
National Trust)

Left

95. The pieces of an
unpicked gown of
c. 1780–5, made
from silk originally
used for a sack dress
of c. 1760. (Gallery
of English Costume,
Manchester
1951.327)

bodice was now solved. In order to avoid joins in her bodice, the eighteenth-century dressmaker had removed two large oblong shapes from the centre back petticoat where they would not have shown, and very neatly filled them in with unpicked straight strips of the pleated trimming [PLATE 98] which had originally decorated the front of the sack dress. They had been pressed carefully and were quite flat. The decorative pinked edges are still visible [PLATE 99]. The dressmaker's ingenuity would have gone unremarked had it not been for the fact that the strips were cut across the grain and show very slightly on the right side of the petticoat. The *compère* or stomacher front of the original 1760s dress still survives with several strips of pleated trimming which were probably too narrow to be used for the remodelled dress. The pattern shape of the *compère* can be seen in the diagram from *L'Art du Tailleur*.

Many fragments of material which were once parts of dresses survive, and these three shapes are a sleeve, with the top elbow ruffle beside it and the bottom ruffle below [PLATE 100]. The fabric

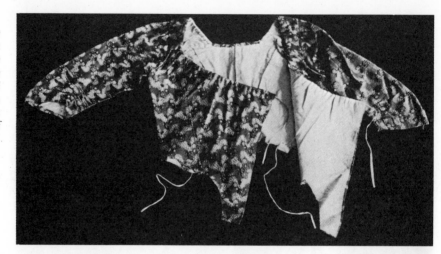

96. *The front bodice of the dress shown in Plate 95 is made from quite large pieces of material without any joins, an unusual feature in this type of remodelling.*

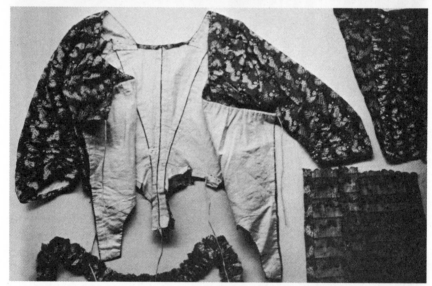

97. *The construction of the bodice is typical of the mid-1780s. The seams are joined together by overhanding and no raw edges can be seen.*

dates from the 1760s. The eighteenth-century sleeve, until the 1780s, was put in differently from those of today. The dressmaker stitched them into the armhole below the arm from the inside of the dress. She then smoothed the fullness of the material onto the linen foundation of the bodice, stitched it down, and then fixed the robings and strips of pleated decoration over the top, to hide the raw edges. In this sleeve some of the tufts of the original stitching remain. The shape of the sleeve is also very different from ours today; the deep curve at the back accommodates the elbow.

Left

98. The back of the petticoat with the panel removed for the front bodice, filled in with unpicked strips of the pleated trimming which originally decorated the front of the sack dress.

Below

99. Detail showing the decorative pinked edges of the trimming strips used to fill in the back of the petticoat. The stitching marks for the gathering lines can still be seen.

The dress in Plate 101, which dates from the 1770s, has been altered in a similar way to the dress shown in Plate 92 from a 1750s silk originally made as a sack, although the back pleating indicates an earlier stage in the evolution of dressmaking processes. The material is pleated down to fit the figure and stitched onto a linen lining, while the later bodice is cut to shape. The crease marks from the pleats of the 1750s sack dress can be seen very clearly, and there are also joins across the top of the bodice where there was not quite enough fabric [PLATE 102]. The skirt material was cartridge pleated and stitched onto the waist of the bodice, while a second line of stitching holds the pleats in position. Once again the silk is really too stiff for the style, and the pleats should be a little deeper to hang properly. The light silks of the 1770s were much more appropriate for this style.

Cotton dresses as well as silks were altered. The print in Plate 103 dates from c.1785 when the dress was originally made. The waistline was raised in c.1793–5 and the little ends were left hanging inside at the back, just in case the dress should need to be altered back again. This is a very characteristic alteration of the period. The drawstring at the neckline remains unaltered.

Sometimes a dressmaker unpicked a dress of the 1780s com-pletely to remake it in c.1800. The skirt lengths were often enough

to make a new dress and the bodice pieces of the original dress still survive. The petticoat was used for the new bodice and sleeves, while the trailing lengths of silk which formed the skirt, looped up *en polonaise*, were long enough to provide a skirt which hung from the new raised waist-level. Occasionally a complete bodice of *c*.1785 with a dress of the same material made in *c*.1800 are preserved together as dress and jacket, though the two items would never have been worn together. Plate 104 shows bodice pieces which were unpicked and not used. The centre fronts face each other with the wide shallow neckline at the top. The waistline is clipped to allow the deep curve to spread round the waist. The two sleeves of *c*.1785 also survive, although little pieces have been cut out of them, possibly for patchwork or to cover buttons [PLATE 105]. The sleeve on the right retains the little cut-out dart shape for the elbow. The pattern shapes of a *c*.1780–90 gown may help to clarify these two shapes [PLATE 106].

Even more complicated deductions had to be made in the case of the dress worn by the seated figure in Plate 107. When it first

101, 102. The back bodice pleats of a 1770s gown are stitched down onto the linen lining, in this alteration from a 1750s sack gown. The crease marks and the joins (right) where there was not quite enough material can be seen clearly. (Gallery of English Costume, Manchester 1947. 828)

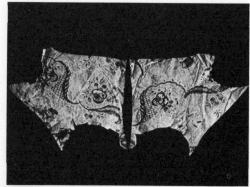

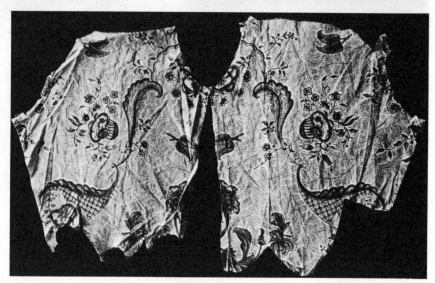

Above left

103. A printed fustian dress originally made in c. 1785 shows the characteristic alteration of c. 1793–5 when the waist level was raised. The ends of the centre back bodice are left hanging inside the skirt. (Victoria & Albert Museum T. 216–1966)

Above right and centre

104, 105. Unpicked bodice pieces of a dress in printed cotton dating from c. 1785. The centre fronts face each other. The sleeves (right) have had small pieces cut out of them possibly for patchwork. The one on the right retains the cut-out shape of the dart for the elbow. (Gallery of English Costume, Manchester, 1938.443/4)

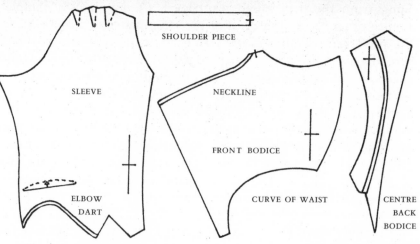

SHOULDER PIECE

SLEEVE

NECKLINE

FRONT BODICE

CURVE OF WAIST

ELBOW DART

CENTRE BACK BODICE

arrived at the Gallery of English Costume the bodice was not joined to the skirt and there were a great many other pieces with it. The embroidered silk dates from the late 1770s when small flower patterns like this were fashionable. They were fashionable again when this gown was remodelled from the earlier sack in c.1800. Plate 108 shows some of the other pieces which were with the gown; two bodice side front panels, the back bodice, the high stomacher front and one sleeve. These all had typical shapes of pattern pieces dating from c.1800. A closer look at the seams revealed holes made by machine stitching. The dress had been remodelled in c.1800 from a sack of the late 1770s. In the late nineteenth century the bodice had been removed and a new one copied carefully for a larger woman to wear as a fancy dress. This bodice would have been made from pieces left over from the original sack or polonaise and matching petticoat. Luckily all the pieces had been carefully preserved. The sewing techniques solved the problem: the even holes in the seams of the unpicked bodice could only have been made by a machine [PLATE 109]. The seams are neatened with oversewing which looks like the work of a court dressmaker – beautiful, neat, precise little stitches, characteristic of

107. The figure seated at the piano wears a gown of c. 1800 made from an embroidered silk dress dating from the late 1770s. (Gallery of English Costume, Manchester, 1961.262)

Opposite below

106. Diagram (scale: $\frac{1}{8}'' \times 1''$) of the bodice and sleeve of a gown with a vandyked collar. c. 1780–90 (Gallery of English Costume, Manchester, 1947.1610)

the late nineteenth and early twentieth centuries. Oversewing seams was certainly done from the 1820s as a method of neatening, but only in this particular way from the 1880s onwards.

Some of the eighteenth-century silks were not really suitable for the later styles into which they were altered. There are six particularly good examples of altered dresses at the Gallery of English Costume, Manchester, of which five can be seen in Plate 110. One dress of striped silk of c.1758–62, originally a sack, was altered in c.1785 and then again in c.1795–1800. In its final form, the front skirt was constructed on the front fall principle and would have tied round the waist with two strings. Although the raised waist-level allowed the pattern of the material to be shown off reasonably well, it was still a bit too stiff to hang properly for the lines of a period when soft clinging muslins were in vogue. This type of alteration can be found in many of the collections listed at the end of the book. Sometimes the dresses do not appear to have been worn after their alteration, perhaps because their owners were not satisfied with the result. Others, like the one described, have obviously been successful, judging from the evidence of wear and tear.

Alterations to eighteenth-century silks continued throughout the nineteenth century. In the centre of Plate 110 is a dress of c.1828 made from a chiné silk of the early 1790s, probably originally a robe à l'Anglaise with fitted bodice and full pleated skirt, which could be looped up en polonaise with a matching petticoat. This would have allowed enough material to make this dress with its full sleeves and the front bodice pieces and deep panel at the hem cut on the cross grain of the fabric. At first sight one might not realise that this was an eighteenth-century silk, but closer examination reveals the original stitching lines, faint creases and little joins in the material. At the back of the skirt, carefully concealed beneath a pleat, is the original eighteenth-century pocket hole.

An embroidered silk of the late 1770s on the right of Plate 110, revealing some of its original crease marks on close examination, was transformed into a dress of c.1835. The original dress was probably a robe à l'Anglaise with a matching petticoat. These cross-cut sleeves needed a lot of fabric and there is a large piece of material, one of the lengths from the skirt still with its pocket hole, which was not used. A piece has been cut away at the hem, probably for cuffs or facings for the new dress of 1835.

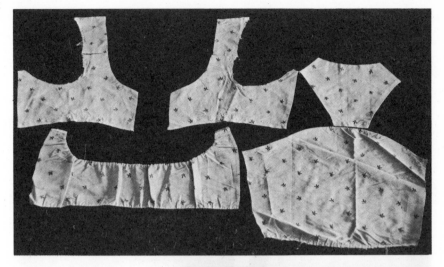

108. Some of the
bodice pieces made up
in the late nineteenth
century for fancy
dress, from material
left over from the
dress in plate 107.
(Gallery of English
Costume, Man-
chester, 1961.262)

109. The even holes
in the seams of the
unpicked bodice
shown above could
only have been made
by a sewing machine.

110. A group of
dresses altered from
eighteenth-century
silks during the
nineteenth century.
From left to right, a
fancy dress of
c. 1840, from silk of
c. 1742–4
(1947.2071), an
evening dress of
c. 1891, in 1750s
silk (1955.253), a
day dress of c. 1828
from a chiné silk of
the early 1790s
(1947.1806), an
evening dress of
c. 1842–4 from the
silk of c. 1775
(A.154) and a day
dress of c. 1835
from an embroidered
silk of the late 1770s
(1938.404). (Gallery
of English Costume,
Manchester)

A beautiful silk of *c.*1742–4, which would originally have been a sack dress with matching petticoat, has been remodelled to provide a fancy dress for *c.*1840 – probably for 'Cinderella at the Ball'; it is on the left of Plate 110. The dress has been decorated down the front, round the neckline and at the ends of the sleeves with plaited cross-cut strips of fine plush, a cotton fabric with a long pile. The bodice has been cut with early 1840s darts running high up over the bust. The front fastens with lacing through eyelet holes. This was probably intended to give an eighteenth-century look to the ensemble. The front of the original petticoat is still used as a petticoat, but the deep flounces have additional trimmings of plaited plush. The back of the bodice shows the seaming of the early 1840s and the waistline is piped, a method not used in the eighteenth century. The front of the skirt is caught back at intervals with piped decorations.

Some of the same features can also be seen in the charming little dress of *c.*1842–4 [PLATE 111], made from a silk of *c.*1775. There are many silks of the 1840s which are very similar in design to those of the eighteenth century and sometimes it is quite difficult to tell them apart at first sight. Once again the bust darts are very long and the waistline is piped. Typical of early 1840s dress

Below

114, 115. *The gored skirt of a dress of c. 1891 (left) is cut from silk dating from the 1750s. The inside of the skirt (right) shows the typical cut and construction of the 1890s. Tapes hold the folds in position at the back. (Gallery of English Costume, Manchester, 1955.253)*

construction are the tiny cartridge pleats with which the skirt fullness is eased onto the bodice [PLATE 112]. The bodice is lined throughout and there are two bones at the centre front to keep the silk from wrinkling [PLATE 113]. This fabric has been remodelled most successfully. The ends of the sleeves and the front ruched strips are bordered with fringe which looks as if it might have been on the original 1775 dress.

The 1840s were the major period for re-using eighteenth-century silks for fashionable dresses, but specimens can still be found after this date, although the majority of the remodelled silks were used for fancy dress. Second from the left in Plate 110 is a dress of c.1891 made from a silk of the 1750s, probably originally a sack dress with matching petticoat, as this would allow enough material to cut this gored skirt [PLATE 114]. The entire cut and construction are typical of the 1890s. The inside of the skirt shows the tapes to hold the folds in position [PLATE 115]. The bodice is boned, and has a petersham waistband labelled *Marshall and Snelgrove*, although this may have been transferred from another dress by a local dressmaker. The neatening of the seams is characteristic of this period.

Perhaps the latest example of a remodelled eighteenth-century fabric may be seen in the Centre de Documentation du Costume in Paris. It is a blue and silver brocaded silk of the early 1760s, which Dior transformed from a sack to a New Look dress of 1947.

These examples of the dressmaker's ingenuity should warn enthusiasts that there is more to dating a dress than at first seems apparent. Once the general outline of the dress, the type of material and the method of construction have been noted, a trained eye will begin to see the tiny details which indicate alterations.

Men's costume is not so difficult to date. The type of fabric, the position of the pockets and seam lines, the width of the sleeves, and the shape of the breeches or trousers provide evidence which is much more easily assessed. The alterations, if any, are usually so slight that they have obviously been made to accommodate the extra inch or two of a man who had put on weight. Although the cut and construction of a man's coat will usually give the date without much trouble, one word of warning is needed. Livery, academic and legal robes are crystallised forms of earlier fashions and this point should be borne in mind when determining the date from the pattern shapes.

III. Costume Conservation, Storage and Display

Many enthusiasts become collectors of costume. They may start with long-hoarded family treasures and build up a collection from the abundance of material still surviving from some periods, particularly the late nineteenth and early twentieth centuries, which can be purchased in antique shops and at sales. The first rule for costume collectors is that, however tempting it may be in the circumstances, beautiful specimens or rare ones in whatever condition should not be worn for fancy dress, theatrical performances or dress shows. If it is necessary to photograph a dress on a living model care should be taken that the right size person is chosen. An anti-perspirant, dress shields and a closely fitting soft cotton slip with sleeves will help protect the dress. Textiles are very fragile and if a dress is exposed to strain and perspiration the material will eventually disintegrate. Photography should take place on a cool day and not in direct sunlight.

In some cases the costume is in perfect condition. It may never have been worn for some reason and remained folded up in a box for many years, packed in quantities of acid-free tissue paper, away from the dusty air, light and damp which cause so much damage. Other specimens may not have been so fortunate and great care must be taken to avoid doing further damage to material already suffering from the depredations of time. In some cases the material is so filthy that the amateur does more damage in trying to remove the dirt than by leaving it alone. Conservation is a specialist's job, needing an incredible amount of patience as well as a knowledge of chemicals, materials, sewing techniques and dress construction. Every specimen presents a new set of problems and the amateur cannot hope to achieve the same results as a fully trained person with a knowledge of weaving and experience of working on different fabrics from many periods.

It is important to remember that in some cases the information provided by an old and slightly grubby costume is invaluable and irreplaceable. If excessive conservation is carried out, all this may be lost. Tiny dirt marks may indicate lines of earlier stitching and show the original shape of the garment. Fragile trimmings, filthy though they are, may be the only surviving specimens of a particular type of fabric. Original stitching should never be removed from a specimen, but when for some particular reason it is absolutely necessary, full notes should be made and close-up photographs taken before it is removed. Often it is better to leave a costume alone or spot clean it than to clean it thoroughly and destroy valuable evidence. A starched linen ruff of the early seventeenth century surviving in the Bayerisches Nationalmuseum, Munich, is a record of the work of a laundress as well as a seamstress. The drops of wax holding the pleats in shape are still in position. Cleaning would have destroyed this evidence.

DRY CLEANING

New methods and chemicals for dry-cleaning are continually being tested in the Dutch Central Laboratory and other conservation departments; reports are available in several publications (see page 170). Sometimes reliable local firms with staff interested in conservation problems are prepared to take time, using these methods and recommended chemicals and will carry out spot cleaning as well as complete dry-cleaning for old materials. While coin-operated dry cleaning machines are now available in most large towns and some large museums have their own special equipment, amateurs must take care that the fabric will stand up to this treatment. Fragile shattered silks of the late nineteenth and early twentieth centuries will disintegrate if treated in this way, and some experts feel that dry-cleaning can make silk fibres brittle. Each item should be considered individually and other examples of the same period studied carefully for additional information before any decision is taken.

Before a costume is treated in any way it should be examined closely. Anything particularly fragile and items like detachable broderie anglaise collars, which would be better cleaned by washing, are removed and notes and photographs are taken, and diagrams made for their replacement afterwards. Strips of muslin or nylon net are stitched over buckles, hooks and any other items which might catch the fabric, unless they can easily be detached. The whole costume is then put inside a muslin or nylon net bag which is sewn up before being put into the dry-cleaning machine. After cleaning, the dress should be carefully removed from the bag as quickly as possible and hung up on a padded hanger for the creases to drop out. Fragile dresses should never be cleaned by this method.

WASHING

Many conservators prefer hand washing to any other method of cleaning, but it can do a great deal of damage if undertaken by inexperienced people. A very large shallow sink is needed to wash textiles properly. Specially designed ones may be seen in the conservation departments of major museums all over Europe. These are very expensive but the amateur can use a large kitchen sink or a bath for small articles after cleaning it carefully to make sure no trace of grease remains. Only cotton and linen materials which are in an extremely good state of preservation should be washed, unless by an expert with the facilities available in a well-equipped conservation room, and a washing machine should never be used. Many experts feel that it is inadvisable to wash eighteenth-century silks as they lose their lustre and stiffness. The fabric should first be checked for colour fastness. Two pieces of damp cotton wool should be held tightly, one on each side of the material, for a few seconds. If any faint trace of colour comes off, it is not safe to wash the material. Each colour must be tested separately.

The washing water must be soft and there should be no impurities. Ideally it should be distilled. Some chemists will supply de-ionised water, which is three times purer than distilled water. In hard water areas rainwater collected in large enough quantities is very good, but it is easier to use a water softener. People living in soft water areas like Plymouth and Manchester are very fortunate.

Household soap and commercial detergents should not be used. It is impossible for the average person to know the chemical contents and many of them contain bleaching agents and can leave deposits in the material which damage the fibres. Special detergents are made for conservation purposes, notably 'Lissapol N'. Pure soap flakes can be purchased at Boots under the trade name 'Kudos'.

In some conservation workrooms small articles such as embroidered collars, bodices or handkerchiefs are washed and rinsed while fixed between two screens covered with nylon mesh and left in a horizontal position for the water to drain away completely. Other conservators prefer not to use screens and lay the fabric on a glass or formica surface to dry flat, thus avoiding the need for ironing. A large piece of stiff polythene should be placed at the bottom of the sink so that the material can be lifted out when the water has drained away. If left flat at a slight angle surplus water can then continue to run away gently instead of streaming through the fragile material and tearing it. It is quite unnecessary to wring the material, which might crease it permanently, and it should never be shaken out vigorously. In the case of a large article, for example a muslin dress, the polythene sheet can be turned over on top of a dry terry towel without disturbing the fragile material and another dry terry towel gently patted over the top, to remove excess moisture. Ordinary starch should not be used to stiffen cotton and linen items as the fabric will eventually rot. Plastic starches are being tested at the Dutch Central Laboratory at the time of writing.

DRYING AND IRONING

Small items can be pressed out flat on a formica or glass sheet to dry. It is unnecessary to iron them afterwards, as they will be quite smooth and it is best to avoid excessive heat wherever possible. Any temperature over $100°$ F can be detrimental. Drying is best done on a well-ventilated rack in a moderately warm place or with a hair dryer, rather than in a hot airing-cupboard or in front of direct heat, which will slightly yellow the fabric. White linen or cotton can be dried quickly in the sun as this has a good bleaching action, although it cannot be done in cities where the air is full of smuts. Never dry coloured or printed materials in the sun as they will fade. Ideally it is better to smooth fabrics out by hand while drying with a hair dryer, to avoid ironing them. This is a lengthy task which cannot be hurried, but the results are worth the trouble.

If ironing has to be done, a cloth should be placed between the iron and the fabric. To avoid the risk of overheating, an old or undependable iron should be switched off while in contact with the material. Embroidered specimens should be ironed very carefully on the wrong side, the right side facing downwards on a terry towel, to prevent the embroidery being flattened – if they have to be ironed at all.

REPAIR WORK

In some cases an extensive amount of repair work is needed. Disintegrating lace, silk cracking on pleat folds, torn muslins, rotting areas caused by perspiration – all need careful treatment. Perhaps one of the safest methods for amateurs is to back the disintegrating fabric with semi-transparent silk organza, crepeline or jap silk, pinned into position with entomologists' butterfly pins (or dressmakers' brass pins for silk) and then to hand stitch with fine silk. At the worst this can be unpicked, and at its best the result is almost invisible, prolonging the life of the fabric for many years. Sometimes a fabric is too brittle to stitch and cracks when a needle is put through it. It is then possible to reinforce the material with a nylon net impregnated with a polyvinyl acetate called Mowilith which is applied to the fabric with a cool iron [PLATE 116]. The amateur should watch an experienced person at work and experiment with scrap material first, until quite confident about the process, as it can do a great deal of damage. Experiments are being carried out continually in the Dutch Central Laboratory to produce better adhesives which will not be subject to chemical changes and which can be easily removed if required.

Careful notes and diagrams or photographs must be made while working on any costume and kept as a record for future reference.

The following points should be noted by anyone attempting conservation. Some people have clumsy hand movements; others have palms which sweat profusely, even in cold weather. Long-sighted people often cannot see the threads in the weave of the fabric they are attempting to mend, except with the aid of a magnifying glass, which can quickly produce eye-strain. These people should not attempt conservation work as they may do damage. Some people have a natural gift for laundering and can

turn a bundle of dirty old muslin into an exquisite 1870s bustle dress trimmed with a mass of frills. Others are exceptionally fine needlewomen and can produce almost invisible repairs to fragile specimens. Good conservation takes time and this is something which cannot be stressed too highly. The white muslin dress [PLATE 117] is a good example of the work which can be done by the amateur conservator. Helen Larson, who owns the dress, took four hours to stitch some of the frills securely into position and another two hours to wash each piece separately. The dress was dried in sunlight and she then took fourteen and a half hours to press it, using a very cool iron and the utmost care, to restore it to its original pristine condition. Altogether twenty and a half hours were needed for conservation. A professional conservator would have had equipment and space to lay the dress out to dry and avoid ironing, or worked with a hairdryer smoothing the dress as it dried. This would have taken even more time.

Other pieces of conservation can take very much longer. A suit worn by Prince Rupert [PLATE 118] which was in a very fragile condition has been restored by Karen Finch. The almost invisible stitching took five hundred hours to complete.

The most important point for the amateur is to study the conservation methods used in leading museums and to practise sewing, washing and ironing on scrap pieces of material, where no damage can be done.

It is hoped that in the near future a National Centre for the Conservation of Textiles, which would be able to offer professional advice on all the latest methods, will be established in or near London.

STORAGE

The problem of storage is one that faces many museums as well as private collectors. In ideal conditions a dress should be kept in an air-conditioned room, flat in a long drawer or box, not folded at all and packed with acid-free, white tissue paper (obtainable from any large stationer or from Woolworths). If hanging in a cupboard it should be on a specially padded hanger and not crushed close to another dress, thus tearing its trimmings.

But how can one store costume cheaply? A padded coat hanger which does not strain the sleeves and shoulders can be made by stitching plastic foam, cotton or nylon wadding over a wooden hanger and covering it with calico. Wads of tissue paper can be used as a temporary measure.

Stiff cardboard boxes like those used for packing dresses in department stores are fairly expensive, but large boxes may be obtained free of charge from florists who are usually pleased to get rid of them [PLATE 120]. These boxes are made of lightweight corrugated card and need reinforcing with thin strips of wood stuck with an impact adhesive at intervals on the base, sides and lid. If this is done they will last quite a long time, if handled carefully. The costume should be packed with plenty of white acid-free tissue paper to prevent creasing and protect the material from the cardboard. Each box should be labelled clearly with a brief description of the costume, the date and accession number, and stored in date sequence for easy access. Woollen garments need some kind of moth deterrent. Many experts feel that any chemical may cause fading and be a health hazard. On the other hand this has to be weighed against the havoc which can be created by a few moths. Paradichlorobenzine crystals seem to be the safest

chemical and can be used in box, store cupboard or display unit in a perforated tin. Old-fashioned but effective moth prevention methods are regular airing and the inclusion of a sheet of newspaper at the top of the box over the tissue paper.

One lesson learned from all collections is that clothes should never be completely sealed in polythene bags, because moulds will grow. Lightweight polythene bags of the type used by dry-cleaners prevent fragile lace on one dress being caught on hooks, beads and sequins of another. They can be slit open on one side and plastic paper clips used to secure the opening. The dress can be removed easily from the hanger beneath the protective covering without an undue amount of handling. Polythene bags and plastic wardrobes set up static electricity and attract dust. Although the costume is inside the bag it can get dirty on removal. Lightweight polythene bags attract less dust than the heavier variety. Both plastic wardrobes and polythene bags can be wiped down with an anti-static fluid to reduce the problem, but this has to be done at fairly frequent intervals.

Cellophane is transparent and allows the object to be viewed easily without excessive handling. It is very useful for small objects, for example shoes, purses and lace, but it has the disadvantage of

tearing easily when used in large sheets to cover dresses. Lightweight dust sheets, made of a closely woven cotton, can be
laundered. Any wardrobe should have rods put across front and
back at the top to support a dust sheet as particles of grit can get in
round the edges of ill-fitting doors opening outwards. Close-
fitting sliding doors can be almost dust-proof, but are much more
expensive to install. Care must also be taken to avoid catching
dress hems when opening the doors.

Unfortunately, if ideal conditions are required and the collection
is a large one, the cost of providing space is almost equalled by the
cost of the storage cupboards, hangers, shelves and boxes. The
problem can only be solved cheaply if the collector is a competent
carpenter, has plenty of space and is prepared to use a great deal of
time and ingenuity.

Some American museums have wonderful storage areas and,
although it is obvious that vast sums of money have been spent, the
ideas can be adapted. The Metropolitan Museum, New York, has
enviable storage space, recently designed. The air is filtered and
conditioned; storage space, conservation department, costume
library, exhibition area and students' working spaces are all contained within the Costume Institute. These are not the conditions
which can be easily copied by the amateur.

At Philadelphia, however, although the costumes are stored in
an air-conditioned room beyond the scope of the average collector,
the method of utilising all the available space could be adapted.
Costumes are suspended on padded hangers from movable rails
at two levels and a whole rack can be pulled out for examination
quickly and easily.

The Museum of the City of New York uses an interesting system
of facing cupboards connected by a rail across an open area the
length of a dress rail. When a cupboard door is opened a whole
dress rail can be moved out for easy access. After a costume has been
selected for study and the dress rail returned to the cupboard, there
is a sizeable area for students to work in [PLATE 119].

In Europe there are several museums which have large textile conservation departments and specially designed storage conditions
for textiles and costume. There are publications available about
some of them (page 170).

Several of the larger collections in Britain, for example the
Gallery of English Costume, the Victoria and Albert Museum and

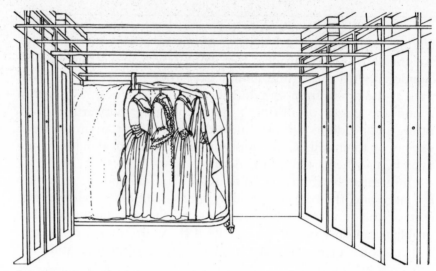

the Welsh Folk Museum, have storage and conservation areas
designed specifically for costume and textiles. Although most of
the equipment would be far too expensive for amateur resources
there are useful and inexpensive ideas to be noted both in these and
in many provincial museums. Among them, for example, are a
chest of drawers [PLATE 121] and an entomological specimen chest
[PLATE 122] utilised for storage of small objects with the aid of a
carpenter's ingenuity at Worcestershire County Museum; at the
Stranger's Hall Museum, Norwich, dresses needing time for
creases to drop out, or waiting for mounting are lifted out of the
way on an ordinary clothes airer [PLATE 123].

All costume collections need a system of records and the larger
the collection the more vital it is to keep consistent and complete
records of each item. It is wise to begin a card index system when
the collection is started. Each card should record the provenance
and type of garment, whether worn by man, woman or child, the
date, a description of the fabric (including the width from selvedge
to selvedge, if possible), and then a full description of the garment
and the way in which it is made, by hand or machine stitching, for
example.

When describing a dress it is best to mount it on a stand to see
how the skirt falls and its length (mini, mid-calf, ankle or floor
length). It is helpful to enter the measurements, taken from the
inside if possible, of bust, waist at raised or natural level, centre
front neck to this waist level and from there to the hem, and the
hip measurement of a tight fitting skirt. These can only be given

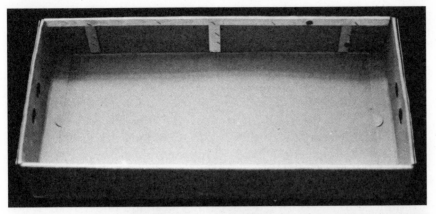

120. Lightweight corrugated cardboard florist's box reinforced with wooden strips, which can be used for packing dresses.

Centre left

121. An ordinary chest of drawers has extra trays fitted inside to take small items like fans and gloves. These can be lifted out easily and the objects seen at a glance. (Worcestershire County Museum)

Centre right

122. The shallow drawers of an entomological specimen chest are divided to store buttons, earrings, brooches and other small trinkets. (Worcestershire County Museum)

Right

123. Dresses waiting for attention suspended out of the way on a clothes airer, saving floor space in a restricted area. (Strangers' Hall Museum, Norwich)

approximately but are useful to give a rough idea of the size of the dress if you need to mount it quickly and have to adapt – or make – a dress stand in a hurry.

A large collection will obviously need more categories than a small one and it is easier to have printed index cards so that a set formula can be followed. The usual divisions are first into male, female and children's clothing and then into different types of garment in alphabetical order. These are then arranged by date within each category. However, a small collection might be divided very simply within the category of female clothing, for example, into accessories, dresses, outerwear and underwear. When a collection grows to any size it is useful to have cross references. A woman's dress could be carded by date and type first, for example 'evening dress 1924', then, if it had the dressmaker's name inside, given a cross reference so that it could be looked up quickly under 'labelled dresses'. It could also be carded under 'chiffon dresses' for easy retrieval when a particular type of fabric was required.

Each costume should be given a number which is usually called the accession number. It is best to give the year when the costume was acquired and then a number to note the order of arrival into the collection, eg. 1970–3. If there are several pieces to the costume, for example a skirt, a day bodice, an evening bodice, matching shoes, and a photograph of it, letters should be added so that each item is labelled individually, e.g. skirt 1970–3a, day bodice 1970–3b, evening bodice 1970–3c, right shoe 1970–3d, left shoe 1970–3e, photograph of wearer in the dress 1970–3f. All these numbers with a full description of the costume and the location within the collection are entered on the index cards and the various pieces can be stored apart for convenience without losing track of them. It is helpful if a photograph can be added to the card; the contact sheets from 35 mm negatives give enough details for this purpose and are relatively inexpensive. A photograph is far more useful than a written description for quick recognition.

Notes can be added to the cards giving the dates when any item is put on display so that it is not used too often. Details of conservation can also be given.

A small label should be stitched to each costume inside the shoulder showing the accession number, which should never be marked with ink on the dress itself; a label can easily be unstitched for a photograph but nothing can remove large unsightly black marks.

DISPLAY

Most private collectors wish to display dresses in temporary exhibitions, and a great deal can be learned from studying the ways in which costumes are shown in various museums in semi-permanent displays. The three great dangers to a costume which is being put on show are dust, light and handling by visitors. Museums deal with dust by having cases fitted with air filters, but the amateur must make sure that if the costumes are not in cases the exhibition is not on long enough for damage to be done. A small hand vacuum cleaner will remove surface dust at the end of each day and the dresses should be covered with acid-free tissue paper or lightweight dust sheets overnight. Country air will do less damage than smutty city air, and the degree of local air pollution should always be borne in mind.

Light can do more damage than dust. Not only can it fade a costume but it can eventually rot the fabric to pieces. A strong north light can do as much damage as sunlight. For this reason costumes should ideally be shown in properly-regulated artificial light. When this is not possible an added safeguard for framed pieces is light-filtering perspex (see page 169) which excludes the damaging ultra-violet rays. If in addition (as is done at the Gallery of English Costume, Manchester, for example) the windows are screened with fine net or voile curtains to exclude the daylight glare, less harm will come to the fragile textiles on display. Special light meters give correct readings of the amount of light in a room and should always be used if textiles are to be on display for longer than a week.

The dress stands present yet another problem. How should the costumes be displayed? Should the models have heads or not? The illustrations show various approaches to the problem. The first is from *The Smart Set*, a temporary display of 1920s and 1930s dresses shown at Los Angeles County Museum in 1969 [PLATE 124]. Here the models were all made to the same pattern with painted hair and faces, thus reducing the cost. In this particular exhibition, in an artificially lit room, the result was most attractive as the

Right

*124. Stylised models
with painted hair
and faces for* The
Smart Set, *an
exhibition of 1920s
and 1930s dresses at
Los Angeles County
Museum, 1969.*

Far right

*125. A model with a
wire support attached
to the body to display
a wig. Hats can be
shown as well as
costume. This is a
good way of dis-
playing men's clothes.
(Royal Scottish
Museum, Edinburgh)*

stylised poses of the models caught the feeling of the twenties and
thirties very well and made the dress fabrics hang correctly. A more
academic approach to the problem is illustrated by the showcase of
models at the Gallery of English Costume, designed by Anne Buck
[PLATES 107, 110]. The framework can be adapted to fit any dress
and is padded to make the correct period shape. This is a useful
method for study purposes. The dummies used in the Costume
Court at the Victoria and Albert Museum are based on the same
principle of padding a framework to the required shape, but are
much more complicated with jointed arms and legs. These would
be too expensive for the amateur to copy. Some of the models at
the Kostuummuseum in The Hague have wigs attached to wires
from the back of the neck to give the effect of heads. A model at
the Royal Scottish Museum, Edinburgh is an acceptable compro-
mise between these two methods [PLATE 125]. It has a wire head
attached to a torso to show wigs, hats and hair ornaments as well
as costume, and is suspended in the air with nylon thread so that
legs are not needed. Realistic effects are achieved with displays of
Dutch regional costume mounted in period settings at the Open-

lucht Museum, Arnhem. The models are of papier-mâché designed by J. Duyvetter.

An exhibition of Heather Firbank's dresses dating from 1908 to 1921 at the Victoria and Albert Museum in 1961 showed some most imaginatively designed models. The heads were made of rubber latex covered with papier-mâché made of reprints of contemporary newspapers. Many different models were used for the exhibition *Fashion: an anthology by Cecil Beaton*, in 1971. One may be seen in plate 224.

The costumes designed for the BBC television series *The Six Wives of Henry VIII* were mounted at very little cost at Bethnal Green Museum in 1970. The stands were based on the metal framework of cope stands loaned by the Victoria and Albert Museum, padded to fit the costumes with sheets of plastic foam, crumpled newspaper, tissue paper and corrugated cardboard [PLATES 126, 127]. Fancy dress costumes in the exhibition *Follies and Fantasies* at Brighton Museum in 1971 were displayed with paper roses massed to give the effect of heads [PLATE 129]; the stands were made of wire, padded to give the correct shape. Experiments have been made with different types of models at the Museum of Costume, Bath. A most attractive one with a skilfully modelled head is shown [PLATE 130]. It is always difficult to display men's costume. Fibre glass legs with cane heads and torsos designed for shop window displays were used for Elizabethan courtiers in the display of costumes from the BBC television series *Elizabeth R* at Hampton Court in 1971 [PLATE 128]. The method where legs are not needed, used by the Royal Scottish Museum provides another solution to the problem [PLATE 125].

The amateur cannot afford to spend a great deal on stands, but a reasonable foundation can be made quite cheaply from galvanised wire netting with a 1 inch (2.54 cm) mesh. A coat of thixotropic (non-drip) enamel paint will prevent any possibility of rust, if the model should be left in a damp place. Plastic coated wire netting can be used instead, but it is much stiffer to handle. The galvanised wire netting can be reinforced with extra wire. With a limited budget for a BBC TV series *For the Sake of Appearance*, I made wire netting torsoes for mounting corsets [PLATES 131, 132], and for dress stands with wooden frames constructed by a carpenter, which were adjustable for different heights [PLATES 133, 134]. These wooden bases were similar in principle to those designed for the

126, 127. Costumes for Anne of Cleves and Henry VIII mounted on the metal frames for cope stands, padded with plastic foam. Exhibition of costumes in 1970 at the Bethnal Green Museum for the BBC TV series The Six Wives of Henry VIII designed by John Bloomfield.

Below left

128. The costume for the Earl of Essex mounted on a model assembled from fibreglass legs and a cane head and torso designed for shop window displays. Exhibition of costumes in 1971 at Hampton Court for the BBC TV series Elizabeth R., designed by Elizabeth Waller.

Below right

129. Fancy dress for 'Folly' (c. 1898) from Castle Howard, displayed on a wire stand padded with wadding to provide the correct period shape. Paper roses massed together give the effect of a head. (Follies and Fantasies Exhibition, Brighton Museum, 1971)

Gallery of English Costume by Anne Buck. Standard wood measurements were used throughout to avoid the expense of cutting [PLATE 135]. (Old standard lamp or dress stand bases can be used, instead of making special stands, as long as the height does not have to be adjusted; the wire netting frame can be stapled into position permanently. It is advisable to wear gloves while handling the wire netting.)

The six dress stands had to be quickly reshaped for fourteen dresses of different sizes and period shapes. I used a rectangle of wire netting which made a shape slightly smaller than the smallest dress (31 inch bust) and added extra pieces of wire netting to broaden the shoulders when needed. The wire netting was stapled to the wooden base and the join at the back was secured with a few pieces of wire. The wire netting was covered with wadding to the required period shape, making it slightly smaller than the measurements of the costume. I dyed cotton stockinette to get a good skin tone and this was darted and seamed to fit each model with very little cutting. Large stitches were easy to unpick when mounting the next dress, to remove or insert wadding and alter the shoulder width. Felt or sateen could also be used to cover the form. Black felt covered the stand for the eighteenth-century corset so that it could be filmed against a black background. The stand was unobtrusive and the corset seemed to float in space [PLATE 132].

Arms were made of doubled lengths of wire hooked in at shoulder level, covered with wadding and muslin and stitched into shape. A quick and easy way of making pliable arms by stuffing nylon stockings lightly with wadding or tissue paper was used for an exhibition at the Royal Ontario Museum, Toronto, when a large number of models had to be mounted quickly. Lengths of wire inside enabled the shapes to bend at the elbows. It is best to keep the arms thin and add tissue paper where more bulk is needed. The stands were finished with necks made of white cardboard cut to the required size and covered with matching stockinette [PLATES 134, 136]. A clear all-purpose adhesive is used for sticking the material. The neck should be slightly smaller than the collar of a tight fitting dress, to avoid straining hooks or buttons.

Perhaps one of the easiest methods is to use a dressmaker's stand of the smallest size available (32 inch bust) with narrow shoulders. The non-adjustable varieties are relatively inexpensive. The modern bust shape can be crushed in slightly and the stand used as

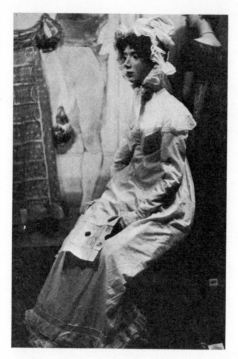

a firm foundation which can be padded to period shape to fit the size of the dress without any strain. The most important thing to remember is that seventeenth, eighteenth and nineteenth-century corsets forced women's figures into very different shapes from those of today. Backs were far narrower, as the shoulder blades were pressed together by whalebone. The shoulder width of a stand should always be adjustable, otherwise too much strain may be placed on a narrow-backed, narrow-shouldered dress, resulting in splitting fabric after a certain length of time. Constant comparison with paintings or photographs of the period will help when padding the dress stand to the correct shape. Stiff brown wrapping paper sellotaped into shape will often provide better support for a skirt than the correct period hooped petticoat, sagging with age, even if one is available. Tissue paper must be placed over it.

One of the most important tasks before arranging an exhibition is to make some rough sketches of the display, with colour schemes. Backgrounds must be chosen which will make the items stand out and not detract from them [PLATE 140]. A ground plan on squared paper with a little model will give an idea of the amount of space available and the finished result. Too small a sample piece of the fabric background may give a false impression of its colour; seen in

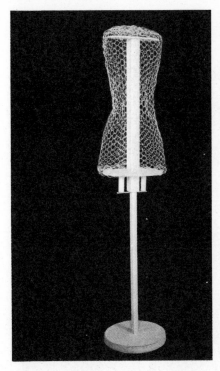
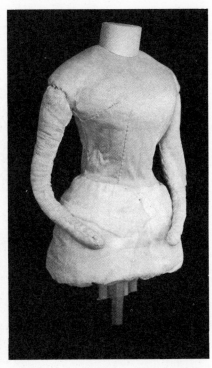

133, 134. A wire netting stand with an adjustable wooden frame, padded with wadding and covered with cotton stocki- nette. The arms are made of doubled lengths of wire covered with wadding and muslin. A dress mounted on the finished stand can be seen in Plate 139.

a large expanse it may turn out to clash badly with the costumes on display. If a model is made first of all, this mistake can be avoided. The texture of the background must also be considered [PLATE 142]. If the exhibition aims to present the costumes in a period setting, the effect of a contemporary wallpaper may be needed. The dresses may be heavily beaded and sequinned and require a dull surface to show off the glitter and sparkle. A dark background will show coloured fabrics off more vividly; a bright background picking up some of the colours in the dresses can produce a very interesting result. An ivory background which reflects all the available light is a help when displaying costumes, as subdued lighting, which is essential, can sometimes give a gloomy effect.

One final important consideration is the labelling, as this can make or mar the appearance of an exhibition. Labels should be unobtrusive; if the background is black, white lettering can be used on black card which will merge into the setting. Large white cards, however attractive the lettering, tend to distract the attention from the dresses on display. It is often better to use small numbers keyed to a catalogue or prominently displayed list, thus avoiding labels altogether.

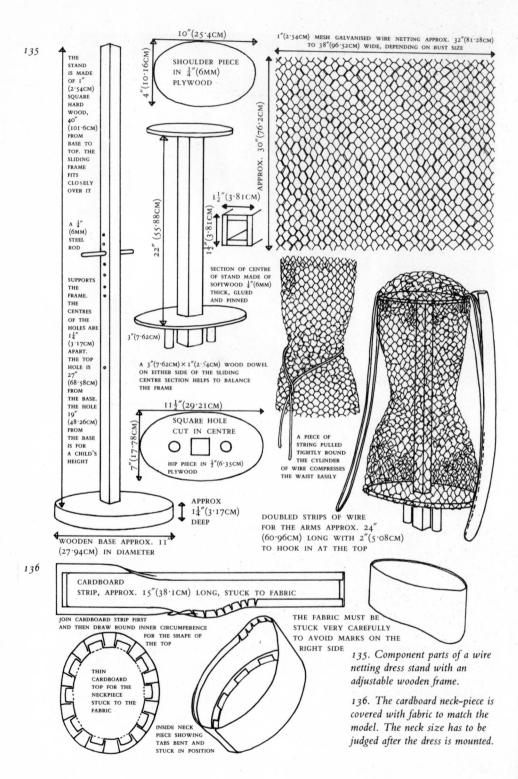

THE STAND IS MADE OF 1" (2·54CM) SQUARE HARD WOOD, 40" (101·6CM) FROM BASE TO TOP. THE SLIDING FRAME FITS CLOSELY OVER IT

A $\frac{1}{4}$" (6MM) STEEL ROD

SUPPORTS THE FRAME. THE CENTRES OF THE HOLES ARE $1\frac{1}{4}$" (3·17CM) APART. THE TOP HOLE IS 27" (68·58CM) FROM THE BASE. THE HOLE 19" (48·26CM) FROM THE BASE IS FOR A CHILD'S HEIGHT

WOODEN BASE APPROX. 11" (27·94CM) IN DIAMETER

10" (25·4CM)

SHOULDER PIECE IN $\frac{1}{4}$" (6MM) PLYWOOD

4" (10·16CM)

22" (55·88CM)

3" (7·62CM)

SECTION OF CENTRE OF STAND MADE OF SOFTWOOD $\frac{1}{4}$" (6MM) THICK, GLUED AND PINNED

A 3" (7·62CM) × 1" (2·54CM) WOOD DOWEL ON EITHER SIDE OF THE SLIDING CENTRE SECTION HELPS TO BALANCE THE FRAME

$1\frac{1}{2}$" (3·81CM)

$1\frac{1}{2}$" (3·81CM)

APPROX. 30" (76·2CM)

$11\frac{1}{2}$" (29·21CM)

SQUARE HOLE CUT IN CENTRE

HIP PIECE IN $\frac{1}{4}$" (6·35CM) PLYWOOD

7" (17·78CM)

APPROX $1\frac{1}{4}$" (3·17CM) DEEP

1" (2·54CM) MESH GALVANISED WIRE NETTING APPROX. 32" (81·28CM) TO 38" (96·52CM) WIDE, DEPENDING ON BUST SIZE

A PIECE OF STRING PULLED TIGHTLY ROUND THE CYLINDER OF WIRE COMPRESSES THE WAIST EASILY

DOUBLED STRIPS OF WIRE FOR THE ARMS APPROX. 24" (60·96CM) LONG WITH 2" (5·08CM) TO HOOK IN AT THE TOP

CARDBOARD STRIP, APPROX. 15" (38·1CM) LONG, STUCK TO FABRIC

JOIN CARDBOARD STRIP FIRST AND THEN DRAW ROUND INNER CIRCUMFERENCE FOR THE SHAPE OF THE TOP

THIN CARDBOARD TOP FOR THE NECKPIECE STUCK TO THE FABRIC

INSIDE NECK PIECE SHOWING TABS BENT AND STUCK IN POSITION

THE FABRIC MUST BE STUCK VERY CAREFULLY TO AVOID MARKS ON THE RIGHT SIDE

135. Component parts of a wire netting dress stand with an adjustable wooden frame.

136. The cardboard neck-piece is covered with fabric to match the model. The neck size has to be judged after the dress is mounted.

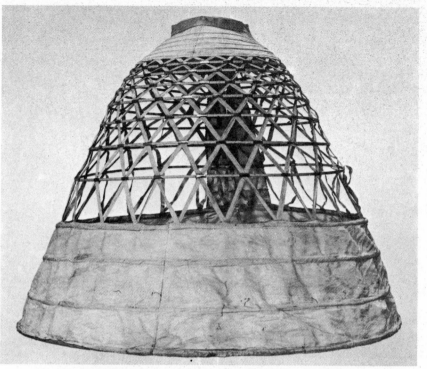

137, 138. It is often
difficult to get enough
dress stands for an
exhibition but some
objects can be dis-
played without them.
The crinoline petti-
coat of c. 1859 (left)
from the London
Museum and the
early bustle petticoat
of c. 1869–70 from
the Helen Larson
Collection (below
left) are suspended
from wooden discs
made to fit the
waist sizes.

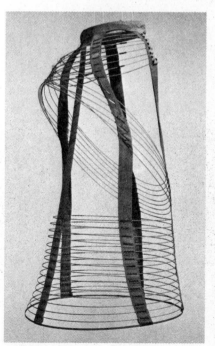

139. A printed
woollen dress of
c. 1856 (Red House
Museum, Christ-
church α12.64) is
mounted on the wire
netting dress stand
seen in plates 133
and 134. A crinoline
petticoat supports the
skirt and the sleeves
are filled out with
tissue paper.

Above left

*140. Added interest
is given to costumes
displayed against a
background made
from a blown–up
photograph or en-
graving, or, as in
this case, a scene in
a park painted by
Pandora Moore:
furniture and other
period accessories
help to set the
costumes in historical
perspective.
(Museum of Costume,
Bath)*

Above right

*141. Stands cheaply
and quickly made
from cylinders of
chicken wire moulded
to period shape,
reinforced with strips
of cane and covered
with tissue paper, to
display costumes for
The Importance of
Being Earnest in a
college exhibition.*

Right

*142. Soft gold slubbed rayon
organza was pleated into
loose folds to provide a rich
background for the Armada
dress in the exhibition of
costumes for the BBC TV
series Elizabeth R., at the
London Museum, 1971.*

Imaginative and informative displays do not always require large sums of money; what they do always need are thought, preliminary planning and plenty of time to carry them out.

ADDRESSES FOR MATERIALS
USED IN CONSERVATION AND DISPLAY

IMPERIAL CHEMICAL INDUSTRIES LTD, General Chemical Sales, Templar House, 81–87 High Holborn, London W.C.1. Tel. (01) 242 9711.
Suppliers of Lissapol synthetic detergent.

IMPERIAL CHEMICAL INDUSTRIES LTD, Plastics Division, Welwyn Garden City, Herts. Tel. Welwyn Garden 23400
Suppliers of ultra violet absorbing grades of perspex for framing textiles to minimise deterioration.

JANSON AND SON, 44 Great Russell Street, London W.C.1.
Suppliers of entomological pins.

MACCULLOCH AND WALLIS LTD, 25 Dering Street, London W.1. Tel. (01) 629 0311.
Suppliers of brass and lace pins. (Where the use of pins for mounting dresses is unavoidable, only rustless brass or stainless steel ones should be used).

PICREATOR ENTERPRISES LTD, 44 Park View Gardens, Hendon, London N.W.4. Tel. (01) 202 8972.
Suppliers of materials for conservation who will send leaflets on request about their own products which have been produced with members of the British Museum Conservation Department.

RUSSELL BOOKCRAFT, Bancroft, Hitchin, Herts. Tel. Hitchin (0462) 3567.
Suppliers of natural silk gauze, also called bookbinders' silk or crepeline.

SIEGEL AND STOCKMAN LTD, 22 Dering Street, London W.1. Tel. (01) 629 3722.
Suppliers of 1890s shaped dress stands designed for boutiques which are useful for museum display, as well as ordinary dress stands made in various styles.

SOME USEFUL BOOKS

BUCK, A. *Costume*. Museums Association, 1958. 5 pages of monochrome plates. A booklet on the development of costume collections, cataloguing, conservation, storage and display of costumes.

CORNFORTH, J. 'Conserving textiles in country houses'. In *Country Life*, 25 January, 1973.

DENMARK: *Report no. 525*, October 1965. Considerations relating to the organisation of conservation work in museums and libraries and the setting up of a training school for conservation. A report presented by the Government Committee set up by the Minister of Cultural Affairs in 1965. Text in Danish.

DUDLEY, D. H. and WILKENSON, I. B. *Museum Registration methods*. The American Association of Museums and the Smithsonian Institution, Washington, 1968 (revised edition).

FINCH, K. 'Conservation'. In *The so-called age of elegance*. Proceedings of the Costume Society Spring conference, 1970.

FINCH, K. 'Conservation of corps de ballet costume designed by Diaghilev for the *Firebird* ballet', in *Costume*, the Journal of the Costume Society no. 4. 1970.

GLOVER, J. *Costume conservation*. In the series of Museums Association Information sheets. 1974.

I.C.O.M. Committee for Conservation: *Natural dyestuffs, origin, chemical constitution and identification* by J'H. Hofenk-de Graaff. Amsterdam, 1969.

I.C.O.M. Committee for Conservation: *Products and instruments suitable for use in museums for protection against damage by light*. Draft no. 2. Compiled by Garry Thompson, July 1969.

INTERNATIONAL INSTITUTE FOR CONSERVATION OF HISTORIC AND ARTISTIC WORKS. Collected reports of the Conference on conservation of textiles. Delft, 1964.

LEENE, J. E. (Ed.) *Textile conservation*. Butterworth, 1972. Numerous monochrome plates and diagrams showing conservation methods in many museums. Wide ranging book with contributions from twenty conservators, all specialists in their own fields, on various aspects of cleaning and repair work.

LEMBERG, R. *Die Textilabeilung der Abegg-Stiftung Bern.* Abegg-Stiftung
Bern, 1970. Text in German. 30 monochrome plates showing ideal
conditions for textile conservation and storage.

MOORE, D. L. 'Costume display', in *The Museums Journal,* 11 February,
1961.

ORGAN, R. M. *Design for scientific conservation of antiquities.* Butterworth,
1968.

PLENDERLEITH, H. J. *The conservation of antiquities and works of art.* O.U.P.
1956. Contains a section on textile conservation.

STUDIES IN CONSERVATION, The Journal of the International Institute for
Conservation of Historic and Artistic Works. Central Research
Laboratory for Objects of Art and Science, Hobbemastraat 25,

IV. Costume for Children and Students

Clothes are the outward visible records of man's tribal characteristics, social position and individual personality. Their changing forms reflect changes of style in art and architecture in a sophisticated society. How should one introduce the subject? At what age is interest first awakened?

The earliest awareness of costume will come with dressing dolls and puppets from the age of four upwards. At this stage the basic differences between everyday dress and the uniform worn by nurse, bus conductor and policeman are recognised. Children begin to get a sense of historical perspective from about eight onwards [PLATE 144] and it is probably between the ages of nine and thirteen that costume can be most usefully employed to give a sense of 'time past'.

Topics for projects like 'The Egyptians', 'The Romans', 'Guy Fawkes' and 'The Battle of Trafalgar' give a great deal of scope and can involve literature, history, geography, drama, art, music and mathematics. Costume may be used to pinpoint differences between one type of society and another, or between various periods in history, since children first gain a sense of historical perspective from a visual understanding of how people looked in the past. Costume detail might be used for collage pictures, paintings or models made of wire, papier-mâché and waste materials painted or dressed with scraps of material [PLATES 143, 145, 146]. In schools boxes of reference material, clearly labelled, should be available (pages 203–5) and the children may work individually or in groups.

Fashions in the past were often restricting and children, who were dressed like miniature adults, suffered the same restrictions as their elders. Modern children can understand a great deal more

CANTEBURY TALES.

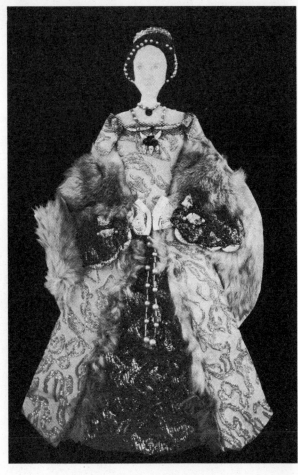

Above

143. Collage figures
designed from
primary sources of
the Tudor period by
a group of student
teachers.

Left

144. A drawing by
a child aged eight.

Right

145. Detail of a
figure from Plate 143.

146. The Three Wise Men, a collage picture by a group of student teachers.

Below

147, 148. A great deal can be learned about other periods when dressing up in copies of the clothes which earlier children wore. The corset and farthingale of the Elizabethan period enforce a stiff posture. The costume was made very cheaply from old curtains by Janet Hoffman, a student teacher.

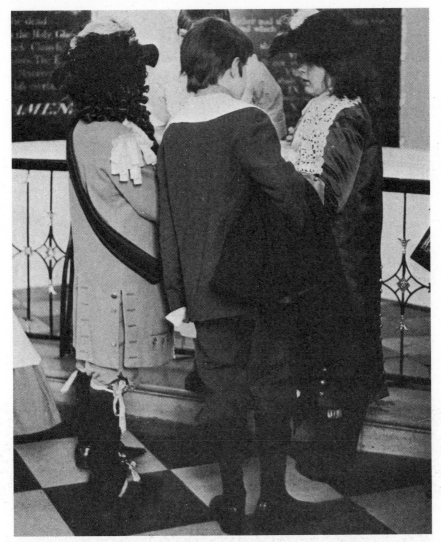

149. Children wearing reproduction period costumes made by Jean Hunnisett over their ordinary clothes for the performance of a play about Samuel Pepys. (Geffrye Museum, Shoreditch, London)

about their predecessors by dressing up in reproductions of period costumes [PLATES 147, 148]. The past begins to come alive as they realise the difficulties of managing hooped petticoats when sitting down or trying to run. All sorts of questions will occur to them and they can often find the answers by observation. Costumes used for this purpose need to be constructed accurately, copying the weight and design of the original fabric and method of fastening as far as possible (pages 231–232) although any teacher with a class of forty would be forgiven for using hooks and eyes and press studs instead of time-consuming pins and laces. The education departments of some museums (the Geffrye Museum, Shoreditch, for example), have a selection of reproduction period costumes available for school [PLATE 149] or other pre-arranged groups visiting the museum. It would also be possible for interested staff and students in any College of Education or Drama School teacher-training department to build up a collection for use with local schools.

Costume may also be used in a different way for improvised drama. Older children of ten and eleven can make their own costumes in simplified form, using imagination and ingenuity, from paper and scraps of old material; pictures of period costume should be used for inspiration and ideas, rather than the children attempting to copy them exactly, a task beyond their powers. Black tights and leotards or dark-coloured jeans with close-fitting jumpers provide the basic costume and the essential features of a period can be added. Elizabethan ruffs and other collars needing lace trimming can be made from paper doilies. Lengths of cheap fabric can be kept on cardboard rolls to avoid creasing and used time and time again for cloaks or skirts, easily adapted to any size with a drawstring put through the waist; different trimmings can be used for each occasion. A basic stock of a few old hats can be redecorated many times.

With older children and students the approach changes. Costume may be used in the same way as already described for project work, and it can also be used for individual studies. These may be within the areas of history (social background), geography (ethnographic studies), home economics (history of fashion and dressmaking), art (history of art) and drama (theatre design). The kind of work will depend on the viewpoint of the staff, the amount and type of preparation done, and the age range and capabilities of the children. The brief generalised outlines which follow describe the sort of work which can be done.

HISTORY (SOCIAL BACKGROUND)

A project can be centred on the study of a well-known person, for example Queen Elizabeth I, Oliver Cromwell, Pepys, Charles II, Jane Austen or Queen Victoria, and the age they lived in. The choice of personality may be suggested by a current film or a historical play seen on television. Other departments might ask for background investigations to be carried out when studying the work of a particular painter, musician, novelist, playwright, poet or scientist. The teacher's first aim is to give a clear visual impression of the person and period under study. A reproduction of a portrait can be used as a starting point for questions. This may only depict head and shoulders, and other pictures will be needed to show contemporary costume (pages 203–5). Perhaps a visit can be arranged to a local museum and art gallery to see real costumes with contemporary furniture and paintings of people who lived at the same time (pages 197–202). Afterwards, work can continue on other aspects of the period with a far greater understanding.

GEOGRAPHY (ETHNOGRAPHIC STUDIES)

The study of primitive people's costume in relation to climatic conditions and the availability of materials is a very obvious idea. The work would form part of a larger scheme and offer a number of possibilities for model-making and experiments with different fabrics.

The influence of geographical factors on the crystallisation of certain types of dress, for example regional costume in Holland, might prove a more difficult topic but would be of interest to sixth formers and necessitate wide reading. Many other influences are involved as well as geographical ones.

The *National Geographic Magazine* provides one of the best sources for photographic material. Local museums often have small ethnographic collections and the Commonwealth Institute, the Horniman Museum and the Museum of Mankind (the British Museum), all in London, have very good displays. While children may not be able to make long journeys from the provinces to visit these three museums, an interested teacher might be able to find time to collect ideas from their displays.

HOME ECONOMICS (THE HISTORY OF FASHION AND DRESSMAKING)

Work in this field can be practical as well as academic, giving a great deal of scope. Here are three ideas: a study of a costume or accessory either seen in a museum or brought in by the teacher; an individual study of cut and construction carried out on a quarter- or half-scale model [PLATE 154]; an illustrated essay on some aspect of costume.

The first may prove an even more valuable starting point than does the study of a reproduction of a portrait. Although the portrait gives an immediate picture of a well-known person, the glimpse of a costume folded carefully, wrapped in masses of tissue paper, never fails to arouse interest. The dress can come to life as it is mounted on a stand (page 159). It is most interesting to see a dress on a student (particularly 1930s bias-cut dresses) and expendable specimens may be set aside for this purpose, where the owner has checked that there are plenty of similar specimens in existence in local and national museums. Older and very rare dresses should of course never be treated in this way as textiles are the most fragile of all museum specimens. Constant handling and perspiration from the human body put additional strain on fibres already weakened by time and may eventually cause complete disintegration.

Detailed observation of a dress is best achieved by drawing it and this will give rise to many questions, for instance:

From what kind of material is it made – wool, silk, linen, cotton, synthetic or mixture?
How was it woven/embroidered/printed?
How has the fabric been cut, and is it on the straight grain of the material?
How has the shaping been achieved?
Has the stitching been carried out by hand or machine?
Are there any darts and if so are they in the same position as dress darts today?
Where are the seams positioned?
Where are the openings?
How does the dress fasten?
How would it have looked when originally worn?
What kind of underwear would be worn to provide the correct foundation?
What sort of accessories are needed?
Would it have been worn for day or evening occasions?
What kind of hairstyle would have been appropriate?

Many of these questions – and more – can be answered by personal observation; the last five can be answered by reference to the books listed in the Costume Bibliography.

The study of an accessory, a glove, a fan, a shoe or a scarf may present problems in dating and involve the question of style and decoration. It will mean a search through books on costume and the other primary sources to find the kind of dress that would have been worn with it. The questions are quickly formulated: when was it used, what material is it made of, and how is it made? Suppose the object to be a mid-eighteenth century shoe, this might lead to an examination of the plates in Diderot's *Encyclopédie* of 1751–72 reprinted in *A Diderot Pictorial Encyclopedia of Trades and Industry* (Dover, 1959) which show details of the equipment needed for shoemaking and the various parts of a shoe.

An illustrated essay on some aspect of costume [PLATES 150, 151] can interest adolescent girls and older students and encourage them to work on their own. It can also lead to practical work. The important point to remember is that a study of costume from the Egyptians to the present day is far too wide. If the choice is limited to one aspect of costume, or to a shorter period of time – perhaps

150. Illustrations for an essay on women's costume from 1920 to 1930 by a schoolgirl of fifteen.

151. Line drawing in white ink from a fashion plate to illustrate an essay, by Margaret Lavelle, a student teacher.

152. Clothes for a paper doll covering the period 1885–1905, made by a schoolgirl of fourteen.

twenty years – the study can cover the evolution of a style and note the relationship of the changing line of dress to the style of painting, furniture and architecture. This is of far more benefit than an unsuccessful attempt to cover a very wide period, with no time to understand it properly. It is also possible to build up a good background knowledge of costume by preparing a series of these essays.

The individual child or student can study cut and construction by making a quarter- or half-scale model doll and dressing it. The idea of a fashion doll is not a new one. Dolls dressed in the latest fashions were exchanged to give three-dimensional news from the mid-sixteenth to the early nineteenth century, when they were superseded by fashion plates. Cut-out paper dolls [PLATE 152] with large wardrobes of interchangeable clothes were very popular as children's toys during the nineteenth century. These ideas can be brought up to date, and the knowledge gained from working on the small scale models can be used for making stage costumes and accessories.

Instructions are given for making wire and papier-mâché models

[PLATE 153], as they possess far more character and period feeling than any mass-produced modern doll. They also give experience of working in another medium and an opportunity for individual work. This craft should be restricted to small groups – a class of not more than eighteen students – as it requires a great deal of individual supervision. It is unlikely to be very successful with children of less than fourteen who are not yet capable of handling all the different materials. The time required to make a doll depends entirely on the student's skill and the amount of detailed work put into it, but roughly $1\frac{1}{2}$–$2\frac{1}{4}$ hours a week for one term of twelve weeks should suffice if some of the sewing can be done in the student's own time. The teacher should make a model first to see where the difficulties lie.

It is advisable to make a thorough study of costume for a short period (not more than twenty years). If possible, the project should be carried out in conjunction with the history course. A selection of books on costume should be borrowed from the school and local libraries, to supplement mounted sheets of reproductions (see page 203). After a preliminary talk about the costume of the period, the student should make a drawing of a dress from the illustrations provided, or design one of her own if she feels confident enough. She should also make drawings of the petticoat and corset to be worn underneath, with details of the hairstyle, shoes, gloves and jewellery.

MAKING A QUARTER SCALE
WIRE AND PAPIER-MÂCHÉ MODEL DOLL

MATERIALS REQUIRED

1 lb coil of 16 gauge soft galvanised wire (approx. 30 yards/28 metres).

1 lb coil of 22 gauge soft galvanised wire (approx. 159 yards/151 metres).

Small pair of pliers.

Hammer.

Box of $\frac{1}{2}$ in. (1.27 cm) wire netting staples.

Small curved modelling tool.

Block of plywood for the base, $3\frac{1}{2}$ in. (8.89 cm) × $3\frac{1}{2}$ in. (8.89 cm) × $\frac{1}{2}$ in. (1.27 cm).

Plastic bowl for mixing papier-mâché.

Cotton wool or wadding for padding.

153. *A wire and papier-mâché model doll, made by a sixteen-year-old girl.*

154. *Wire and papier-mâché model dolls.*

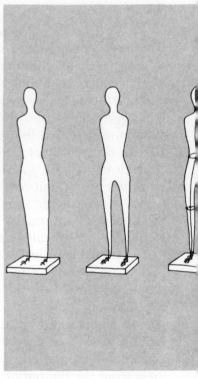

Newspapers.
Packet of 'Polycell' or cold water paste.
Powder paints, mixing palettes, brushes.

STAGES IN CONSTRUCTION
1. Cut one piece of 16 gauge wire 36 in. (91.44 cm) long for the body and one piece 34 in. (86.36 cm) long for the spine. Cut one piece of 16 gauge wire 17 in. (43.18 cm) long for the legs and two pieces of 16 gauge wire 17 in. (43.18 cm) long for the arms.
2. Cut the 22 gauge wire into a variety of lengths, e.g. 3 in. (7.62 cm) long for securing joins, 12 in. (30.48 cm) for twisting round the figure.
3. Bend the 36 in. (91.44 cm) length of wire in half and shape it into a silhouette figure, keeping the head fairly small.
Bend 1 in. (2.54 cm) forwards for the feet.
4. Bend the 17 in. (43.18 cm) length of wire for the legs in half and then bend 1 in. (2.54 cm) forwards for the feet.
5. Gently hammer the staples into the plywood block, leaving a space to tuck in the wire.

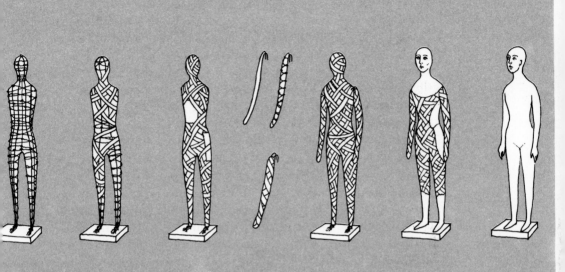

6. Fold the 34 in. (86.36 cm) length of wire in half. Shape it to form the spine and diaphragm and secure it with 22 gauge wire at the head, neck, waist, knees and feet. Bend 1 in. (2.54 cm) forwards for the feet.

7. Hammer the staples firmly into the plywood block to secure all the pieces of wire.

8. Twist the lengths of 22 gauge wire round the figure to form a framework. Twist each piece round the 16 gauge wire to secure it. Do not pull the 16 gauge wires close together.

9. Tear the newspaper into long strips approximately $\frac{1}{2}$ in. (1.27 cm) wide.

10. Brush the strips of newspaper with 'Polycell' or cold-water paste. Take each piece as it is pasted and twist it firmly round the model, turning the model round to see it from all angles, until the model is built up adequately into the shape of the corseted figure of the selected period. Cotton wool or small pieces of paper, folded and pasted to form padding, may be used where necessary for the hips, diaphragm and legs. Do not build up the head yet.

11. Fold the two 17 in. (43.18 cm) lengths of wire in half for the arms, bending over the ends for 1 in. (2.54 cm). Shape them, making the rounded ends for the hands fairly small. Twist 22 gauge wire round them to make a framework.

12. Stick layers of newspaper and padding round the arms until they are shaped. Do not put more than one layer of newspaper on the hands or they will look too big. Leave the model and the arms to dry away from direct heat for four days.

13. Prepare the papier-mâché while the model is drying. Shred newspaper into tiny pieces and leave them to soak in a bowl of water to become soft and malleable. When the paper has been soaked for several days it disintegrates. Rub it very gently between the hands in the water to aid this process. Strain the contents of the bowl through muslin and add some 'Polycell' until it becomes almost like modelling clay to handle. The papier-mâché can be boiled in a galvanised bucket for half an hour before straining it, stirring frequently. This method reduces the paper to pulp more quickly and removes any lumps, and the paper need not be soaked for more than twenty-four hours.

14. Stab holes on either side of each shoulder and hook in the arms. Twist some paper strips over them and stick firmly to make the shoulders smooth. The arms are capable of a little movement.

15. Model the head, shoulders and feet with papier-mâché, adding more 'Polycell' until it sticks firmly. Keep turning the model round to see it from all angles. Leave it to dry as before.

16. The face, neck and hands may need building up by pasting small pieces of paper over the papier-mâché, to give a smooth surface.

17. When completely dry, paint the model all over with powder paint, mixing it fairly thickly and avoiding air bubbles. Two coats may be needed to conceal the newsprint.

18. Paint the features with powder paint or poster paints using a fine sable brush. Try to capture the characteristic appearance of the cosmetics of the chosen period.

The teacher may prefer to prepare the models as far as stage 5, to save time in the classroom. The dolls may be made in any size, but the $\frac{1}{4}$ scale model simplifies the pattern cutting and dressmaking instructions. The quantities of wire given above make a $\frac{1}{4}$ scale model with these measurements: height $16\frac{1}{2}$ in. (41.91 cm), waist 6 in. (15.24 cm)–$6\frac{1}{2}$ in. (16.51 cm), length of shoulder $1\frac{1}{4}$ in. (3.17

cm), bust $8\frac{1}{2}$ in. (21.59 cm)–9 in. (22.86 cm), hips $8\frac{1}{2}$ in. (21.59 cm)–
9 in. (22.86 cm), length of front neck to waist $3\frac{3}{4}$ in. (9.52 cm),
length of back neck to waist $4\frac{1}{8}$ in. (10.47 cm). It is best to keep the
figure fairly slim. The model may be lightly padded with cotton
wool before dressing it.

Models may also be made from strips of white cotton material
twisted over a wire framework and covered with old nylon
stockings, felt or other fabrics seamed together, but the papier-
mâché variety is firmer for sticking in pins.

The wire framework may also be constructed from 1 in. (2.54 cm)
mesh galvanised wire netting; it can be made quickly but is a little
more difficult to handle as the wire is stiff (see page 19 *Patterns of
Fashion 1860–1940* by Janet Arnold).

For patterns and diagrams showing construction see the books
listed on page 231. Petticoats should be made to provide the
correct shape for the skirt. The dress should always be cut in
cheap cotton, fitted on the model and adjusted. If marked carefully
and then unpinned, the pieces can be used as a pattern, cutting the
dress material on the same grain.

The fabric and trimmings must be chosen carefully. They must
be fairly light in weight and the design must be in scale with the
model. The fabric must resemble the original material in miniature
in texture, weave and pattern. Silk, fine wool, cotton lawn, striped
poplin, nylon gauze, velvet and taffetas with small patterns in
lurex thread are particularly suitable. Narrow lampshade braid,
silk and cotton fringing, cotton and nylon lace, Russian braid and
tiny beads may be obtained cheaply in most large department and
chain stores. Narrow crossway or straight strips of the same material
as the dress may be pinked and pleated up to resemble eighteenth-
century trimmings.

It is best to dress the model completely before arranging the
hair. Wigs may be made from plumbers' tow, unravelled silk, or
wool stitched securely on a skull cap of cotton lawn, which is then
stuck on the head with Copydex, rubber solution or all-purpose
clear adhesive. Crepe hair, which may be obtained in plaits of
various shades can also be used. It should be unplaited and steamed
if it is to be straightened, and cut and stuck straight onto the
papier-mâché head. For piled-up eighteenth-century wigs a rolled
and stitched base of cotton wool or wadding should be pinned
securely onto the head; crepe hair may then be stuck on top.

Hats may be made from 'Vilene' interlining or some other stiff fabric covered with material and secured with adhesive, or from strip straw. Narrow ribbons, little coloured feathers and artificial flowers, in proportion to the rest of the costume, may be stitched on for trimming. Keep a large box well stocked with beads, scraps of ribbon and other materials which can be used for making jewellery, hats and wigs.

It is important to keep the model in a polythene bag when not working on it. When it is finished you can make a transparent box of stiff acetate with a cardboard base and top, for display purposes.

ART (HISTORY OF ART) AND DRAMA (THEATRE DESIGN)

The art teacher may have an interest in costume as it relates to the history of art and style, or as the subject matter of a painting, in the treatment of the fabric or the way the costume has forced a particular pose for a portrait.

Probably the most general use for costume study in the art department is for designing and making costumes for stage productions, sometimes in co-operation with the home economics department. The different ways of using costume for this purpose are treated on pages 206–16, and the work is sometimes done entirely by the drama department.

The teacher must be prepared to do a considerable amount of groundwork before embarking on a project of this type. The same stages of preparation as in the professional theatre must be carried out to achieve reasonable results, although obviously they can be simplified for amateur work. An actual worksheet and reading list of the kind given to College of Education students for six months' study away from college gives some idea of the amount of help which is needed. In a school the children would study the play in their English lessons and be familiar with plot and characters, and would work on the costume design during their art lessons.

THE TAMING OF THE SHREW—WORKSHEET

Read the play thoroughly and make a brief synopsis of the action in each scene.

Read the notes given by the producer and set designer on Elizabethan period style and the colour schemes they have in mind.

Make a list of the characters.

Make rough sketches from the primary sources, ie. paintings, engravings, tapestries etc. for ideas for the costumes.

Work out colour schemes for all the characters.

Use little scraps of fabric to give the texture as well as the colour. If you do not have enough material, use paint or coloured paper from magazines. If these are arranged on separate cards, you can move them about to see how the colour schemes will change in each scene.

Using the sketches made from the primary sources, make rough sketches, on separate sheets of paper, for the costumes needed for each character.

Make the final designs for costumes with samples of fabric you would like to use. Remember the producer's note that the designs can be inspired by the Elizabethan period. They do not need to be exact copies.

TEMPORARY EXHIBITIONS OPEN AT THE TIME

The Elizabethan Image   Tate Gallery
Costumes for the BBC television series *The Six Wives of Henry VIII*   Bethnal Green Museum

PLATES 155 TO 164 ARE PHOTOGRAPHS TAKEN AT INTERVALS DURING TWELVE WEEKS SHOWING STUDENTS AT WORK ON A PRODUCTION OF 'NOYES FLUDDE', AN OPERA BY BENJAMIN BRITTEN BASED ON THE CHESTER MIRACLE PLAY, PRODUCED AT AVERY HILL COLLEGE OF EDUCATION IN 1970

Below left

155. Preliminary drawings from medieval primary sources by Judy Hindle.

Below right

156. Designs by Judy Hindle for costumes using colours and shapes seen in stained glass windows.

157. Simplified costume shapes with a limited colour range based on medieval costume but with a view to using existing material. Susan Urry.

158. Masks were needed for eighty singers playing the animals entering the Ark. Many children were involved both in singing and mask making for the production.

159. Design for Mr Japhet by Jill Pooley, giving a lively interpretation of the medieval period with highly textured fabric surfaces.

160. *A series of designs by one student was finally selected, and here she compares the colour range and shapes with the design. Small adjustments are often carried out during fittings, affecting for example the amount of material in a sleeve or the shape of a neckline, and sometimes a design is completely changed while the costume is being made.*

161. *Thick paper shapes masked the cotton tunic while dye was applied with a plastic foam roller. This was quicker than fabric collage but gave less surface texture.*

Above left

162. *The folds in the fabric shown in the designs were freely interpreted with a collage of nets, and other materials mounted on basic T-shaped cotton garments dyed to the required colours. Newspaper patterns were used to cut the different pieces of fabric, which were then zig-zag machined to the cotton bases.*

Above right

163. *As the costumes were simple T-shapes little fitting was required, but adjustments for length were necessary.*

Right

164. *One of the Gossips on stage in a finished costume in shades of flame, orange and dark red.*

BOOK LIST (SELECTED FROM BOOKS
AVAILABLE IN THE COLLEGE LIBRARY)

AUERBACH, E.	*Nicholas Hilliard*, Routledge & Kegan Paul, 1961
BENTIVEGNA, F. C.	*Abbigliamento e costume della pittura Italiana Vol I: Rinascimento*, Carlo Bestetti, 1962
BOUCHER, F.	*History of Costume in the West*, Thames & Hudson, 1968
CAMDEN, C.	*The Elizabethan Woman*, Cleaver Hume, 1952
CUNNINGTON, C. W. & CUNNINGTON, P.	*Handbook of English Costume in the Sixteenth Century*, Faber, 1954
DAVENPORT, M.	*The Book of Costume*, Crown Publishers Inc., New York, 1948
DIGBY, G. W.	*Elizabethan Embroidery*, Faber, 1963
LAVER, J.	*Early Tudor 1485–1558* (Costume of the Western World Series), Harrap, 1951
LEVI-PISETZKY, R.	*Storia del costume in Italia* Vol. III, 16–17th centuries: Instituto Editoriale Italiano, Milan, 1964
MORSE, H. K.	*Elizabethan Pageantry*, Studio, 1934
REYNOLDS, G.	*Elizabethan and Jacobean 1558–1625* (Costume of the Western World Series), Harrap, 1951
ROSSARO, M.	*The Life and Times of Elizabeth I* (Portraits of Greatness series), Paul Hamlyn, 1967
STRONG, R.	*Portraits of Queen Elizabeth I*, O.U.P., 1963
STRONG, R.	*The English Icon*, Routledge & Kegan Paul, 1969
STRONG, R.	*Tudor & Jacobean Portraits*, 2 vols. H.M.S.O., 1969

One common need, whatever the approach or the subject within which costume is being studied, is for a great deal of preparatory work by the teacher to make sure that the children or students can find most of the answers to their questions by their own efforts. The first and quickest sources of information on any aspect of costume are the books in the school or college library, and the local public lending or reference library. Many of those on costume written specifically for children are illustrated with

over-simplified drawings which do not give any indication of
period style, but books on other aspects of social history provide
plenty of illustrations from primary source material. A collection
of reproductions, preferably in colour, showing costume has
the additional advantage of familiarising children with works of
art (see page 203). Museum publications make a good basis for a
section on costume in the school library as they are usually inexpensive and well illustrated with photographs of actual specimens.

Work of this type may be undertaken on the school or college
premises with material provided by the teacher. Additional interest
can be given by material supplied by the local city or county
museum schools loan services. These are rapidly expanding in size
and number and often welcome ideas for displays and suggestions
for projects from teachers. Although the initial display may take
time, the same material may be used over and over again by many
different schools which are too far from a museum to make visits
a practical possibility.

For the schools near a museum, regular visits can provide an
impetus or further stimulus to work (page 197).

THE USE OF THE LIBRARY

It is most important to do some background reading before trying
to use the primary sources. Obviously it is perfectly possible to go
into a museum, art gallery or country house and enjoy looking at
all the objects on display, but if children and students are to get the
most out of a visit, some preparation should be done beforehand.

The card index drawers in the library are the place to start, and
it is essential to be familiar with the various systems of cataloguing
books so that no time is wasted. The school library may only
consist of a few shelves of books, grouped under subject titles and
arranged in alphabetical order according to the author's name. The
local public library will have thousands of books arranged on the
open shelves in a similar way, and in many the Dewey Decimal
system of cataloguing will be used. In both it is possible to browse
and to examine the books individually. In the reference library
the majority of the books are stored away from the general public
and a hunt through the card index drawers becomes an essential
part of the process of finding a book.

All books printed since 1950 are listed in *The British National Bibliography* which is available in the local public reference library. This is a subject list in annual volumes of British books published since 1950, based upon the books deposited in the Copyright Office of the British Museum with full author, title and subject indexes. The bibliography is in two sections: in the first (classified) section, the entries are arranged according to the Dewey Decimal system of subject classification with full details of title, price, number of pages, illustrations, size, series and publisher; in the second (author and title) section, the entries are arranged alphabetically, giving the author and the short title of the book, and the publisher and price. Hints for tracing information are given in the front.

Costume covers dress and fashion and is listed with Social Customs and Folklore under the classification numbers 390–398 as follows:

390 General Works
391 Costume
392 Family, marriage customs
394 Social customs
395 Etiquette
396 Women
398 Folklore

Clothing is listed as a separate subject and includes books on the manufacture of garments and the economics of the dress trade. It is also worth looking under Textiles and Local History for books which have useful information on costume.

Libraries will give advice on using *The British National Bibliography*, *The Aslib Directory*, *The Costume Index*, *The Art Index*, and *The British Union Catalogue*. *The Aslib Directory* is a guide to sources of information in Great Britain and Ireland. It lists national libraries, university libraries, public and county libraries, and libraries and information departments of societies and other organisations capable of providing specialised information. *The Costume Index* by Munro and Cook provides a subject index to plates and illustrated texts. *The Art Index* is a cumulative author and subject index to a selected list of fine arts periodicals and museum bulletins from 1933 onwards. *The British Union Catalogue* provides a record of the periodicals of the world from the seventeenth century to the present day in British libraries.

In the larger reference libraries and specialised libraries like that of the Victoria and Albert Museum, the books are given shelf numbers and entered in both subject and author catalogues so that they can be located easily. The reader enters the title, author's name, date of publication and accession (shelf) number on a form, and the staff obtain the book for him. These libraries may at first seem a little intimidating with serried rows of desks and catalogues and it takes a little time to get used to working in them, but one is soon accustomed to the routine and further catalogue searching can be done while waiting half an hour for the books to arrive. The staff will explain the catalogue system to newcomers.

Lists of books illustrated with photographs of primary sources which show costume follow each section in the chapter on Primary Sources (page 11). An introductory bibliography for teachers and students who are beginning to study costume is given on page 217. Many of these books are available from the local public lending or reference library. Some of the more rare or foreign publications may not be so easy to obtain but it is possible to borrow many of them through the National Central Library Service at any local public library. This may take some weeks, so the books should be ordered well in advance and postage must usually be paid by the borrower. These books can always be consulted by the serious student in the specialised libraries, for example the Victoria and Albert Museum and the British Museum Reading Room, where admission tickets are required. Accommodation is limited and admission is restricted to those readers who need facilities for research and reference which are not readily available in other libraries normally accessible to them.

The British Museum subject and author catalogues are printed and available in some other reference libraries as well as in the Reading Room, so that the enthusiast can work away from London, listing books for use when time permits, if they are not available locally. *The Subject Index* published by the Trustees in 1965, notes under Costume, 'See also Dress; tailoring; toilet; brooch; buttons; embroidery; fans; feathers; fur; jewellery; lace; masks; weapons; and under individual articles of apparel e.g. girdles; gloves; hats; shawls; etc. For stage and cinema costumes see Drama; scenic art and cinematography. For Hairdressing see hair.' This list may prove helpful for students as it gives some idea of the categories under which costume may be found.

The Victoria and Albert Museum Library has a general catalogue of costume books and *Costume*, an index to the more important material in the library with annotations and shelf marks, compiled by C. H. Gibbs-Smith in 1936.

Many source books with contemporary information and illustrations are listed in the foot notes and bibliographies of the costume books in the Costume Bibliography starting on page 217, and in the primary source lists on pages 115–18. These form a good starting point for a search in the catalogue. Accident, simple guesswork and luck can often produce an interesting selection of books when neither authors nor titles are known. On one occasion, information was required on costume worn for physical education in the nineteenth century. There seemed to be no books on the subject, but a search through the *Subject Index of Books published before 1880* compiled by R. A. Peddie in 1933 produced this series of illustrated books listed under calisthenics and gymnastics: *An elementary course of Gymnastics* by Peter Henry Clias, 1823; *An Elementary Course of Gymnastic Exercises . . . including swimming* by Captain P. H. Clias, 1825; *The Elements of Gymnastics for Boys and of Calisthenics for Young Ladies* by Gustavus Hamilton, 1827, and *The Gymnastic Polymachinon* by Captain Chiosso, 1855. The illustrations for gymnastics were invaluable and swimming costumes were noted for future reference.

This searching does take time and the enthusiast must read quickly, cultivating the art of skimming a page and picking out the essential words. A note should also be made of all books used, with their accession numbers in different libraries, to save searching the catalogue more than once. One can keep a small card index file, or write the titles in a series of looseleaf notebooks.

THE USE OF MUSEUMS

LETTERS TO MUSEUMS

The collections of costume in museums are obviously a wonderful source of information, but a great deal of work must be done by teachers, children and students before asking museum staff for help.

The method of teaching through personal discovery is used in schools all over the country. Unfortunately a great many teachers do not realise how much material they must have available in the classroom and how much preparation is necessary for this type of work, so that children can learn how to find things out for themselves. Almost inevitably they allow the children to write letters, asking for information which could quite easily be obtained from books and by visiting the local museum, using it as an extension of the classroom for discovery purposes.

To the Victoria and Albert Museum

Dear Sir,
Please could you send me various information on costume through the ages.
Yours faithfully,

This genuine letter from a ten-year-old child gives some idea of the problem which increasingly faces museum staff. The teacher had done little or no preparation and the 'various information' requested could have been looked up in the school or local public library. If teachers and lecturers encourage children and students to write to museums they should vet the letters and make sure that the request is for a list of museum publications or for specific information, perhaps following a museum visit.

To the Victoria and Albert Museum

Dear Sir,
I am a student of the ——— Technical College and I am required to prepare a paper on ——— (space provided for student to fill in the subject).
Your name has been given to me as a specialist in this field and I would appreciate any information that you care to send me.
None of this information will be published but will be used for academic purposes only.
Yours faithfully,

This letter is included here as a warning and to discourage other lecturers and teachers from producing similar documents. It was typed and duplicated by a member of staff for students to fill in. Students must be trained to think for themselves and to carry out their own research. This point must be repeated many times, however elementary it seems.

One important point which emerges after reading a selection of students' letters is that it is foolish for a lecturer to encourage a student living on a small grant in Newcastle to undertake a subject for which all the relevant material is in London or Paris. Unless the student can afford to travel, disappointment is the usual result. If the student is really enthusiastic, then ways of working on inaccessible material will be found, but most students would be well advised to discover what is available locally and find a topic of interest which is within the bounds of possibility. A study of the primary sources of costume may suggest some new ideas and fields of study.

> To the Victoria and Albert Museum
> Dear Madam,
> I am studying 'Ladies' Riding Habits in the Nineteenth Century' for my special study. I have taken notes from articles in *Myra's Journal* and made sketches from the illustrations. Do you have any riding habits in the reserve collection? I have found several fashion plates which show riding habits but I would like to look at some real ones to see what kind of material was used. Would it be possible to draw them or take photographs?
> Yours sincerely,

The student has a clear idea of what she is doing and has asked for specific information, of the sort that museum staff can usually supply quickly and easily.

To summarise, a letter asking for help with a costume study should give its title, some idea of the background reading already done and other material studied, if any. The request should relate specifically to the collections and publications of the particular museum to which the letter is addressed. Time is limited and museum staff have many other duties apart from replying to hundreds of letters asking for 'some information on costume from the Egyptians to the present day'.

ARRANGING A MUSEUM VISIT

Work in a museum must be planned carefully to integrate it with class projects or the individual student's work, otherwise the whole point of the visit may be lost.

Ideally the teacher or lecturer should make a preliminary visit to the museum to select the costumes which relate to the work at hand. She may prepare a worksheet with questions which lead the children or students from case to case allowing them time to examine objects carefully, read the attached labels and make drawings and notes for themselves. She may prefer to talk to the group on arrival at the museum, ask them questions and rely on their memories. The second method has obvious disadvantages if the museum is crowded and the group is large, since half of them will not be able to hear the instructions properly.

It is only courteous for a teacher to write in advance notifying the museum of the intended visit. In a small museum it may be impossible to cater for more than one party of forty children at the same time. Some museums have education services. If a teacher needs help, she should write in advance to arrange for a museum teacher to talk to a group of children or students and help to start them working afterwards.

Sometimes the costumes the teacher would like to use are not on display. In most museums approximately a quarter of the objects are on show and three-quarters are in the reserve collection. If material which is not on show is needed and a request is made sufficiently far in advance of a visit, the museum may be able to produce examples from store and sometimes even set up a special display.

Where the school or college is too far from a museum for visits to be practical, there are often schools loans services organised by the city or county museum.

These are general observations about planning museum visits which might apply to any subject. Let us now be specific and look at some schemes for the study of costume.

This is an example of a very basic worksheet which could be adapted to suit different age ranges.

1. Look at the portrait of the lady, painted in 1860, which is in the front hall. Describe her dress and make a drawing of it. Who painted it?
2. Draw and/or describe a similar dress on display in Room 3. Was it worn for day or evening?
3. Choose a parasol, a pair of shoes, a shawl and a fan which are of the same date. Draw and describe them. At what time of day would they have been used?

4. What are the differences between the dress shown in case 6 and the one in case 7? Make notes and sketches. Put down the date of each dress.

5. How was the skirt of the dress in case 5 supported? Make notes and drawings from case 2, which shows underwear.

This worksheet can be extended to involve work in other galleries, for example relating furniture styles to dress shapes; questions can be asked about the costumes worn by people in a story, novel or play which the group have been studying, for example *The Railway Children, Pride and Prejudice, She Stoops to Conquer.*

This method allows individual work. A choice of questions can be given and large groups need never be gathered round the same object, obscuring the view for the general public and elbowing each other for space in which to draw.

The study of costume in a museum may lead to the study of many other things – the textiles used for a costume, and the way in which the designs were printed, woven or embroidered, the processes involved in making a dress, the tools which were used and how they were made. Or it might awaken an interest in one of the primary sources, rather than in costume itself and hence lead to other studies.

The most important task is to encourage curiosity, to train the questioner to observe an object carefully, to record it accurately, to relate other material to it and finally to answer for him or herself the question which he or she has asked.

It is always difficult to give adequate individual attention to large numbers of students in a museum when time and space are limited. One solution is to give a talk with plenty of coloured slides showing enlargements of the objects which are to be seen later. Another method is to prepare a written commentary on the objects, with particular details to be noted. Many people need training to look carefully and simply do not see things unless they are pointed out. The best way of observing an object is to draw and write a detailed description of it, but if time is limited and older students are embarrassed about their drawing ability a slide lecture and a written commentary are better than nothing.

The commentary should give as much detailed information as possible that is not already on the labels in the museum. This is a specimen from a series of notes giving information on the cut and

construction of costumes displayed at the London Museum for a
special study session titled *La Belle Epoque 1890–1914* (the full
commentary was published in *La Belle Epoque*, Costume Society
1967).

1. 34/61/2 *c*.1892–3
Lemon ottoman silk evening dress. Label on waistband of
bodice – *Madame Bishop, 19 Sussex Place, Queens Gate, S.W.*

Fully boned bodice lined with lemon cotton sateen and
opening at the centre front with hooks and eyes.

The treble puffed sleeve is mounted on top of a straight close
fitting foundation sleeve in lemon cotton sateen.

Leaver's lace sleeve flounces and gathered frill round the neck.

Note the arrangement of the pleats at centre front and centre
back bodice.

The skirt has a smooth centre front panel slightly gored with
three gores on each side (see diagram 1).

The two gored side panels are eased in to the waistband. The
remaining four gores are gathered tightly in at the centre back.
This fullness is held in position with tapes tied across the centre
back, fifteen inches down from the waistline. The hem is
interlined for twelve inches at the front and eighteen inches at
the centre back. Coarse Leaver's lace is mounted on a stiff
pleated muslin frill inside the hem. The hemline is padded to hold
it out.

There were seventeen items, and diagrams were provided to
explain the cut of the dresses. This amount of detailed information
is needed to cater for the wide range of interest of a large group of
people.

It is possible to talk about a costume quite easily to five
students and be certain that everyone can see and hear properly;
with more than this number problems arise. A group of ten can
be halved and individual attention can be given to one group at a
time, while the others work on their own. This is still possible up
to twenty although the time for individual attention has decreased.
More than this number and it is better to provide a written commentary or give a slide lecture.

Students will need time to look for and study the primary
sources at first hand. The guide which follows was given to a group

of theatre costume students for use with a worksheet after a lecture at college. It applies specifically to the Victoria and Albert Museum, London, but it provides useful pointers for a visit to any major Museum.

SOURCES FOR COSTUME STUDY
AT THE VICTORIA AND ALBERT MUSEUM

1. *The Costume Court* provides a permanent exhibition of costumes from *c.*1600–*c.*1950 with accessories. Related fashion plates and photographs of paintings are also on display. Guide pamphlet available.

2. *The Library* – Books and periodicals on the subject of costume may be seen in the specialist library on the first floor. The catalogue is in the end room.

3. *Department of Prints and Drawings, Room 71* – Drawings and engravings showing dress and theatrical costume designs are often exhibited. If not, they may be studied in the department. Ask to be shown the catalogue. Space is limited so please make sure that your request is specific.

4. *Primary sources*, e.g. paintings, carvings, tapestries, etc. all over the Museum.

Metalwork Department, by the Library –

(a) English warming-pan *c.*1650, no. 1462–1870. Shows a man and woman in costume of the period.

(b) Indicating lock in case on the wall, signed Johannes Wilkes, *c.*1680, no. M.109–1926. Shows a man walking, wearing costume of the period.

(c) Memorial brasses on the wall.

Textile Study Room 101 –

(a) Valances for a bed, *c.*1580–90 in case on the wall. Shows people in Elizabethan costume.

(b) English domestic embroideries in case just outside Room 101, in the corridor. Seventeenth-century stump work embroidery with little figures in contemporary costume, padded and raised from the surface of the fabric. Casket 1678, no. T.43–1954. English embroidered picture *c.*1680–90, no. T.49–1954.

Tapestry Rooms, near the Restaurant – Two rooms with tapestries all over the walls showing hunting scenes etc. of the fifteenth and sixteenth centuries.

Room 24, near the Restaurant – A case with an altarpiece, English, late fourteenth-century, nos. A.48, 49, 50, 51 and 52–1946. Figures in costume.

Room 20 – Pearwood altarpiece, Piedmontese, early sixteenth century. Crowds of figures with good details of dress.

Staircase by the Exhibition Road Entrance – Two designs for theatrical costume by Bernardo Buontalerdi (1536–1608). Florentine, c.1589, no. E.614–1936.

First room by the Exhibition Road Entrance – Two marble busts by Ridolfo Sirigatti, of his parents Niccolo and Cassandra Sirigatti, dated 1578. Florentine.

On staircase leading up from the Exhibition Road Entrance – Two bed valances, late sixteenth century, show people in Elizabethan costume.

Room 53 – Cases of coifs, jackets and gloves, lace trimmed collars and purses, all early seventeenth century.

Room 54 – Cravat of carved limewood c.1680 by Grinling Gibbons.

Room 55 – Miniature paintings from the sixteenth century to the early eighteenth century, by Nicholas Hilliard, Isaac Oliver, Samuel Cooper etc.

Room 58 – Two paintings by Devis –
   (a) The Duet, 1749.
   (b) Miss Elizabeth Hemyng, c.1740.

Room 57A – Miniature paintings from the mid-eighteenth century to the early nineteenth century.

Staircase leading down to the Jones collection – Paintings of 1616 showing the Ommeganck annual procession at Brussels, commemorating the translation of the Miraculous Image of the Virgin from Antwerp to the Church of Notre Dame de Sablon, Brussels. These paintings show early stage settings as well as costume.

Music Gallery over the Costume Court – A painted lid from the outer case of a spinet, sixteenth century, Italian. Shows costume of c.1540–50

Objects are often moved and temporary exhibitions arranged; the teacher should always visit the museum prior to sending students, if it is at all possible, as the work or guide sheet prepared six weeks before may need alteration. This applies to every museum and art gallery.

THE COLLECTION OF PRIMARY SOURCE MATERIAL REPRODUCTIONS

One of the essential aids for studying costume is a collection of reproductions showing primary source material, which can be handled easily.

Obviously it is possible to spend a lot of money on glossy photographs ordered specially from museums. However, articles in weekend newspaper colour supplements, art magazines, calendars, greeting cards and catalogues from sale rooms, e.g. Christie's and Sotheby's, often provide large coloured, as well as black and white, reproductions of paintings showing costume.

165. These light card-mounts include a reproduction from a calendar, post cards from various museums, pages from a booklet and part of an article from a weekend newspaper colour supplement, all of which show costume detail, the majority in colour. Enclosed in polythene bags they will withstand constant handling.

Museums and art galleries produce postcards of items in their collections at very reasonable prices and illustrated museum booklets like those from the Gallery of English Costume, Manchester, or inexpensive art books – for instance the Fontana-Unesco series – can be purchased specifically in order to obtain reproductions for mounting. Some of the publications from the Metropolitan Museum, New York, and the Geffrye Museum, London, are produced with perforated pages and are obviously intended to be used in this way. If reproductions are mounted on stiff card, enclosed in a closely-fitting polythene bag and stored in heavy cardboard boxes for further protection, they will last a long time and withstand continual handling [PLATE 165].

An elementary cataloguing system is required for easy access and as a start a box can be allocated for each century. The reproductions can be sorted into categories of 'men', 'women' and 'children', or the century can be divided into shorter periods of ten or twenty years, with pictures of all types of dress within the same period in one box. I have found this second method to be the easier one for use with students. There are many paintings of family groups and one would need three reproductions to show 'men', 'women' and 'children' for one painting, which means an increase in cost as well as volume. It is also easier to sort the cards back into their correct boxes after use, if one only has the date to consider.

Individual college students should make a collection of reproductions of primary source material including their own drawings and photographs for reference purposes. This is absolutely essential for the theatre designer, amateur or professional, particularly if working away from London.

The following museums and art galleries provide particularly wide ranges of postcards, colour slides and booklets of items in the collections showing costume. In addition many costume collections have their own publications.

Bodleian Library, Oxford OX1 3BG
Illuminated manuscripts

British Museum, Great Russell Street, London, W.C.1.

Engravings, wall paintings, sculpture, illuminated manuscripts, jewellery, coins, medals and seals.

The National Gallery, Trafalgar Square, London W.C.2.
Paintings.

The National Portrait Gallery, St Martin's Place, London W.C.2.
Paintings, silhouettes, daguerrotypes and *cartes-de-visite*. These are all portraits of well-known people and are useful for details of hairstyles and wigs as well as clothes.

Victoria and Albert Museum, South Kensington, London S.W.7.
Fashion plates, engravings, jewellery, miniatures, carvings, porcelain figures, silhouettes, reproductions of brass rubbings.

Lists of publications and prices should be sent for as new items are continually being added.

Filmstrips which can be cut up as individual slides are available in the categories of Fine Arts, Social History, Textiles etc. from Visual Publications, 197 Kensington High Street, London W86 BB. A list of publications and prices will be sent on request.

V. Costume for the Stage

Designing costumes for theatrical productions of any kind involves a certain routine. Occasionally the producer of a play or opera is also the designer of both set and costumes, but it is more usual to find the design work done separately and often by two people. This chapter is concerned with the work of the costume designer. The amateur or student cannot do better than follow some of the methods used in the professional theatre and for television; the increasing use of closed circuit television in schools and colleges makes the careful presentation of designs for this medium very necessary.

Exhibitions of designs and costumes from the professional theatre and television are often on display; for example *Staging the Romans* at the Hayward Gallery, London, in 1973 showed costumes for the RSC productions of *Antony and Cleopatra, Julius Caesar, Titus Andronicus*, and *Coriolanus*.

The costume designer's first job is to read the play thoroughly and make a list of the characters, with rough notes of his ideas. Usually the two designers work fairly closely together in the early stages until their ideas have been formulated and the producer has decided on the overall look of the play.

The costume designer needs to know fairly early on if there are to be many walkers-on (ladies-in-waiting and soldiers for example) as all these people will need costumes as well as the leading characters. Amateur producers should be discouraged from adding extra members to the cast, once the budget has been allocated.

There seem to be four main approaches to costume design. A play can be presented as an accurate historical reconstruction, copying contemporary evidence as faithfully as possible, an approach which is most successful for films and television; it can be designed as an accurate historical representation, exaggerated a little and interpreted to provide extra visual interest, an approach needed on the stage, where fine detail is lost; or the designer can capture the style or mood of a period, taking the essential lines and details to indicate it; or finally it can be a purely imaginative work.

In the first approach the designer tries to costume the characters as they would have been dressed in the period in which the producer wishes the play to be set, taking into consideration the type of people – rich or poor, old or young – and working with great attention to detail to provide the correct atmosphere. Portraits, drawings, engravings and other primary sources of the period are carefully studied and every effort is made to cut the costumes correctly using the right weight of fabric. The jewellery is also copied as exactly as possible.

It is most important for this type of production that the actors should know how to wear their costumes properly, as the stance can make or mar the final effect. If the limitation of movement imposed by the substructure of a dress – for example the rigid corset and wide hooped petticoat of the mid-eighteenth century – is properly understood, the actress will move in the correct way for the costume. Hairstyles and head-dresses are also most important for this kind of production and need great care and attention.

For the second approach the designer uses all the historical evidence and studies the primary sources but the designs will be interpreted in a theatrical way. The fabrics are sprayed with bleach and dye, and built up with rubber solution and collage methods to texture the surface more boldly than contemporary evidence shows. This method can make the costumes seem 'more real than real' when seen at a distance, but it can create problems when cleaning is needed. The colour scheme may be limited, producing an effect of gloom or gaiety in keeping with the mood of the play.

The third approach can offer considerable scope to the designer, and is seen more in ballet than other fields. Details of costume which indicate a period are worn with tights and leotards, rather than complete period costumes. For example, a ruff might indicate the Elizabethan period, a mask with voluminous domino the eighteenth century. The whole production can be carried out in exotic colours and fabrics or dark and subdued ones to capture the atmosphere which the producer wishes to create.

166. Ondine *Act III, designed by Lila di Nobili for the Royal Ballet in 1958. The velvet dresses worn by the court ladies and the paillette trimmed dresses of the dancers are based on the fashions of c. 1810–15.*

167. The costumes designed by David Walker for the 1971 Royal Shakespeare Company production of London Assurance *showed an understanding of the appropriate weight of fabric for use with the fashions of the early 1800s. The cut, based on a close study of costumes in museums, emphasised the period style.*

The purely imaginative style may be inspired by historic costume, natural forms or geometric shapes. Masks can be used to convey the characters of the actors to the audience; shapes and colours of fabrics may provide the mood of the play and improvisations will emerge. As a programme note for the 1955 Stratford-on-Avon production of *King Lear*, designed by Isamu Noguchi, read, 'Our object in this production has been to find a setting and costumes which would be free of historical or decorative associations so that the timeless and mythical quality of the story may be clear.'

Some productions may not exactly fit any of these categories or may have aspects of all four, but usually one approach predominates. It is important to remember that completely accurate historic costuming is not always the intention of the producer and designer. What is right for Piero Tosi designing the films *The Leopard* and *Death in Venice* is not necessarily the approach for Cecil Beaton's designs for the Ascot scene in *My Fair Lady*, or Lila di Nobili working on the ballet *Ondine* at Covent Garden [PLATE 166]. What is important is that in all four the audience is immediately aware of the period style and can enjoy the visual beauty of the production. In *The Leopard* and *Death in Venice* a sense of complete authenticity was achieved; in the musical *My Fair Lady* an exaggerated and delightful view of an exaggerated period was given, using the historical fact of the black and white Ascot race meeting of 1910 in Act II, but elaborating on it; the ballet *Ondine* adapted accurately researched historical costume into one of the most visually beautiful ballet productions ever mounted.

There are some plays where accurate historic costuming is necessary to give the sense of period style. *Hay Fever* has dialogue which could only have been spoken in the 1920s, while *The Importance of Being Earnest* belongs very firmly to the mid-1890s with the atmosphere of town house and country house, muffins and cucumber sandwiches. Other plays can be shifted in time quite happily. For example *Twelfth Night*, although usually dressed in late sixteenth-century costume, was interpreted very beautifully and appropriately by Lila di Nobili in the styles of the 1630s at the Royal Shakespeare Theatre in 1962.

This chapter describes the costume designer's task, particularly for productions with historical rather than purely imaginary designs.

Once the producer and designers have agreed on the desired visual effect, the costume designer carries out a considerable amount of research among the primary sources. He will, particularly if working away from London, have a file of drawings and reproductions (see page 203) for making sketches.

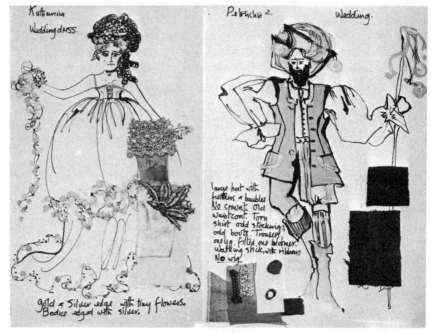

168, 169. Designs (above) by Hilary Coote for the wedding clothes for Katharina and Petruchio in The Taming of the Shrew, *presented as a musical set in the 1780s. Fabric samples are attached. The design for Katharina's dress in the first scenes (below) was carried out in red and orange striped cotton, giving a waspish effect. Cutting diagrams are given.*

When he has decided on the general shape of the costumes, he must consider the colour scheme most carefully. The lighting will change the colour of the fabrics and the colour schemes should be discussed with the producer well beforehand to avoid bad mistakes, as the visual effect can be enhanced or destroyed by the colour of the lighting. The designs should be pinned up on the wall with suggested fabrics attached, so that the overall effect may be seen. A design should be produced for each character, even if it is to be a very simple costume put together from existing stock, as it is very easy to arrive at the dress rehearsal only to discover that two minor characters have nothing to wear. The designs can be moved about so that the colour scheme for each scene can be studied.

Shopping for fabrics may be done locally, although the London shops and street markets offer a wider and cheaper range of materials than it is possible to find elsewhere. The texture of the fabric – rough or smooth, shiny or matt – is most important. Quite often old sheeting dyed or cheap calico sprayed or printed will give

170, 171. A limited range of black, white, grey and shades of brown was specified for a production of The Rivals *(left) and proved extremely effective. Design for Captain Absolute by Chris Bevin. The design can convey character, and should provide details of hair or wig styles and accessories, as well as the cut of the costume. Tattle, in* Love for Love, *(right) in an exaggerated period style designed by Marilyn Mowbray.*

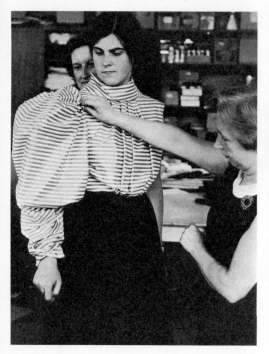

172, 173. Careful fitting is as important for the amateur as for the professional actress. Adjustments are made to a sleeve to allow more comfortable movement for Miss Prism in a scene from The Importance of Being Earnest *designed by Kate Ward.*

a better effect theatrically than a more expensive cloth. The amateur with limited funds can unpick old evening dresses and coats and press, dye and spray them, to use them again.

Once the producer has seen the rough sketches and agreed on the proposed colour schemes work goes ahead on the finished designs. The designer will by this time know all the cast and be able to work with particular actors in mind. He will be researching not only the costume, its cut and construction, but also the accessories, jewellery, hats, shoes, wigs and gloves. The general appearance of the character is most important.

The designer will usually do his own shopping as it is most important to choose the right texture, colour, design and weight of fabric. Quick decisions have to be reached about its possibilities; if it would dye successfully, if it could be shaped in the right sort of way, if it is heavy enough to take the kind of trimmings required, if it will light well. The designer also has to worry about the budget and may have to practise economies by cutting down on the cost of one fabric so that another can be more expensive.

Once the designs are completed and the fabrics purchased, the wardrobe mistress takes the measurements of the entire cast, listing them in her notebook for easy reference, and the costumes

174–177. Jewellery made from hardware and various adhesives can look more convincing than the real thing. Rich surface textures are given with appliqué motifs of Nottingham lace and trails of rubber latex, sprayed with gold paint and French enamel varnish. Soft green velvet dress for Jane Seymour (above), and (below) a dress with fur-lined sleeves for Catherine Howard, both designed by John Bloomfield for the BBC TV series The Six Wives of Henry VIII.

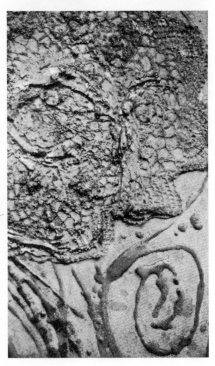

178, 179. It is
interesting to compare
the original design by
John Bloomfield for
one of the costumes
for Henry VIII for
The Six Wives of
Henry VIII, *with
the costume on
display* (right) *at
Bethnal Green
Museum.*

180, 181. *Glenda
Jackson is wearing a
boned corset and hip
pads to give the
correct shape for the
Phoenix costume for
Elizabeth R.
designed by Elizabeth
Waller. The
jewellery, make-up
and wig complete
the picture.*

are ready to be cut. A good designer should be able to cut, fit and sew a costume completely himself, even though he may only supervise in the wardrobe, so that he can explain how he wants his sketches to be interpreted.

In the professional theatre the designer usually sees at least one fitting of each costume and listens to the actors' comments. The costume is examined from every angle and the actor will make sure that he can make all the movements plotted in the play comfortably.

The cut and construction of the costume are vitally important. An incorrectly cut fabric, worn without the right foundation, will always look wrong, however good the fabric and trimmings. In the amateur theatre costumes are usually made at home by a large team of workers. The wardrobe mistress should give clear instructions and diagrams with a Xerox copy of each design so that the dressmaker can assemble the pieces correctly.

The designer, wardrobe mistress and properties department will also make sure that all the accessories are provided, and that the actor can cope with them. Sometimes it can be difficult to persuade an actress to wear the correct hairstyle but the wrong one can so easily spoil the whole effect.

The actors usually see the designs in the wardrobe, those of the rest of the cast, as well as their own, as soon as they have been approved by the producer. The costumes will have an effect on the way they think about their parts and they may wish to change some detail they are not happy about.

The final problem which remains after each production and is the same for both amateurs and professionals, is that of storage. Certain stock (for example petticoats and corsets) can be used over and over again in other productions. Some of the costumes which have a good basic shape can be stripped of their trimmings, dyed and re-used. The others can be unpicked and stored as flat pieces of material ready for re-cutting on a later occasion. Many amateur theatres with their own premises make quite a useful profit from hiring out their costumes, but this requires good organisation and plenty of storage space.

BOOKS ON THE HISTORY OF
THEATRICAL COSTUME

BEAUMONT, C. *Ballet design: past and present.* Studio publications, 1946.
Numerous monochrome and 50 colour plates, many of which show
ballet costume.

LAVER, J. *Costume in the theatre.* Harrap, 1964.
165 monochrome plates.

NEWTON, S. M. *Renaissance theatre costume.* André Deutsch, 1973.
A discussion of the sense of historic past in Renaissance theatre
costume.

READE, B. *Ballet Designs and Illustrations. 1581–1940.* H.M.S.O., 1967.
173 monochrome plates of costumes and performances from contemporary prints in the collection at the Victoria and Albert Museum.

STRONG, R. *Festival designs by Inigo Jones.* Victoria and Albert Museum,
1969.
Catalogue of an exhibition of drawings for scenery and costume
from the Devonshire Collection, Chatsworth.

BOOKS ON COSTUME DESIGN AND MAKING

See also Technical Works, pages 231–232 for information on the cut of
period costumes.

FERNALD, M. and SHENTON, E. *Costume design and making.* A. and C. Black,
1937. 24 monochrome plates from primary sources and 51 pages of
simplified pattern diagrams.

JACKSON, S. *Simple stage costumes.* Studio Vista, 1968. Line drawings
and 36 monochrome and colour plates of stage costumes. Useful for
costuming school plays on a limited budget.

MOTLEY. *Designing and making stage costumes.* Studio Vista 1964. 55
monochrome and colour plates of costume designs for the theatre.

An optical sound, 16 mm educational film *Staging a design* made in
ektachrome colour at the Geoffrey Whitworth Theatre, Crayford, and
running for 22 minutes is available from the Bexley Arts Council. For
further details write to the Bexley Arts Council, Town Hall, Bexley, Kent.

VI. Costume Bibliography

This selection of books and articles, mainly published after 1900, deals primarily with the history of Western European Costume. A few especially useful foreign publications are included as they can be borrowed through the National Central Library Service in Britain. Some specialised categories of costume require separate bibliographies, for example military uniform, but a few basic books are listed. Little has been written on occupational costume (clothes worn in particular trades, e.g. butchers, miners) and working dress (general clothing belonging to no specific trade); the main sources of information are the drawings, photographs etc. for each period. Most books on European regional (peasant, folk) costume are written in the language of their country and are only obtainable in specialist reference libraries; the *National Geographic Magazine* has occasional articles and a selection of the large number of books on the subject are listed in *A Bibliography of European Folk Dress*, compiled by James Snowden for the Costume Society, 1973.

Books in this section and under Primary Sources, should both be consulted. For instance, information on costume for a Restoration Comedy might first be sought in BRITISH ISLES (page 223), GENERAL (page 220) and SOCIAL HISTORY (page 219). The main visual primary sources will be found under SEVENTEENTH CENTURY (page 16), SCULPTURE (page 49), PAINTINGS (page 37), DRAWINGS and ENGRAVINGS (page 60), and MINIATURES (page 67). Information on fabric, cut and construction will be found under TEXTILES (page 232) and TECHNICAL WORKS (page 231). Some of the museums listed in Part VII have specimens of seventeenth-century costume on display for further study. Books marked † are particularly suitable as the basis of a costume library for schools. They are well illustrated and in many cases inexpensive.

BIBLIOGRAPHIES, ENCYCLOPAEDIAS, GLOSSARIES, DICTIONARIES

BIBLIOGRAPHIES
Many other works will be listed in bibliographies in the books referring to your particular subject of study and these should also be consulted.

ANTHONY, P. and **ARNOLD, J.** *Costume.* The Victoria & Albert Museum in association with the Costume Society, 1966. Revised edition, 1974.†

BERLIN. *Katalog der Freiherrlich von Lipperheid'schen Kostumbibliothek.* 2 vols. Berlin, 1896–1901. New edition by E. Nienholdt and G. Wagner Neuman, 2 vols. 1965. The catalogue of a German costume library.

BURSTON, W. H. and **GREEN, C. W.** (eds). *Handbook for History Teachers.* Methuen, 1962, new edition 1971. Useful guide to sources of information.

CENTRE INTERNATIONAL D'ETUDE DES TEXTILES ANCIENS, LYON. *Bulletin,* bi-annually. Lists of recent publications on textiles and costume.

GINSBURG, M. 'Hosiery Bibliography', in *Costume,* no. 2, 1968.

HILER, H. and **M.** *Bibliography of Costume. A dictionary catalog of about eight thousand books and periodicals.* H. W. Wilson, New York, 1939. Reprinted 1967.

MONRO, I. S. and **COOK, D. E.** (eds). *Costume Index. A subject index to plates and to illustrated text.* H. W. Wilson, New York, 1937. Supplement 1957.

NORTHAMPTON PUBLIC LIBRARIES. *Catalogue of the Leather and Footwear Collections in the Northampton Central Reference Library and the Library of the Northampton Central College of Further Education.* 1968.

VICTORIA AND ALBERT MUSEUM LIBRARY. 'Costume', 1936. Typescript index to the more important material in the Victoria & Albert Museum Library with annotations and shelf marks, compiled by C. H. Gibbs-Smith.

ENCYCLOPAEDIAS
glossaries and dictionaries. Standard works of reference, e.g. Oxford English Dictionary, Encyclopaedia Britannica, etc., should first be consulted. Early dictionaries define obsolete terms.

BECK, S. W. *The Drapers' Dictionary. A manual of textile fabrics, their history and applications.* The Warehousemen and Drapers' Journal, 1886.

CUNNINGTON, C. W. and **P.**, and **BEARD, C.** *A Dictionary of English Costume, 900–1900.* A. & C. Black, 1960. Line drawings in the text.

GAY, V. *Glossaire archéologique du Moyen Age et de la Renaissance.* 2 vols. Vol. I. A–G. Librairie de la Société Bibliographique, Paris, 1882. Vol. II. H–Z. Auguste Picard, Paris, 1928.

LELOIR, M. *Dictionnaire du costume et ses accessoires, des armes et des étoffes des origines à nos jours.* Librairie Gründ, 1951. Numerous line drawings and four colour plates.

GUIDES TO MUSEUMS, ART GALLERIES, COUNTRY HOUSES

AUTOMOBILE ASSOCIATION. *Treasures of Britain.* Drive Publications, 1968. Useful, well-illustrated guide to museums, country houses and churches in Britain.

CENTRO INTERNAZIONALE DELLE ARTE E DEL COSTUME, Palazzo Grassi, Venice. *Guida Internazionale ai musei e alle collezione pubbliche di costumi e di tessuti.* 1970. International guide to collections of costume and textiles, compiled from questionnaires.

CORBETT, E. (ed.). *The Libraries, Museums and Art Galleries Year Book 1971.* Lists every library, museum and art gallery in Great Britain and Ireland.

HISTORIC HOUSES, CASTLES AND GARDENS IN GREAT

BRITAIN AND IRELAND. Index Publishers, annually.
HUENFELD, I. P. *International Directory of Historical Clothing.* The Scarecrow Press, Inc., Metuchen, N.J., 1967.
MUSEUMS AND GALLERIES IN GREAT BRITAIN AND IRELAND. Index Publishers, annually.
WISE, T. *A Guide to Military Museums.* Bellona Publications, 1969.

JOURNALS PUBLISHING ARTICLES ON COSTUME

CIBA. *Review* (1937–). The Society of Chemical Industry in Basle, Switzerland. Articles mainly on aspects of the textile industry but some on costume.
COSTUME SOCIETY. *Costume.* The Journal of the Costume Society, published by the Society, c/o Department of Textiles, Victoria & Albert Museum, London S.W.7 (1965–). Illustrated articles on aspects of costume, bibliographies, etc.
COSTUME SOCIETY OF SCOTLAND. *Bulletin.* Published by the Society, c/o 5 Abbotsford Park, Edinburgh 10 (1966–).
KUNGL. LIVRUSTKAMMAREN, Stockholm. *Livrustkammaren.* The Journal of the Royal Armoury (1937–). Well-documented articles on costume and armour.
NEEDLE AND BOBBIN CLUB, New York. *Bulletin* (1917–). Illustrated articles on various aspects of costume, textiles and embroidery.
WAFFEN-UND KOSTÜMKUNDE. *Zeitschrift der Gesellschaft für historische Waffen-und Kostümkunde* (1959–). Deutscher Kunstverlag, Munich. Well-documented articles on costume and armour.

SOCIAL HISTORY

BENTLEY, N. *The Victorian Scene, 1837–1901.* Weidenfeld & Nicolson, 1968. Over 400 monochrome and 40 pages of colour plates
BOTT, A. (ed.). *Our Fathers (1879–1900): manners and customs of the ancient Victorians: a survey in pictures and text of their history, morals, wars, sports, inventions and politics.* Heinemann, 1931. Numerous monochrome plates.
BOTT, A. (ed.). *Our Mothers: a cavalcade in pictures, quotation and description of late Victorian women 1870–1900.* Gollancz, 1932.
BURGESS, A. *The Age of the Grand Tour.* Elek, 1967.
CARPENTER, E. *A House of Kings: the official history of Westminster Abbey.* John Baker, 1966. Illustrations of coronation processions and funeral cortèges.
CLEPHANE, I. *Ourselves, 1900–1930.* Lane, 1933. Monochrome plates.
DE VRIES, L. *Panorama 1842–1865.* John Murray, 1967. The world of the early Victorians as portrayed in the *Illustrated London News*.
EDWARDS, R. and **RAMSEY, L. G. G.** *The Connoisseur Period Guides: Tudor, 1500–1603* (1956): *Stuart, 1603–1714* (1957); *Early Georgian, 1714–1760* (1957); *Late Georgian, 1760–1810* (1956); *Regency, 1810–1830* (1956); *Early Victorian, 1830–1860* (1958).
ERLANGER, P. *The Age of Courts and Kings. Manners and Morals 1558–1715.* Weidenfeld & Nicolson, 1967. Numerous monochrome plates, many showing costume.
FOWLER, K. *The Age of Plantagenet and Valois.* Elek, 1967. Numerous monochrome and colour plates of French and English life from 1328 to 1498.

The study of costume is part of the study of social history. Much information may be found in books which do not deal specifically with costume but describe the social background of a period.

GATTEY, C. N. *The Bloomer Girls.* Femina, 1967. 33 monochrome plates and contemporary description of 'Bloomer' costume.

HARTLEY, D. R. and **ELLIOT, M. A. V.** *The Life and Work of the People of England.* Batsford, 1925–31. Six volumes, each with about 150 monochrome plates, covering the 11th to the 18th centuries.

HUSSEY, M. *Chaucer's World: a pictorial companion.* Cambridge University Press, 1967. Numerous monochrome plates.

LAVER, J. *The Age of Optimism. Manners and Morals 1848–1914.* Weidenfeld & Nicolson, 1966. 96 pages of monochrome plates.

MAYHEW, H. *London Labour and the London Poor 1861–7.* 4 vols. Enlarged photographic reprint. Frank Cass, 1967. Numerous plates.

RICKERT, E. *Chaucer's World.* Oxford University Press, 1948. 39 pages of monochrome plates. Contemporary descriptions of costume.

ROSSARO, M. *The Life and Times of Elizabeth I,* trans. C. J. Richards. Hamlyn, 1967. 30 monochrome and 75 colour plates.

SMITH, P. *The Turnpike Age.* Luton Museum, 1970. Numerous plates of engravings, useful for occupational and working dress.

WILDEBLOODE, J. and **BRINSON, P.** *The Polite World. A guide to English manners and deportment from the thirteenth to the nineteenth century.* Oxford University Press, 1965. Details about dress and movement in quotations from contemporary sources.

GENERAL

Some of the best known and most useful reference books on costume are listed in this section. They cover all countries, all periods of time and contain many illustrations.

D'ASSAILLY, G. *Ages of Elegance: five thousand years of fashion and frivolity.* Macdonald, 1968. Numerous monochrome and colour plates, mostly undated.

BOEHN, M. VON. *Modes and Manners,* trans. J. Joshua. Harrap, 1932–5. Numerous monochrome and a few colour plates. Vol. 1, *From the Decline of the Ancient World to the Renaissance*; vol. 2, *The Sixteenth Century*; vol. 3, *The Seventeenth Century*; vol. 4, *The Eighteenth Century.*

BOEHN, M. VON and **FISCHEL, O.** *Modes and Manners of the Nineteenth Century,* trans. M. Edwardes. Revised edition, Dent, 1927. Numerous monochrome and a few colour plates. Vol. 1, *1790–1817*; vol. 2, *1818–42*; vol. 3, *1843–78*; vol. 4, *1879–1914.*

BOUCHER, F. *A History of Costume in the West.* Thames & Hudson, 1967. 817 monochrome and 335 colour plates. A standard work.†

BRAUN-RONSDORF, M. *The Wheel of Fashion: costume since the French Revolution, 1789–1929,* trans. O. Coburn. Thames & Hudson, 1964. 415 monochrome and 28 colour plates.

BRUHN, W. and **TILKE, M.** *A Pictorial History of Costume; a survey of costume of all periods and peoples from antiquity to modern times including national costume in Europe and non-European countries.* Zwemmer, 1955.

DAVENPORT, M. *The Book of Costume.* Crown Publishers, New York, 1948. 3,000 monochrome plates. A comprehensive history of costume up to 1860, covering dress, accessories, coiffure, etc. A standard work on the subject.†

GARLAND, M. *The Changing Face of Beauty.* Weidenfeld & Nicolson, 1957. Illustrated with portraits showing types of beauty in various periods.

HANSEN, H. H. *Costume Cavalcade.* Methuen, 1956. 685 examples of costume in colour, redrawn from original sources.†

HOTTENROTH, F. *Le costume chez les peuples anciens et modernes.* 2 vols.

Armand Guerinet, 1884–91. Reprinted E. Weyhe, New York, 1947. Colour plates with line drawings and diagrams.

KELLY, F. M. and **SCHWABE, R.** *Historic Costume: a chronicle of fashion in Western Europe 1490–1790*. Batsford, 1925. Monochrome and colour plates, with many line drawings and some patterns. A standard work.

KELLY, F. M. and **SCHWABE, R.** *A Short History of Costume and Armour Chiefly in England, 1066–1800*. 1931, reprinted David & Charles, 1972. Monochrome and colour plates, with many line drawings.†

KLEPPER, E. and **LAVER, J.** *Costume through the Ages*. Thames & Hudson, 1963. Numerous line drawings.†

KÖHLER, C. and **SICHART, E. VON.** *A History of Costume*, trans. A. K. Dallas. Harrap, 1928. Dover, New York, 1963. 600 monochrome and 16 colour plates with patterns of costumes.†

KYBALOVA, L., HERBEYOVA, O., LAMAROVA, M. *Pictorial Encyclopedia of Fashion*, trans. C. Rosoux. Hamlyn, 1968. Numerous useful monochrome and colour plates, unfortunately undated in some cases.†

LAVER, J. *A Concise History of Costume*. Thames & Hudson, 1969. 275 monochrome and 58 colour plates from a wide variety of primary sources.†

LELOIR, M. *Histoire du costume de l'antiquité à 1914*. Ernst. Vol. VIII, *1610–1643* (1933); vol. IX, *1643–1678* (1934); vol. X, *1678–1715, 1715–1725* (1935); vol. XI, *1725–1774* (1938); vol. XII, *1775–1795* (1949). Numerous plates from contemporary sources, with many drawings and diagrams of cut. Series incomplete.

PAYNE, B. *History of Costume from the Ancient Egyptians to the Twentieth Century*. Harper & Row, New York, 1965. 375 plates, 241 line drawings and diagrams of cut.

RUPPERT, J. *Le costume*. 5 vols. Librairie d'Art. R. Ducher, 1930–1. Reprinted Flammarion, 1958.

ŜROŇKOVÁ, O. *Fashions through the Centuries: Renaissance, Baroque and Rococo*, trans. T. Gottheiner, Spring Books, 1959. Numerous plates.

TILKE, M. *Costume Patterns and Designs: a survey of costume patterns and designs of all periods and nations from antiquity to modern times*. Zwemmer, 1956.

WILKERSON, M. *Clothes*. Batsford, 1970. 67 monochrome plates of primary source material. Useful for children from 13–18 years.†

THEORY AND PSYCHOLOGY OF DRESS

BELL, Q. *On Human Finery*. Hogarth Press, 1948.

CUNNINGTON, C. W. *Feminine Attitudes in the Nineteenth Century*. Heinemann, 1935.

CUNNINGTON, C. W. *Why Women Wear Clothes*. Faber, 1941. Some interesting theories and entertaining extracts from contemporary sources.

FLUGEL, J. C. *The Psychology of Clothes*. Hogarth Press, 1950. A basic work with a particularly full bibliography.

LAVER, J. *Style in Costume*. Oxford University Press, 1949. 32 plates relating costume to the architecture and décor of different periods.

LAVER, J. *Taste and Fashion*. Revised edition, Harrap, 1945. 60 monochrome and 12 colour plates. Covers from the French Revolution to the present day.

LAVER, J. *Dress: how and why fashions in men's and women's clothes have changed during the past 200 years*. Murray, 1950. 106 monochrome plates.

THE ANCIENT WORLD

This section covers races and countries up to the time of the fall of the Roman Empire.

BIEBER, M. *Greichische Kleidung*, Berlin, 1928. Useful book with 64 pages of monochrome plates and diagrams for draping Greek costume.

BROHOLM, H. C. and **HALD, M.** *Costumes of the Bronze Age in Denmark.* Oxford University Press, 1940. A scholarly work with monochrome plates.

EVANS, M. M. and **ABRAHAMS, E.** *Ancient Greek Dress.* New edition, Argonaut Inc., Chicago, 1964. 40 monochrome plates and line drawings.

HEUZEY, L. A. and **HEUZEY, J.** *Histoire du costume dans l'antiquité classique, l'Orient, Egypte, Mésopotamie, Syrie, Phénicie.* Société d'Edition Les Belles Lettres, 1935. The most scholarly work on the costume of the period.

HILER, H. *From Nudity to Raiment: an introduction to the study of costume.* W. G. Foyle, 1929. 12 monochrome, 12 colour plates and 141 line drawings.

HOUSTON, M. G. *Ancient Egyptian, Assyrian and Persian Costumes and Decorations.* A. & C. Black, 2nd edition, 1954. 9 colour plates and over 250 drawings and diagrams of cut in the text.

HOUSTON, M. G. *Ancient Greek, Roman and Byzantine Costume and Decoration.* A. & C. Black, 2nd edition, 1947. 8 colour plates and over 200 line drawings and diagrams of cut in the text.

HOPE, T. *Costume of the Ancients.* 1st edition, 1809. Reprinted as *Costumes of the Greeks and Romans.* Dover, New York, 1964. Line drawings.

KLEPPER, E. and **LAVER, J.** *Costume in Antiquity.* Thames & Hudson, 1964. Numerous line drawings.†

LUTZ, H. *Textiles and Costumes among the Peoples of the Ancient Near East.* Leipzig, 1923. Monochrome plates and line drawings.

WILSON, L. M. *The Roman Toga.* Johns Hopkins Press, Baltimore, 1924. Scholarly work, with 73 plates, diagrams of primary source material and reconstructions.

WILSON, L. M. *The Clothing of the Ancient Romans.* Johns Hopkins Press, Baltimore, 1938. Scholarly work with 103 plates and diagrams.

AMERICA

Further information on American costume may be found in The Book of Costume *by Millia Davenport and similar works listed under General.*

BOSTON MUSEUM OF FINE ARTS. *Great Costumes 1550–1950.* 1963. 24 colour plates of French, English and American costumes in the collection.

EARLE, A. M. *Two Centuries of Costume in America, 1620–1820.* 2 vols. Macmillan, 1903. Monochrome plates. Many interesting quotations from original sources.

HORAN, J. D. and **SANN, P.** *Picture History of the Wild West.* Spring Books, 1954. Over 250 plates of desperadoes, rustlers and outlaws.

McCLELLAN, E. *History of American Costume 1607–1870.* 1904. Reissued Tudor Publishing, New York, 1969. Over 700 plates and line drawings.

McGARVEY, E. 'The Fashion Wing', in *Philadelphia Museum of Art Bulletin*, vol. LVII, no. 217, 1961. 70 monochrome plates.

METROPOLITAN MUSEUM OF ART; *Bulletin*, vol. XXX, no. 1, August/September 1971. Issue devoted to articles on costume and the Costume Institute.

WARWICK, E. and **PITZ, H. C.** *Early American Costume.* The Century Co., London and New York, 1929. Reprint Benjamin Blom, New York, 1965. Monochrome plates and line drawings. Covers *c.* 1600–1800, including early European background.

AUSTRALIA

FLOWER, C. *Duck and Cabbage Tree. A pictorial history of clothes in Australia 1788–1914.* Angus & Robertson, 1968.

BRITISH ISLES

BRADFIELD, N. *Costume in Detail, 1730–1930.* Harrap, 1968. 360 pages of line drawings and 12 colour plates.
CUNNINGTON, C. W. and **P.** *A Picture History of English Costume.* Vista Books, 1960. Many monochrome plates of portraits, miniatures, engravings and other primary sources.†
CUNNINGTON, P. *Costume in Pictures.* Dutton Vista pictureback, 1964. Monochrome plates.†
STRUTT, J. *The Dress and Habits of the People of England.* 2 vols, first printed 1842. Reprinted Tabard Press, 1970. Illustrations redrawn from primary sources. Dated but useful for quotations from manuscript sources.

BRITISH ISLES General. Further information may also be found in many of the books listed under General (page 220).

CUNNINGTON, C. W. and **P.** *Handbook of English Medieval Costume.* Faber, 1952. Revised edition, 1973. Line drawings.
DRUITT, H. *A Manual of Costume as Illustrated by Monumental Brasses.* Alexander Moring, 1906. 110 monochrome plates.
HARTLEY, D. *Medieval Costume and Life.* Batsford, 1931. Monochrome plates and diagrams showing how to reconstruct the costumes for theatrical purposes.
HOUSTON, M. G. *Medieval Costume in England and France.* A. & C. Black, 1939. 350 line drawings and 8 colour plates. Covers the 13th, 14th and 15th centuries with an account of construction and diagrams of patterns.

BRITISH ISLES Mediaeval.

CUNNINGTON, C. W. and **P.** *Handbook of English Costume in the Sixteenth Century.* Faber, 1954, revised edition, 1970. Line drawings.
KELLY, F. M. *Shakespearean Costume for Stage and Screen.* A. & C. Black, 1938. Monochrome plates and 93 line drawings.
LAVER, J. *Early Tudor, 1485–1558.* Costume of the Western World series, Harrap, 1951. Monochrome and colour plates.
LINTHICUM, M. C. *Costume in the Drama of Shakespeare and His Contemporaries.* Oxford University Press, 1936. 22 plates of photographs. Useful for colours and textiles used in clothing during the 16th and early 17th centuries.
MORSE, H. K. *Elizabethan Pageantry: a pictorial survey of costume and its commentators from 1560–1620.* Studio, 1934. Special spring number of the *Studio.* Monochrome plates and useful contemporary descriptions.
REYNOLDS, G. *Elizabethan and Jacobean, 1558–1625.* Costume of the Western World series, Harrap, 1951. Monochrome and colour plates.

BRITISH ISLES Sixteenth century

BUCK, A. 'Variations in Englishwomen's Dress in the Eighteenth Century', in *Folk Life,* Journal of the Society for Folk Life Studies, vol. 9, 1971, pp. 5–28. Monochrome plates.
CUNNINGTON, C. W. and **P.** *Handbook of English Costume in the Seventeenth Century.* Faber, 1955, revised edition 1967. Line drawings.
CUNNINGTON, C. W. and **P.** *Handbook of English Costume in the Eighteenth Century.* Faber, 1957, revised edition 1972. Line drawings.†
HALLS, Z. *Women's Costumes 1600–1750.* H.M.S.O., 1969. A catalogue of the collection at the London Museum with 21 monochrome plates.†

BRITISH ISLES Seventeenth and eighteenth centuries.

LENS, B. *The Exact Dress of the Head, 1725–1726.* Introduction by J. L. Nevinson. Costume Society, 1970. Monochrome plates.
MANCHESTER CITY ART GALLERIES. *Women's Costume in the 18th Century.* Manchester City Art Galleries, 1954. Monochrome plates.†
NEVINSON, J. L. 'New Material for the History of Seventeenth-century Costume in England', in *Apollo* 20, 1934, pp. 315–19.
VICTORIA AND ALBERT MUSEUM. *Costume Illustration: seventeenth and eighteenth century.* Introduction by J. Laver. H.M.S.O., 1951. Monochrome plates.

BRITISH ISLES
Nineteenth and twentieth centuries

ADBURGHAM, A. *A Punch History of Manners and Modes, 1841–1940.* Hutchinson, 1961. Illustrated with cartoons from *Punch* magazine.
BUCK, A. 'The Costume of Jane Austen and Her Characters', in *The So-called Age of Elegance.* The Costume Society, 1970. 6 monochrome plates.
BUCK, A. *Victorian Costume and Costume Accessories.* Herbert Jenkins, 1961. 51 monochrome plates of portraits and costume and 29 line illustrations.†
CUNNINGTON, C. W. and **P.** *Handbook of English Costume in the Nineteenth Century.* Faber, 1959, revised edition, 1970. Line drawings.†
CUNNINGTON, C. W. *English Women's Clothing in the Nineteenth Century.* Faber, 1937. Descriptions of costume from contemporary sources.
CUNNINGTON, C. W. *English Women's Clothing in the Present Century.* Faber, 1952. 66 monochrome, 3 colour plates and many line drawings.
GERNSHEIM, A. *Fashion and Reality 1840–1914.* Faber, 1963. 235 monochrome plates from period photographs.
GIBBS-SMITH, C. H. *The Fashionable Lady in the Nineteenth Century.* H.M.S.O., 1960. Fashion plates for each fifth year from 1800 to 1900.†
HOPE, T. and **MOSES, H.** *Designs of Modern Costume Engraved for Thomas Hope of Deepdene by Henry Moses 1812.* Introduction by J. L. Nevinson. Costume Society: extra series no. 4, 1973. 20 facsimile line engravings.
MANCHESTER CITY ART GALLERIES. *Women's Costume, 1800–35* (1952); *Women's Costume 1835–70* (1951); *Women's Costume 1870–1900* (1953); *Women's Costume 1900–30* (1956). Series of booklets, each with 20 pages of monochrome plates.†
MOORE, D. L. *The Women in Fashion.* Batsford, 1949. 108 pages of photographs of costume *c.* 1800–1927.

EUROPE

FRANCE

BLUM, A. *The Last Valois, 1515–1590.* Costume of the Western World series, Harrap, 1951. Monochrome and colour plates.
BLUM, A. *Early Bourbon, 1590–1643.* Costume of the Western World series, Harrap, 1951, Monochrome and colour plates.
EVANS, J. *Dress in Medieval France.* Oxford University Press, 1952. Monochrome plates.
HARMAND, A. *Jeanne d'Arc, ses costumes, son armure.* Ernest Leroux, 1929. Monochrome plates, line drawings and diagrams showing the cut of costumes from reconstructions.
MAUROIS, A. *The Women of Paris,* trans. Norman Denny. Bodley Head, 1954. 143 plates of photographs of everyday life in Paris from fashion world to factory.
MUSÉE DU COSTUME DE LA VILLE DE PARIS (Annexe du Musée Carnavalet), 11, Avenue du President Wilson. Booklets illustrated with monochrome plates of costume and accessories in the collection.

PITON, C. *Le costume civil en France du XIIIe au XIXe siècle.* Flammarion, 1913. Over 700 plates of illustrations from primary sources, including some coloured plates. A standard work.

REISET, G. A. H. Comte de. *Modes et usages au temps de Marie Antoinette. Livre-journal de Mme Éloffe, marchande de modes, couturière lingère ordinaire de la Reine et des dames de sa cour.* 2 vols. Paris, 1885.

VANIER, H. *La mode et ses métiers. Frivolités et luttes des classes, 1830–70.* Armand Colin, 1960. Monochrome plates. Social background as well as costume detail.

WEIGERT, R. A. Series: *Costumes et modes d'autrefois.* Rombaldi, 1955–8. Seven books, each containing 24 hand-stencilled plates of costume illustrations by artists including Bosse, Bonnart, Saint-Aubin, Leclère, Watteau de Lille, Debucourt, Vernet and Devéria.

FRANKFURT AM MAIN. *Frankfurter modenspeigel.* Austellung des Historichien Museums, 1962. Exhibition catalogue. GERMANY

NIENHOLDT, E. *Kostümkunde.* Klinkhardt & Biermann, 1961. 203 monochrome and 23 colour plates. A source book of samples of costume in museum collections.

STAATLICHE KUNSTSAMMLUNGEN. Dresden. *Historische Prunkkleidung.* 1963. 32 monochrome plates. State costumes in Dresden State Museum *c.* 1550–early 18th century.

BENTIVEGNA, F. C. *Abbigliamento e costume nella pittura Italiana.* Carlo Bestetti, Rome. Vol. 1, *Rinascimento* (1962) covers the 15th and 16th centuries; vol. 2, *Baroco e Impero* (1964) covers the 17th and 18th centuries. Many monochrome and a few colour plates. ITALY

LEVI-PISETZKY, R. *Storia del Costume in Italia.* Instituto Editoriale Italiano. 5 vols., 1964–9, each containing a large number of superb monochrome and colour plates.

HAAGS GEMEENTEMUSEUM (MUNICIPAL MUSEUM OF THE HAGUE). *Een gala japon omstreeks 1760. A gala dress about 1760.* 1957. 15 monochrome plates and a scale diagram of cut. English text. NETHERLANDS

NEDERLANDS KOSTUUMMUSEUM DEN HAAG (NETHERLANDS MUSEUM OF COSTUME). *Vrouwenkostuum 1800–1820. Women's dress 1800–1820.* 1960. 26 monochrome plates. English text.

THIENEN, F. VAN. *The Great Age of Holland, 1600–50.* Costume of the Western World series, Harrap, 1951. Monochrome and colour plates.

CEDERSTROM, R. *Gustavus II Adolphus vid Lützen.* Livrustkammaren, Stockholm, 1944. Monochrome plates with scale diagrams of cut. SCANDINAVIA

CHRISTENSEN, S. F. *De Danske kongers kronologiske samling paa Rosenborg, Kongedragterne fra 17 og 18 aarhundrede.* 2 vols. København, i kommission hos Ejnar Munksgaad, 1940. Danish monarchs' costumes from the 17th and 18th centuries.

EKSTRAND, G. *Karl X Gustavus dräkter.* Livrustkammaren, Stockholm, 1959. 52 monochrome plates with 4 pages of patterns. The costumes of King Charles X Gustavus of Sweden (1622–60). English summary.

EKSTRAND, G. 'Nils Nilsson Brahes Spanska drakt', in *Livrustkammaren,* the Journal of the Royal Armoury, Stockholm. May 1968. 23 monochrome plates. Nils Brahe's Spanish Costume of 1655. English summary.

HAZELIUS-BERG, G. *Modedräkter, 1600–1900.* Nordiska Museet, Stockholm, 1952. 64 monochrome plates of costumes in the collection.

NYLEN, A. M. 'Stureskjortna' in *Livrustkammaren*, the Journal of the Royal Armoury, Stockholm, vol. IV, pp. 8–9, 1948. Article on the Sture shirts, *c.* 1567, with monochrome plates and diagrams; English summary.

PYLKKÄNEN, R. *Säätyläispuku Suomessa vanhemmalla Vaasa-ajalla, 1550–1620.* Helsinki, 1955. Monochrome plates. Costume of the earlier Vasa period. English summary.

PYLKKÄNEN, R. *Barokin pukumuoti Suomessa 1620–1720.* Helsinki, 1970. Monochrome plates. Fully documented study of Baroque costume in Finland. English summary.

SPAIN

BERNIS MADRAZO, C. *Indumentaria medieval española.* Instituto Diego Velásquez del Consejo superior de Investigaciones cientificas. Serie Artes y Artistas, Madrid, 1956. 182 monochrome plates. Covers 7th century A.D.–1500.

BERNIS MADRAZO, C. *Indumentaria española en tiempos de Carlos V.* Serie Artes y Artistas, Madrid, 1962. 230 monochrome plates from contemporary sources. Covers the period *c.* 1500–1560.

GOMEZ-MORENO, M. *El panteón real de las Huelgas de Burgos.* Instituto Diego Velásquez, del Consejo superior de Investigaciones cientificas, Madrid, 1946. 143 monochrome plates with patterns of medieval Spanish royal costumes.

READE, B. *The Dominance of Spain, 1550–1660.* Costume of the Western World series, Harrap, 1951. Monochrome and colour plates.

CHILDREN'S DRESS

CUNNINGTON, P. and **BUCK, A.** *Children's Costume in England from the Fourteenth to the End of the Nineteenth Century.* A. & C. Black, 1965. 32 plates.

GARLAND, M. *The Changing Face of Childhood.* Hutchinson, 1963. Monochrome plates.

GEFFRYE MUSEUM, Shoreditch. *Children at Home* series. London County Council. 16th century, no. 4426 (1964); 17th century, no. 4241 (1964); 18th century, no. 4271 (1965); 20th century, no. 125E (1967). Illustrated with monochrome plates.†

LAVER, J. *Children's Fashions in the Nineteenth Century.* Batsford, 1951. Monochrome and colour plates of fashion plates.

MACQUOID, P. *Four Hundred Years of Children's Costume from the Great Masters, 1400–1800.* Medici Society, 1923. 34 colour plates of contemporary portraits.

MANCHESTER CITY ART GALLERIES. *Children's Costume.* 1959. Monochrome plates of costumes from the collection at the Gallery of English Costume.†

MOORE, D. L. *The Child in Fashion.* Batsford, 1953. 51 plates of children in original costumes, many now at the Museum of Costume, Bath.

MEN'S DRESS

GENERAL
See also Technical Works. Chapters on men's dress will be found in many of the books listed under General.

AMIES, H. *ABC of Men's Fashion.* Newnes, 1964. 8 monochrome plates.

BARNEY, S. D. *Clothes and the Man: a guide to correct dress for all occasions.* Pitman, 1951. Line drawings.

BENNETT-ENGLAND, R. *Dress Optional.* Peter Owen, 1967. Monochrome plates.

HALLS, Z. *Men's Costume 1580–1750.* H.M.S.O., 1970. Catalogue of costume at the London Museum with 21 monochrome plates.†

LAVER, J. *Dandies.* Weidenfeld & Nicolson, 1968. Monochrome plates.

MOERS, E. *The Dandy.* Secker & Warburg, 1960. 15 monochrome plates. Covers from Brummell to Beerbohm.

CARMAN, W. Y. *British Military Uniforms from Contemporary Pictures.* Spring Books, 1968. 109 monochrome and colour plates. Tudor period to the present day. MILITARY AND NAVAL UNIFORM
See note on page 217.

DICKENS, ADMIRAL SIR G. *The Dress of the British Sailor.* H.M.S.O., 1957. 24 monochrome plates of paintings and costumes.

JARRETT, D. *British Naval Dress.* Dent, 1960. 86 monochrome and 1 colour plate.

MAY, COMMANDER W. E. *The Dress of Naval Officers.* H.M.S.O., 1966. 69 monochrome plates.

MELEGARI, V. *Great Regiments,* trans. R. Strom. Weidenfeld & Nicolson, 1969. Numerous monochrome and colour plates.

MOLLO, J. and **B.** *Uniforms and Equipment of the Light Brigade.* Historical Research Unit, 1968. 61 plates of regiments at Balaclava in 1854.

MOLLO, J. and **B.** *Uniform of the Royal Navy during the Napoleonic Wars.* Hugh Evelyn, 1965. 20 colour plates, redrawn from primary sources.

HARGREAVES-MAWDSLEY, W. N. *A History of Legal Dress in Europe until the End of the Eighteenth Century.* Oxford University Press, 1963. 21 monochrome and 1 colour plate. Scholarly work. LEGAL AND ACADEMICAL DRESS

HARGREAVES-MAWDSLEY, W. N. *A History of Academical Dress in Europe until the End of the Eighteenth Century.* Oxford University Press, 1963. 21 monochrome and 1 colour plate. Scholarly work.

HAYCRAFT, F. W. *The Degrees and Hoods of the World's Universities and Colleges.* Revised by E. W. Scobie Stringer. Cheshunt Press, 1948.

SPECIALISED COSTUME

BUCK, A. 'The Countryman's Smock', in *Folk Life,* Journal of the Society for Folk Life Studies, vol. 1, 1963. OCCUPATIONAL *costume, working dress, regional costume and traditional dress. See note on page 217.*

CUNNINGTON, P. and **LUCAS, C.** *Occupational Costume in England, from the 11th century to 1914.* A. & C. Black, 1967. 64 plates and over 300 line drawings.†

ELLIS, M. *Welsh Costume and Customs.* Picture Book no. 1, National Library of Wales, 1951. 14 monochrome and 6 colour plates.

HENSHALL, A. and **SEABY, W.** 'The Dungiven Costume', *Ulster Journal of Archaeology,* vols 24 and 25, 1961 and 1962. A study of 17th century dress in Ulster.

HESKETH, C. *Tartans.* Weidenfeld & Nicolson, 1961. 85 monochrome and 34 colour plates.

LANSDELL, A 'A Guide to Collections of Occupational Costume'. In *Costume,* the Journal of the Costume Society, 1973.

MAXWELL, S. and **HUTCHINSON, R.** *Scottish Costume 1550–1850.* A. & C. Black, 1958. Line drawings. Useful list of sources.

MICHAELSON, K. 'Newhaven Fishwives' Costume' in *Bulletin V.* The Costume Society of Scotland, 1970. Line drawings and diagrams of patterns.

RUBENS, A. *A History of Jewish Costume,* 1967, revised edition, Weidenfeld & Nicolson, 1973. 264 monochrome and colour plates.

WHITE, W. J. *Working Class Costume from Sketches of Characters by William Johnstone White*, **1818**, ed. P. Clabburn. Costume Society, 1971

SPORTS COSTUME

BUGGE, A. *Touristinder og andre sportspiker*. Norsk Folkemuseum, Oslo, 1961. Many plates showing sports clothes from the 18th century to *c.* 1960, worn in Norway.

CUNNINGTON, P. and **MANSFIELD, A.** *English Costume for Sports and Outdoor·Recreations from the Sixteenth to the Nineteenth Centuries*. A. & C. Black, 1969.†

FOSTER, I. 'The Development of Riding Costume *c.* 1880–1920' in *Costume*, no. 3, 1969.

KIDWELL, C. *Women's Bathing and Swimming Costume in the United States.* Smithsonian Institution, United States National Museum Bulletin 250, 1968.†

MANCHESTER CITY ART GALLERIES. *Costume for Sport*, Manchester City Art Galleries, 1963. 20 pages of monochrome plates.†

WEDDING DRESS
AND MOURNING
DRESS

ANDERSON, E. *Brudekjolen*. National Museum, Copenhagen, 1967. 28 plates.

AUDIAT, P. *Vingt-cinq siècles de mariage*. Hachette, 1963. Monochrome and colour plates of weddings through the ages.

BUCK, A. 'The Trap Re-baited. Mourning Dress 1860–1890' in *High Victorian*. The Costume Society, March 1968.

CUNNINGTON, P. and **LUCAS, C.** *Costume for Births, Marriages and Deaths*. A. & C. Black, 1972. 64 plates and over 100 line drawings.

DENEKE, B. *Hochzeit*. Prestel-Verlag, Munich, 1971. 127 monochrome and colour plates. Wedding costume and customs in Germany.

THE FASHION WORLD

A more detailed list of books is given in Costume by Anthony and Arnold. See page 218.

ADBURGHAM, A. *Shops and Shopping*, 1800–1914. Allen & Unwin, 1964. 16 monochrome plates and 100 line engravings from original sources. A standard work.

AMIES, H. *Just So Far*. Collins, 1954. Autobiography of Hardy Amies.

BEATON, C. *The Glass of Fashion*. Weidenfeld & Nicolson, 1954. 16 photographs and many line drawings by the author.

BERTIN, C. *Paris à la mode. A voyage of discovery*, trans. Marjorie Deans, Gollancz, 1956. The story behind a model dress.

BROOKLYN MUSEUM. *The House of Worth*, 1962. 20 monochrome photographs of dresses from the House of Worth, *c.* 1860–1908.

CHASE, E. W. and **I.** *Always in 'Vogue'*. Gollancz, 1954. Written by a former editor of *Vogue* and illustrated with photographs and drawings from *Vogue*.

CHILLINGWORTH, J. and **BUSBY, H.** *Fashion*. Lutterworth Press, 1961. Monochrome plates.

DIOR, C. *Dior by Dior*, trans. A. Fraser, Weidenfeld & Nicolson, 1957. An account of the founding and organisation of the House of Dior.

FAIRCHILD, J. *The Fashionable Savages*. Doubleday, 1965. The world of fashion from the viewpoint of the publisher of the American trade paper *Women's Wear Daily*.

GARLAND, M. *Fashion*. Penguin, 1962. Covers *c.* 1900–60.†

GINSBURG, M. *Fashion: an anthology by Cecil Beaton*. H.M.S.O., 1971. Exhibition catalogue illustrated with monochrome photographs and line drawings of couturiers and dresses *c.* 1900–71.

GORDON, L. W. D. *Discretions and Indiscretions.* Jarrolds, 1932. The autobiography of Lucile, the founder of the Couture House.

HARTNELL, N. *Silver and Gold.* Evans, 1955. 14 plates of monochrome photographs, sketches, with descriptions of dresses made for the Coronation in 1953.

HOLME, B., TWEED, K., DAVIES, J. and LIBERMAN, A. *The World in Vogue.* Secker & Warburg, 1963. Plates of photographs, drawings and articles from *Vogue* magazine 1893–1963.

LATOUR, A. *Kings of Fashion.* Weidenfeld & Nicolson, 1958. 26 monochrome plates. Covers the history of the couturier from Rose Bertin to Christian Dior.

LOS ANGELES, COUNTY MUSEUM. *A Remembrance of Mariano Fortuny 1871–1945.* 1967–8. Small exhibition catalogue, not illustrated.

LYNAM, R. (ed.) *Paris Fashion. The great designers and their creations.* Michael Joseph, 1972. Numerous monochrome and colour plates.

MARSHALL, C. *Fashion Modelling as a Career.* Arthur Barker, 1957. Illustrated with 15 monochrome plates of photographs of fashion models of the mid-1950s.

MARSHALL, F. *Fashion Drawing.* The Studio Publications, 1955. Describes the work of a fashion artist.

NOUVION, T. DE and LIEZ, E. *Ministre des modes sous Louis XVI. Mademoiselle Bertin, marchande de modes de la reine, 1747–1813.* Paris, 1911. The life of Rose Bertin, Marie Antoinette's dressmaker. Descriptions of dresses with prices.

PICKEN, M. B. and MILLER, D. L. *Dressmakers of France. The who, how and why of French couture.* Harper, 1956. Monochrome plates of couturiers, workrooms, etc.

POIRET, P. *En habillant l'Époque.* Bernard Grasset, 1930. Reminiscences by the couturier, illustrated with 16 monochrome plates. (Unillustrated English edition, *My First Fifty Years,* trans. S. H. Guest, Gollancz, 1936.)

POIRET, P. *King of Fashion, the autobiography of Paul Poiret,* trans. S. H. Guest, Lippincott, 1931.

QUANT, M. *Quant by Quant.* Cassell, 1966. 16 monochrome plates.

SAUNDERS, E. *The Age of Worth, couturier to the Empress Eugénie.* Longmans, 1954. Monochrome plates.

SPANIER, G. *It Isn't All Mink.* Collins, 1959. Account of the couture house of Balmain by the Directrice.

STEWART, M. and HUNTER, L. *The Needle Is Threaded.* Heinemann, 1964. A history of the National Union of Tailors and Garment Workers, from the medieval guilds to the present day.

THAARUP, A. *Heads and Tales.* Cassell, 1956. Autobiography of the Danish milliner.

WORTH, J. P. *A Century of Fashion.* Little, Brown, 1928. An account of the founding and history of the House of Worth.

UNDERWEAR AND ACCESSORIES

CUNNINGTON, C. W. and P. *The History of Underclothes.* Joseph, 1951. Monochrome plates and line drawings.

LIBRON, F. and CLOUZOT, H. *Le corset.* Paris, 1933. 85 monochrome and colour plates with some line drawings.

UNDERWEAR

Chapters on underwear will be found in many of the works listed under General.

ST LAURENT, C. *A History of Ladies' Underwear*. Michael Joseph, 1968. 216 monochrome and colour plates.

WAUGH, N. *Corsets and Crinolines*. Batsford, 1954. Reprinted 1972. 115 plates of primary source material and 24 patterns of garments.†

ACCESSORIES *including hats, hairstyles, jewellery and footwear.*

D'ALLEMAGNE, H. R. *Les accessoires du costume et du mobilier depuis le treizième jusqu'au milieu de dix-neuvième siècle*. 3 vols. Schemit, 1928. 393 monochrome plates.

ANDERSON, R. M. 'The Golilla. A Spanish collar of the seventeenth century', in *Waffen-und Kostumkunde*, no. I, January 1969.

ANGELOUGLOU, M. *A History of Make-up*. Studio Vista, 1970. Numerous monochrome and colour plates.

ARNOLD, J. *Perukes and Periwigs: a survey c. 1660–1740*. H.M.S.O., 1970. 27 monochrome plates of paintings from the National Portrait Gallery.†

BALLY SCHUHMUSEUM, Felsgarten, Schoenwerd, Switzerland. *Catalogue of the Collection*. Wilhelm Sulser, 1948. Monochrome plates of items in the collection.

BECK, S. W. *Gloves, their Annals and Associations*. Adams, 1883. Dated but useful work on the trade and social history of gloves.

BOEHN, M. VON. *Modes and Manners. Ornaments*. Dent, 1929. 241 monochrome and 16 colour plates.

BRAUN-RONSDORF, M. *The History of the Handkerchief*. F. Lewis, 1967.

BRIGHTON MUSEUM AND ART GALLERY. *Vanity*. 1972. A useful exhibition catalogue listing items from many museums.

CORSON, R. *Fashions in Hair*. Peter Owen, 1965. A history of 5000 years of hairstyles with numerous monochrome plates and 2500 line drawings.

CORSON, R. *Fashions in Eyeglasses from the 14th century to the Present Day*. Peter Owen, 1967. 120 monochrome plates and 500 line drawings.

CRAWFORD, T. S. *A History of the Umbrella*. David & Charles, 1970. Monochrome plates.

EVANS, J. *A History of Jewellery 1100–1870*. Faber, 1953. 1970. 176 plates.

FLOWER, M. *Victorian Jewellery*. Cassell, 1951. 118 pages monochrome, 10 colour plates.

FREEMAN, C. *Luton and the Hat Industry*. Luton Museum and Art Gallery, 1953. 31 monochrome plates.

GARDNER, A. 'Hairstyles and Head-dresses 1050–1600', in *The Journal of the British Archaeological Association*, 3rd series, vol. XIII, 1950.

GARSAULT, F. A. DE. *The Art of the Wigmaker*, trans. J. Stevens-Cox. Hairdressers Technical Council, London, 1966. Translation of *L'Art du Perruquier*, 1767.

GRASS, M. N. *History of Hosiery*. Fairchild Publications, 1955. Monochrome photographs of examples of knitting and machinery.

GREGORIETTI, G. *Jewellery through the Ages*, trans. Helen Laurence. Hamlyn, 1970. 400 plates from primary sources, over 200 in colour.

HUGHES, G. *Modern Jewelry*. Studio Vista, 1964. 415 monochrome and colour plates. An international survey covering 1890–1964.

IRWIN, J. *Shawls: a study in Indo-European influences*. H.M.S.O., 1955. Plates of specimens in the Victoria & Albert Museum.

LINKS, J. G. *The Book of Fur*. James Barrie, 1956. 15 monochrome and 1 colour plate. A brief history of the fur trade.

LUSCOMB, S. C. *The Collectors' Encyclopedia of Buttons*. Crown Publishers, New York, 2nd edition, 1968. Over 3000 monochrome plates of buttons.

NORTHAMPTON MUSEUM. *Picture Book of Boots and Shoes,* 1964.†

RHEAD, G. W. *History of the Fan.* Kegan Paul, 1910. Egypt to the early 20th century. This was a limited edition of 500 copies.

ROCK, C. H. *Paisley Shawls.* Paisley Museums and Art Galleries, 1966. A guide to the collection.†

SEELEY SERVICE. *The Book of Public School, Old Boys, University, Navy, Army, Air Force and Club Ties.* Introduction by James Laver. Seeley Service, 1968. Numerous colour plates.

SMITH, A. L. and **KENT, K.** *The Complete Button Book.* Doubleday and The World's Work, 1949. Illustrates more than 5700 buttons.

STEINGRUBER, E. *Antique Jewellery. Its history in Europe from 800–1900.* Thames & Hudson, 1957. 341 monochrome and 8 colour plates.

STEVENS-COX, J. *An Illustrated Dictionary of Hairdressing and Wig Making.* Hairdressers Technical Council, London, 1966.

TWINING, LORD. *A History of the Crown Jewels of Europe.* Batsford, 1960. 800 plates. Covers 17 centuries.

WELLS, F. A. *The British Hosiery Trade.* Allen & Unwin, 1935. An account of the industry with an extremely useful bibliography.

WOODFORDE, J. *The Strange Story of False Teeth.* Routledge & Kegan Paul, 1968. 76 monochrome plates. Many entertaining anecdotes.

WOODFORDE, J. *The Strange Story of False Hair.* Routledge & Kegan Paul, 1971. 52 monochrome plates, mainly from primary sources.

TECHNICAL WORKS

ARNOLD, J. *Patterns of Fashion 1. Englishwomen's dresses and their construction c. 1660–1860.* Wace, 1964. Macmillan, 1972. Drawings of dresses showing their construction, with 30 detailed patterns.†

ARNOLD, J. *Patterns of Fashion 2. Englishwomen's dresses and their construction c. 1860–1940.* Wace, 1965. Macmillan, 1972. Drawings of dresses showing their construction, with 40 detailed patterns.†

ARNOLD, J. 'Sir Richard Cotton's Suit', in *The Burlington Magazine,* May 1973. Article with a pattern of a suit of 1618.

DIDEROT, D. *A Diderot Pictorial Encyclopedia of Trades and Industry; manufacturing and the technical arts in plates selected from 'L'Encyclopédie, ou Dictionnaire Raisonné des Sciences, des Arts et des Métiers' of Denis Diderot* (1751––65). 2 vols. Ed. C. C. Gillespie. Dover, New York, 1959.

MAXWELL, S. 'Two Eighteenth-century Tailors', in *Hawick Archaeological Society Transactions,* 1972. Two Scottish tailors' account books.

PETRASHECK-HEIM, I. *Die meisterstuckbucher des schneiderhandewerks in Innsbruck.* Museum Ferdinandeum, Innsbruck, 1970–. An account of the master tailors of Innsbruck and their pattern books from the 16th to the 18th century.

TAILOR AND CUTTER, London (1866–). Students are recommended to study past and present numbers of this publication.

WAUGH, N. *The Cut of Men's Clothes, 1600–1900.* Faber, 1964. 29 pages of plates, 42 cutting diagrams, 27 tailor's patterns and bibliography.†

WAUGH, N. *The Cut of Women's Clothes, 1600–1930.* Faber, 1968. 71 monochrome plates, 75 cutting diagrams, 54 tailor's patterns and bibliography.†

COOPER, G. *The Invention of the Sewing Machine.* The Smithsonian Institution Press, 1968, 137 monochrome plates.

TECHNICAL *works on pattern cutting, dressmaking and tailoring.*

SEWING *equipment, dry cleaning and laundry work.*

GILBERT, K. R. *Sewing Machines.* H.M.S.O., 1970. A Science Museum booklet.†
GRAY, J. *Talon Inc. A romance of achievement.* Meadville, Pa., 1963. History of the Talon zip-fastener company.
GROVES, S. *The History of Needlework Tools and Accessories.* Country Life, 1966. 199 monochrome plates of needlework tools and paintings showing them in use.†
MANSFIELD, A. 'Dyeing and Cleaning Clothes in the Late Eighteenth and Early Nineteenth Centuries', in *Costume*, no. 2, 1968.
WILKINSON, A. 'Conversation at Castle Howard', in *Costume*, no. 3, 1969. The work of a laundry maid at the turn of the century.

PRINTED & WOVEN TEXTILES, EMBROIDERY, LACE

BAIN, R. *The Clans and Tartans of Scotland.* Collins, 1938. Colour plates of tartans. Revised edition, 1959.
DIGBY, G. W. *Elizabethan Embroidery.* Faber, 1963. Monochrome plates.
EMERY, I. *The primary structures of fabrics: an illustrated classification.* The Textile Museum, Washington, 1966. Numerous monochrome plates.
FELKIN, W. *Felkin's History of the Machine Wrought Hosiery and Lace Manufacturers.* 1867. Centenary edition, David & Charles, 1967.
HALLS, Z. *Machine-made Lace in Nottingham in the 18th and 19th Century.* Nottingham Museum and Art Gallery, 1964. Monochrome plates.
HARTLEY, M. and **INGILBY, J.** *The Old Hand-Knitters of the Dales with an Introduction to the Early History of Knitting.* The Dalesman Publishing Company, 1951. 4 monochrome plates and many line drawings.
IRWIN, J. and **BRETT, K. B.** *Origins of Chintz.* H.M.S.O., 1970. 158 monochrome plates, some of chintz for clothing.
KLESSE, B. *Seidenstoffe in der Italienischen Malerei des 14 Jahrhunderts.* Schriften der Abegg-Stiftung, 1967. 211 monochrome, 12 colour plates of paintings and textiles with 519 line drawings of silk designs.
LEVEY, S. M. *Discovering Embroidery of the 19th Century.* Shire Publications, 1971. 30 monochrome plates of embroidery, including examples on dress.†
MEULEN-NULLE, L. W. VAN DER. *Lace.* Merlin Press, 1963. 49 monochrome plates of portraits and specimens of lace.†
PALLISER, F. B. *A History of Lace.* Revised edition by M. Jourdain and A. Dryden, Sampson Low, 1902. Dated, but still useful work on the subject with many plates of portraits and specimens from many countries.
ROTHSTEIN, N. *The English Silk Industry, 1700–1825.* Adams & Dart, 1974. 50 monochrome and 4 colour plates of contemporary silks and designs. Invaluable for dating silks.
SCHUETTE, M. VON. *Alte Spitzen.* Klinkhardt & Biermann, 1963. 179 monochrome plates of lace. A standard work.
THORNTON, P. *Baroque and Rococo Silks.* Faber, 1965. 119 monochrome plates of silks, designs, costumes and paintings.
WALKER, B. G. *A Second Treasury of Knitting Patterns.* Pitman, 1971. Monochrome plates of many early knitting patterns.
WARDLE, P. *Victorian Lace.* Herbert Jenkins, 1968. 82 monochrome plates.

VII. Collections of Costume and Costume Accessories in England, Scotland and Wales

This guide has presented several problems in compilation. Costume collections are being built up in museums all over the country and this survey includes over eighty of them. Many of the collections have not yet been fully catalogued and in some cases the specimens are in boxes, sometimes in inaccessible stores, so that it is difficult to get a really adequate idea of the contents. It means very little to know how many items there are unless the quality and date of each individual specimen is also known. There is little point in recording the fact that there are twenty women's dresses of the 1860s in a collection unless the fact that eighteen of them have been altered for fancy dress at the end of the nineteenth century is also recorded. Fully illustrated catalogues are needed for each collection, but there are very few available.

All the collections reflect the taste and individual interests of the collectors who formed them and some museums have definite policies for collecting material of certain types. This should be borne in mind when looking at or working in any collection.

For these reasons I have attempted to describe the collections briefly to give an idea of their scope. I visited seventy-five of the museums listed between September 1970 and January 1972 and contacted the curators of the others by letter and telephone. During this time I noted over 1,500 items of particular interest in the costume collections: good examples of fashionable dress and accessories, usually complete and unaltered, often with their makers' labels and made from good quality fabrics; rare examples of occupational or working clothes; items of local interest, perhaps with documentary evidence. Unfortunately lack of space has prevented mention of more than a few of them, but over 50 illustrations are included. Special categories of costume, for example ethnographic costume, oriental costume, armour and uniform, require separate source books, as the fields are so large. However, I have listed a few collections where the enthusiast can start research. There are small groups of costume on display in many English country houses, for example Burghley House, Hatfield House, Longleat House and Woburn Abbey; some are privately owned and others belong to the National Trust. A few firms, such as Clark's of Street (shoes), Fownes of Worcester (glove manufacturers), Butterick (paper patterns) and Jantzen (swimwear) keep a small collection of related material in their archives. Some examples of cricketing costume are kept in the Cricket Memorial Gallery at Lord's while the Wellcome Museum of Medical Science in Euston Road, London, has a few doctors' academic robes as well as a collection of prints and books relating to dress.

It is important to remember that in many cases the museum staff dealing with costume may not necessarily be specialists in the field. In a small museum they may have to deal with enquiries about ceramics, painting, archaeology and local crafts as well. For this reason enthusiasts wishing to look at items closely should be prepared to do their own background reading and to try and answer for themselves the questions which arise from their study. Great care must be taken when handling costume; many specimens are in a very fragile state and can easily be damaged beyond repair by careless or clumsy hands. I have indicated the number of visitors for whom there is sufficient study space in each museum. An advanced student may require several specimens and plenty of room for items to be spread out, while a group of children drawing one mounted dress will take up the same area.

LIST OF ADDRESSES

Telephone

ABERDEEN (0224)23942

ABINGDON 3703

ABERDEEN: Art Gallery and Regional Museum, Schoolhill, Aberdeen AB9 1FQ

ABINGDON: Borough Museum, Market Square, Abingdon, Berks OX14 3JE

Telephone

AYLESBURY: Buckinghamshire County Museum, Church Street, Aylesbury, Bucks HP20 2QP — AYLESBURY (0296)82158

BARNARD CASTLE: The Bowes Museum, Newgate, Barnard Castle, Co. Durham DL12 8NP — BARNARD CASTLE (08333)2139

BATH: The Museum of Costume, The Assembly Rooms, Alfred Street, Bath BA1 2QH — BATH (0225)28411

BEDFORD: Cecil Higgins Art Gallery, Castle Close, The Embankment, Bedford MK40 3NY — BEDFORD (0234)53791

BIRMINGHAM: City Museum and Art Gallery, Congreve Street, Birmingham B3 3DH — BIRMINGHAM (021)235 9944

BOLTON: Bolton Museum and Art Gallery, Civic Centre, Bolton BL1 1SE — BOLTON (0204)22311

BRADFORD: Bolling Hall Museum, Brompton Avenue, Bradford, Yorkshire BD4 7LP — BRADFORD (0274)25974

BRIGHTON: Art Gallery and Museum, Church Street, Brighton BN1 1UE — BRIGHTON (0273)63005

BRISTOL: Blaise Castle Folk Museum, Henbury, Bristol BS10 7QY — BRISTOL (0272)625378

CARDIFF: Welsh Folk Museum, St Fagan's Castle, Cardiff CF5 6DX — CARDIFF (0222)561357

CHELMSFORD: Chelmsford and Essex Museum, Oaklands Park, Moulsham Street, Chelmsford CM2 9AQ — CHELMSFORD (0245)53066

CHERTSEY: Chertsey Museum, The Cedars, Windsor Street, Chertsey, Surrey KT16 8AT — CHERTSEY (09328)65764

CHESTER: Grosvenor Museum, 27 Grosvenor Street, Chester CH1 2DD — CHESTER (0244)21616

CHRISTCHURCH: The Red House Museum and Art Gallery, Quay Road, Christchurch, Hants BH23 1BU — CHRISTCHURCH (02015)2860

CLAYDON: Claydon House, Middle Claydon, Buckingham MK18 2EY — STEEPLE CLAYDON (029673)349

COLCHESTER: The Holly Trees (Later Antiquities), 87 High Street, Colchester CO1 1UG [Branch of Colchester and Essex Museum] — COLCHESTER (0206)77475

COVENTRY: Herbert Art Gallery and Museums, Jordan Well, Coventry CV1 5QP — COVENTRY (0203)25555

DUMFRIES: Burgh Museum, The Observatory, Corberry Hill, Dumfries DG2 7SQ — DUMFRIES (0387)3374

DUNFERMLINE: Carnegie Dunfermline Trust, Abbey Park House, Abbey Park Place, Dunfermline, Fife KY12 7PB — DUNFERMLINE (0383)23638/9

DUNFERMLINE: Pittencrief House Museum, Pittencrief Park, Dunfermline, Fife KY12 8QH — DUNFERMLINE (0383)22935

EDINBURGH: National Museum of Antiquities of Scotland, Queen Street, Edinburgh EH2 1JD — EDINBURGH (031)556 8921

EDINBURGH (031)225 7534	EDINBURGH:	The Royal Scottish Museum, Chambers Street, Edinburgh EH1 1JF
EXETER (0392)56724	EXETER:	Royal Albert Memorial Museum, Queen Street, Exeter EX4 3RX
GLASGOW (041)334 1134/5/6	GLASGOW:	Art Gallery and Museum, Kelvingrove, Glasgow G3 8AG
GLASGOW (041)632 1350	GLASGOW:	Burrell Collection, Camphill Museum, Queen's Park, Glasgow G41 2EW
TARFSIDE 254	GLENESK:	Glenesk Trust Folk Museum, The Retreat, Glenesk, Brechin, Angus DD9 7YT
both GLOUCESTER (0452)24131	GLOUCESTER:	City Museum and Art Gallery, Brunswick Road, Gloucester GL1 1HP
	GLOUCESTER:	Folk Life and Regimental Museum, Bishop Hooper's Lodging, 99–103 Westgate Street, Gloucester GL1 2PG
HALIFAX (0422)54823	HALIFAX:	Bankfield Museum, Ackroyd Park, Booth Town Road, Halifax HX3 6HG
HARTLEBURY (02996)416	HARTLEBURY:	Worcestershire County Museum, Hartlebury Castle, Kidderminster, Worcs DY11 7XX
both HEREFORD (0432)2456	HEREFORD:	Hereford City Library and Museums, Broad Street, Hereford HR4 9AU
	HEREFORD:	Churchill Gardens Museum, Venn's Lane, Hereford HR1 1DE
HITCHIN (0462)4476	HITCHIN:	Hitchin Museum and Art Gallery, Paynes Park, Hitchin, Hertfordshire SG5 1EQ
HULL (0482)27625	HULL:	The Georgian Houses, 23–4 High Street, Hull HU1 1NE
IPSWICH (0473)213761	IPSWICH:	Ipswich Museums and Art Galleries, High Street, Ipswich, Suffolk IP1 3QH
KINGUSSIE 307	KINGUSSIE:	The Highland Folk Museum, Duke Street, Kingussie, Inverness-shire PH21 1JG
LEEDS (0532)755821	LEEDS:	Kirkstall Abbey House Museum, Abbey Walk, Leeds LS5 3EH
ABERFORD (097332)259	LEEDS:	Lotherton Hall, Aberford, Leeds LS25 3EB
LEICESTER (0533)28354	LEICESTER:	Wygston's House, 25 St Nicholas Circle, Leicester LE1 5LD
LIVERPOOL (051)207 0001	LIVERPOOL:	City of Liverpool Museum, William Brown Street, Liverpool L3 8EN
LONDON (01)980 2415	LONDON:	Bethnal Green Museum, Cambridge Heath Road, London E2 9PA
LONDON (01)636 1555	LONDON:	The British Museum, Department of Prints and Drawings, Great Russell Street, London WC1B 3DG

Telephone

LONDON: The Museum of Mankind (British Museum), 6 Burlington Gardens, London WIX 2EX — LONDON (01)437 2224/8

LONDON: City of London Police Museum, Wood Street Police Station, London EC2V 7HN

LONDON: The Guildhall Museum, Gillett House, 55 Basinghall Street, London EC2V 5DU — LONDON (01)606 3030

LONDON: Horniman Museum and Library, 100 London Road, Forest Hill, London SE23 3PQ — LONDON (01)699 2339

LONDON: The London Museum, Kensington Palace, London W8 4PX — LONDON (01)937 9816

LONDON: Metropolitan Police Museum, Bow Street Police Station, Bow Street, London WC2E 7AT

LONDON: National Army Museum, Royal Hospital Road, Chelsea, London SW3 4SR — LONDON (01)730 0717

LONDON: National Maritime Museum, Romney Road, Greenwich, London SE10 9NF — LONDON (01)858 4422

LONDON: Permanent Exhibition of Judicial and Legal Costume, Royal Courts of Justice, Strand, London WC2A 2LL

LONDON: Vestry House Museum of Local History and Antiquities, Vestry Road, Walthamstow, London E17 9NH — LONDON (01)527 5544

LONDON: Victoria and Albert Museum, South Kensington, London SW7 2RL — LONDON (01)589 6371

LUTON: Museum and Art Gallery, Wardown Park, New Bedford Road, Luton LU2 7HA — LUTON (0582)36941

MAIDSTONE: Museum and Art Gallery, St Faith's Street, Maidstone, Kent ME14 ILH — MAIDSTONE (0622)54497

MANCHESTER: The Gallery of English Costume, Platt Hall, Wilmslow Road, Rusholme, Manchester M14 5LL — MANCHESTER (061)224 5217

MARKET HARBOROUGH: The Symington Collection of Period Corsetry, R. & W. H. Symington & Co. Ltd., Church Square, Market Harborough, Leicestershire LE16 7NB — MARKET HARBOROUGH (0645)2211

NEWCASTLE-UPON-TYNE: Laing Art Gallery and Museum, Higham Place, Newcastle-upon-Tyne NE1 8AG — NEWCASTLE (0632)26989/27734

NORTHAMPTON: Central Museum and Art Gallery, Guildhall Road, Northampton NN1 IDP — NORTHAMPTON (0604)34881

NORTHAMPTON: Abington Park Museum, Abington Park, Northampton NN1 5LW — NORTHAMPTON (0604)31454

NORWICH: Strangers' Hall Museum of Domestic Life, 4 Charing Cross, Norwich NOR 20J — NORWICH (0603)22233

Telephone		
NORWICH (0603)22233	NORWICH:	Bridewell Museum of Local Industries and Rural Crafts, Bridewell Alley, Norwich NOR 02H
NOTTINGHAM (0602)43615	NOTTINGHAM:	City of Nottingham Museum and Art Gallery, The Castle, Castle Place, Nottingham NG1 6EL
OXFORD (0865)57522	OXFORD:	Ashmolean Museum, Beaumont Street, Oxford OX1 2PH
PADIHAM (0282)72177	PADIHAM:	Gawthorpe Hall, Habergham Drive, Padiham, Burnley, Lancs BB12 8UA
GLASGOW (041)889 3151	PAISLEY:	Museum and Art Galleries, High Street, Paisley, Renfrewshire PA1 2BB
PETERBOROUGH (0733)3329	PETERBOROUGH:	Museum and Art Gallery, Priestgate, Peterborough PE1 1LF
PRESTON (0772)53989	PRESTON:	Harris Museum and Art Gallery, Market Square, Preston, Lancs PR1 2PP
READING (0734)55911	READING:	Museum and Art Gallery, Blagrave Street, Reading RG1 1QL
READING (0734)85123	READING:	Museum of English Rural Life, University of Reading, Whiteknights, Reading RG6 2AG
RUFFORD 254	RUFFORD:	Rufford Old Hall, 200 Liverpool Road, Rufford, Ormskirk, Lancs L40 1SG
SALISBURY (0722)4465	SALISBURY:	Salisbury and South Wiltshire Museum, 42 St Ann Street, Salisbury SP1 2DT
SHREWSBURY (0743)54876	SHREWSBURY:	Borough Museum and Art Gallery, Castle Gates, Shrewsbury SY1 2AS
BROADWAY (038681)2410	SNOWSHILL:	Snowshill Manor, Snowshill, Broadway, Worcs WR12 7JU
ROADE (0604)862229	STOKE BRUERNE:	Waterways Museum, Stoke Bruerne, Towcester, Northants NN12 7SB
TAUNTON (0823)3451	TAUNTON:	Somerset County Museum, Taunton Castle, Taunton, Somerset TA1 4AA
TRURO (0872)2205	TRURO:	Royal Institution of Cornwall, County Museum and Art Gallery, 25 River Street, Truro, Cornwall TR1 2SJ
	WALTHAMSTOW:	See London: Vestry House
WARWICK (0926)43431	WARWICK:	St John's House, Coten End, Warwick (Branch of County of Warwick Museum)
WESTON-SUPER-MARE (0934)24133	WESTON-SUPER-MARE:	Public Library and Museum, The Boulevard, Weston-super-Mare, Somerset BS23 1PL
WEYBRIDGE (0932)43573	WEYBRIDGE:	Weybridge Museum, Church Street, Weybridge, Surrey KT13 8DE
WINCHESTER (0962)66242	WINCHESTER:	Hampshire County Museum Service, Chilcombe House, Chilcombe Lane, Bar End, Winchester, Hants

WOODSTOCK:	Oxford City and County Museum, Fletcher's House, Park Street, Woodstock, Oxford OX7 1SN	WOODSTOCK (0993)811456
WORCESTER:	See Hartlebury	
WORTHING:	Museum and Art Gallery, Chapel Road, Worthing, Sussex BN11 1HD	WORTHING (0903)39189
YORK:	Castle Howard, York YO6 7DA	CONEYSTHORPE (065384)333
YORK:	Castle Museum, Tower Street, York YO1 RY	YORK (0904)53611

182. Glenesk Folk Museum. Winter dress of c. 1878 in brilliant blue ribbed silk and wool mixture, trimmed with white swansdown, worn by a girl aged 6–8 years. (57.122DRCX10)

ABERDEEN

ABERDEEN ART GALLERY AND REGIONAL MUSEUM

The small collection of costume was acquired locally or from people with connections with Aberdeen, and dates mainly from the late nineteenth and early twentieth centuries.

There are a few dresses, including a skirt, waistcoat and cape of c.1889–91 labelled *Romanes and Paterson, Manufacturers to the Queen, 62 Princes St., Edinburgh*, which is in soft blue/grey twill weave, heavy woollen cloth, very firm in texture (71.64d). An ivory satin wedding dress of c.1934 is also of interest. The centre front panel is cut on the cross, the skirt has cross-cut panels at the hem and the train falls in seven petal shapes (64.63.8).

The collection also includes a few petticoats, stockings, chemises, blouses, hats, shoes, gloves, and other small accessories, with several pieces of men's uniform and a few items of children's wear. The costumes are hanging in cupboards, protected by polythene bags. Fragile items and underwear are packed in boxes.

At the moment there is a small area for costume display in the decorative arts gallery but it is hoped to extend this in the future when the new premises are opened.

Each item is entered in an accessions book and then in a card index. Colour transparencies of several costumes can be duplicated on request but are not available commercially.

Parties of not more than twenty-five children can see costumes on request; there will shortly be a schools service. Up to six college students at a time can work in the costume store. Appointments should be made well in advance.

ABINGDON

BOROUGH MUSEUM

The very small collection of costume here is being built up gradually. It consists of a few eighteenth-century accessories, a group of nineteenth-century baby clothes, women's dresses and accessories, and two prize-winning smocks made for the Great Exhibition of 1851.

At the moment the costumes are in store; it is hoped that there will be display cases in the near future. A card index is being prepared. Not more than five older children or students can work in the reserve collection at any one time because of limited space. Appointments should be made in advance.

AYLESBURY

BUCKINGHAMSHIRE COUNTY MUSEUM

The collection of costume has been acquired mainly from donors having some connection with Aylesbury or the county. Displays of lace-making, with particular reference to Buckinghamshire, should be noted, as almost all the specimens are for trimming clothes.

There is a selection of over fifty, mainly nineteenth and twentieth-century women's day dresses, several evening dresses, a few nineteenth-century hats and bonnets, a small group in each category of skirts, blouses and bodices, all mainly twentieth-century. Women's underwear includes a few petticoats, dressing gowns, camisoles, brassières, chemises, a bustle petticoat, drawers, stockings and undersleeves, all nineteenth or early twentieth-century. A small range of accessories includes gloves, parasols, fans, aprons, handkerchiefs, collars, bags, boots and shoes. Fragments of footwear which date from the Tudor period are specimens from archaeological sites in the City of London. There is a small collection of mainly nineteenth and early twentieth-century babies' clothes and children's wear, and a specialised wear section which includes twenty smocks. There are a few items of mens' wear, among them a banyan of 1775–80, worn by John Baker Holroyd, 1st Earl of Sheffield (1735–1821), in brown satin damasked in a large foliage design. The gown is double breasted, fastening with eight buttons covered in brown silk (11AS.48).

Each item in the collection is entered in an accessions book with a full description and then in a card index, with the location.

The museum has two small rooms for costume displays, with space for ten or more dresses. Accessories are exhibited in two large glass cases. The museum education service caters for groups of up to forty children aged between ten and eighteen. A room is planned for students' use, but at the time of writing only two advanced students can work in the costume section at any one time, as space is limited. Reference books on costume are available for students working in the collection. Appointments should be made well in advance.

PUBLICATIONS AVAILABLE FROM THE MUSEUM

A selection of postcards and colour slides is in preparation.

BARNARD CASTLE

THE BOWES MUSEUM

The costume collection is part of the textile section, which includes a large number of tapestries, pieces of embroidery and lace. It has been built up mainly through gifts, usually from donors with local connections.

There are over 150 dresses, some of very good quality, ranging from the early nineteenth to the early twentieth century. A few of the best specimens are from the 1820s including an exquisite, unaltered dress of c.1820, too fragile to handle, in white gauze with a woven pattern of blue leaves in flossed silk. The small puffed sleeves are trimmed with pale turquoise blue satin to match the leaves, with little decorative tassels. (CST 843). The great majority of the dresses date from the mid-nineteenth century, and include a purple shot silk taffeta dress of c.1837–8 with full sleeves ruched over the sleevehead. It was made by a travelling dressmaker who stayed at the house for a week at a time (CST1132/1966.92). A maternity gown of c.1845–55 is in white cotton with a tiny purple sprig print. The front is open, with drawstrings at the waist and there is a matching cape with the dress (CST726/1963.756). Also probably for maternity wear was a brown shot silk dress of c.1845–50 with a full cartridge-pleated skirt. The fitted elbow-length sleeves have bell-shaped ends, and there are a pair of detachable engageantes to match. This dress was also made by a travelling dressmaker (CST1133/1966.93). A lilac cotton dress of c.1845 has a most interesting back fastening. It consists of two cotton strips with metal eyelet holes punched on one side and brass hooks attached to eyelet holes punched on the other. The fastening seems to be of the same period as the dress but no manufacturer's name or patent mark is visible (CST 743/1963.774).

Among several labelled dresses of the early twentieth century is an evening dress of 1911, in white satin with a black net overdress heavily beaded with jet bugle beads, white opaque bugle beads, with a crimson velvet sash. It is labelled *Paquin Paris 3 Rue de la Paix London 39 Dover Street. Hiver 1911* (CST511).

There is a good selection of wedding dresses and the large collection of underwear includes many exquisite hand-made petticoats and chemises worn by Lady Liverpool, Lady Dainford and Lady Ridley. There are a few, mostly good quality, corsets and bustles, and a small selection of children's and babies' clothes.

Men's costume includes uniforms which belonged to the Bowes family, a few suits and three smocks.

Each item is entered in a general accessions book; a card index is being prepared.

The dresses are mounted on padded hangers, then covered with polythene bags. They are stored on movable dress rails covered with dust sheets. One rack has a representative selection of fairly sturdy dresses which are easily accessible for children and students to study closely. Fragile items and underwear are packed in boxes.

At present there is one large gallery with several dresses, suits and children's costumes displayed with examples of lace, embroidery and tapestry. A party of thirty children can work here at a time, and groups of six children can be taken to see items in the reserve collection. Advance notice of an intended visit should be given. Three older students can be accommodated at a time for more detailed work; appointments should be made well in advance.

BATH

THE MUSEUM OF COSTUME

The museum was founded by Doris Langley Moore O.B.E. and is housed in the Assembly Rooms. It contains a very comprehensive collection, primarily of clothes worn by fashionable people, with many specimens of extremely high quality and is so well known that it needs little introduction.

The earliest items of women's dress are embroidered coifs and bodices of the late sixteenth and early seventeenth centuries and a superb silver tissue dress of c.1660. A fair proportion of specimens are from the early eighteenth century and the number of items increases from c.1750 onwards, culminating in a large range of twentieth-century dresses from couture houses. Among the many couturiers represented are Balenciaga, Pierre Balmain, Callot Soeurs, John Cavanagh, Christian Dior, Doeuillet, Doucet, Hartnell, Jacques Fath, Lanvin-Castillo, Lucille, Molyneux, Paquin, Pucci, Maggy Rouff, Schiaparelli, Victor Stiebel, Yves St Laurent and Worth. Some of the most elegant dresses in the collection were worn by Lady Curzon when Vicereine of India, the Ranee of Pudukota, Dame Margot Fonteyn de Arias, Martita Hunt, Vivien Leigh and the Hon. Mrs John Ward.

Among a good range of men's wear, the sixteenth-century embroidered shirts, the eighteenth-century embroidered court suits and the waistcoats are particularly fine.

The collection of babies' and children's clothes includes seventeenth and eighteenth-century layettes, which are on semi-permanent display. There are four cabinets of dressed dolls of the nineteenth and twentieth centuries and a 'Dolls' Tea Party' exhibit.

A selection of items from the very comprehensive range of underwear which includes corsets, bustles, brassières, drawers, petticoats and chemises is always on show. There are separate small displays of sportswear, including bathing costumes, and selections of stockings and shoes, of which there are particularly good collections from the eighteenth century to the present day. Accessories for dressmaking, goffering irons, glove stretchers and instruments for grooming top hats are exhibited near the costumes. One room contains millinery and head-dresses, breakfast caps and hair ornaments.

A very large display area allows approximately five hundred costumes and over fifteen hundred accessories and trinkets to be exhibited, often in a period setting. In December and January each year numerous specimens are changed, but some of the rarer ones are left on show permanently.

A full description of each item is entered in the card index and every Easter a 'Dress of the Year' is put on view; this is selected by some well-known fashion writer to represent one of the current trends.

Costumes are hung in date sequence in several store rooms, except for fragile specimens, which are in boxes. Preparations are being made to extend the storage to another building. Underwear and babies' clothes are stored in boxes in date order. Woollen specimens are packed separately and the date of the last moth-proofing is marked on the outside of the box. Conservation is carried out on the premises, but on the whole the dresses accepted are in very good condition and do not require a great deal of work.

A library and study room, is housed at No. 4, The Circus, and a great deal of material has already been accumulated. This includes 1830s French fashion plates still in the magazines, and fashion photographs from *The Sunday Times* from c.1960–70.

School parties of any size with an adequate number of teachers and a museum guide can work in the exhibition area. Until more accommodation is available there are facilities for two advanced students or a group of up to fifteen college students working on a special topic at any one time. Appointments to work in the collection should be made in advance.

PUBLICATIONS AVAILABLE FROM THE MUSEUM

The Museum of Costume, Assembly Rooms Bath. Guide to the exhibition and a commentary on the trends of fashion by Doris Langley Moore, Founder of the Museum.
A Picture Book from the Museum of Costume.
A large selection of black and white and colour postcards of costumes in the collection.
The bookstall has a selection of publications dealing with costume. A list of these and the postcards may be obtained free of charge from the museum by sending a stamp for postage.

BEDFORD

CECIL HIGGINS ART GALLERY
Two collections of textiles are housed in the museum, the Corporation collection of costume with some examples of lace, and the Trustees' collection, consisting almost entirely of lace.

Opposite

183. *Museum of Costume, Bath. Silver tissue dress of c. 1660 trimmed with cream lace enriched with thin strips of parchment completely covered with ivory silk thread. The bodice is heavily boned and laces up at the centre back.*

The lace collections are particularly fine, covering all periods and types, providing examples of cuffs, collars, lappets, caps, flounces and other trimmings. The work of Thomas Lester, a local man who designed many prize-winning items in nineteenth-century exhibitions, should be noted. His designs were passed out to cottage workers who made the lace. A large number of the specimens directly related to dress are in Bedfordshire Maltese lace and Buckinghamshire point ground lace.

The costume collection reflects local taste, as it has been acquired mainly from donors living in Bedford. Some of the labelled dresses were made by dressmakers working locally, and there are many purchased in London. There is a comprehensive selection of women's dress dating mainly from the nineteenth and twentieth centuries. Over seventy-five of the twentieth-century dresses and costumes were donated by Miss P. Burnaby, many worn by herself and others collected from her friends. A small group of bodices, blouses and skirts date from the late nineteenth and twentieth centuries. There is a larger selection of coats, jackets and mantles of the same period and quite a number of shawls, mainly nineteenth-century. The underwear section includes nightdresses, bustles, corsets and a bathing costume of c.1913.

There is a fair selection of mainly nineteenth-century headwear with some eighteenth-century specimens. Accessories are divided into those worn and those carried; a small group of those worn in the nineteenth and twentieth centuries includes combs, ostrich plumes, fichus, aprons and sashes. A larger collection of parasols, umbrellas, fans, purses and handkerchiefs etc., also mainly nineteenth and twentieth-century, are in the group of accessories carried, and there are small selections of nineteenth and twentieth-century gloves, mittens and footwear.

The very small collection of mainly twentieth-century men's clothes is divided into suits, waistcoats, trousers and breeches, coats, cloaks, smocks, underwear, shirts, headgear and accessories (worn and carried). The sizeable group of mainly nineteenth- and twentieth-century children's and babies' clothes is catalogued under robes and frocks, coats and cloaks, underwear, headwear, gloves, footwear and accessories.

A large selection of lace and a few costumes are on display in the museum. The reserve collection of costumes is hanging on rails in date sequence, with fragile specimens packed in boxes. An extension to the museum is being built and plans for 1975 include new display and storage areas.

Each item is entered in an accessions book; the two collections are indexed separately. A collection of colour transparencies of costume taken by the museum could be copied for students on request, but they are not available commercially. For an article 'Thomas Lester's Lace' by Margaret Greenshields, see *Embroidery*, Spring 1968.

A room is available for study sessions; three advanced students or groups of up to thirty children or ten sixth-formers can be accommodated at a time. Appointments should be made well in advance.

BIRMINGHAM

CITY MUSEUM AND ART GALLERY

The major part of the large collection of costume and accessories was acquired from local people. There are a few plain, women's everyday dresses; most of them are very fashionable. They date from the late eighteenth to the mid-twentieth century but most are from the nineteenth century. There are about fifteen late eighteenth-century gowns, the majority altered from earlier silks, and particularly good ranges of dresses from c.1838–45, the late 1860s, the early 1870s and the 1950s. A dress of c.1898–9 made from a William Morris fabric, and labelled *Sarah Fullerton-Monteith Young, Grosvenor Square 21 Mount Street* (M36'48A) is of particular interest. Among the accessories, which are divided into groups of underwear (with a selection of nightgowns, petticoats, chemises and a few corsets) handbags, gloves, fans, bonnets, hats and shoes, is a quilted down petticoat of c.1865 in red printed cotton, labelled *Booth and Fox's. London 1862. Dublin 1865. Patent (No 8162) Down skirt. Size 34 in. Warranted pure arctic down. Wash with down inside. Shake well whilst drying.* There are also a pair of sleeve supports of c.1830–4 made of cotton sateen with wire to stiffen them (M75'38).

The children's costume category, although not comprehensive, contains many good, mainly nineteenth-century, individual specimens and includes accessories, underwear, babies' clothes and a large group of christening robes.

Men's costume is catalogued under coats, footwear, headgear, neckwear, shirt fronts, smocks, suits, trousers and waistcoats. Among several eighteenth and nineteenth-century suits there is one in rich tan cut and uncut patterned velvet with a satin ground, consisting of coat, waistcoat and breeches. This was originally worn by Lord Riverstone who ordered it from Paris and paid £27.10.3. The tailor's bill is also in Birmingham Museum. There are also some civil and military uniforms, a group of more than ten smocks and a few ecclesiastical vestments dating from the seventeenth century.

Dresses are all protected by polythene bags and hung in cupboards in chronological order, except for very fragile specimens, which are in boxes.

Each item is entered in an accessions book and then in a card index.

The museum displays are undergoing reorganisation at the time of writing. There is limited space for costume cases and the exhibits are

arranged for a year or eighteen months at a time, usually around a theme such as '1920s Dresses', 'Tennis Clothes', 'A Gentleman's Wardrobe'.

The schools service has a selection of expendable specimens for children aged eight to fourteen to handle. Groups of not more than six or seven children aged fifteen to eighteen, or College of Education or art students can be accommodated in the reserve collection at any one time, to work under supervision. There is working space for two advanced students. Appointments should be made well in advance.

PUBLICATIONS AVAILABLE FROM THE MUSEUM

18 monochrome photographic cards in three sets (6 cards in each set) illustrating the change in fashion from 1745 to 1908 from examples in the collection. Each set is supplied in a folder containing descriptive notes.

Set A. 1745 to 1785 photographs 1 to 6
Set B. 1820 to 1870 photographs 7 to 12
Set C. 1872 to 1908 photographs 13 to 18.

12 monochrome photographic cards in two sets (6 cards in each set) illustrating Victorian and Edwardian dolls dressed in fashions of the period. Each set is supplied in a folder containing descriptive notes.

Set A. photographs 1 to 6
Set B. photographs 7 to 12.

Opposite

184. City Museum and Art Gallery, Birmingham. Wedding dress of c. 1888–90 in soft lightweight ivory silk, with draperies inspired by Greek statuary super-imposed on typical 1880s dress construc-tion. It is labelled 'Liberty Costumes'. (M68'68)

BOLTON

BOLTON MUSEUM AND ART GALLERY

Bolton Museum has built up in recent years a small collection of about a thousand items of costume and accessories in very good condition.

There is an interesting collection consisting of dresses, shoes, hats, underwear etc. from a local family, donated by the last of the line, Miss Walker. There are many items of clothing, some unworn and with the prices still attached, dating from the early 1890s to the 1920s.

Among the small selection of dresses from c.1810–1870 is a maternity gown of c.1845–50 in turquoise blue and yellow silk, patterned with a striped design and large flowers, and with a yellow quilted soft silk lining (T136.1967).

Most of the dresses in the general collection date from c.1870 onwards and include a maid's uniform in blue and white striped cotton of c.1893–1900. There are two large white cotton aprons with little embroidered bibs and long straps to tie at the back. Two embroidered strips which would have been ruched up to form caps, (one being laundered while the other was in use), still have a pair of long plain cotton streamers to be pinned on at the back (T272.1967).

Among the twentieth-century dresses is a court dress of c.1910, worn by the donor's aunt at Holyrood Palace, made of cream net over ivory satin, with black net embroidered in cream. A contemporary photograph is a most valuable record (T20.1964). A dinner dress of c.1916 is of shot green and yellow silk giving the effect of bronze (T31.1963), and one of c.1918 is in mauve and navy chiffon over pink voile, with shot blue and pink taffeta giving the effect of mauve (T219.1967). A dress of c.1919 in kingfisher blue satin, with chiffon of the same colour is embroidered with black beads and sequins (T129.1967). A characteristically straight dress of c.1926-7 is made of deep beige crepe satin with the reverse side of the material used for the side skirt panels for a contrast of surface texture (T20.1966).

The collection also contains a few specimens in each of the following categories: aprons, collars, blouses, bodices, skirts, hats, shoes, bonnets, parasols, jabots, scarves, capes, shawls, feather flowers for hat trimmings, feather boas, infants' and children's clothes, all dating mainly from the late nineteenth and early twentieth centuries. A selection of women's underwear includes nightgowns, camisoles, bed jackets, combinations, petticoats and corsets.

There are a few items of men's clothing, waistcoats and morning coats, mainly from the late nineteenth century. Present-day items include a good selection of the Borough Police Force uniforms.

Each item is entered in an accessions book with a full description, and its location is noted in a card index file.

The costumes are stored in a small room on dress rails, in protective wardrobes or in cardboard boxes clearly labelled.

The museum has attractive displays of costume, and groups of thirty children can be catered for. Twelve older students or four advanced students can be accommodated at a time, depending on the amount of material needed. Appointments should be made well in advance.

BRADFORD

BOLLING HALL MUSEUM
The major part of the costume collection, which is stored in Bolling Hall, a seventeenth-century house, was acquired from local donors and reflects the taste of middle-class Bradford society from the mid-nineteenth to the mid-twentieth century.

There are some 150 dresses, over half of them twentieth-century, but they include three dresses from c.1775-1818 which belonged to the Rawson family of Bradford. The first is a sack gown in lemon silk, with

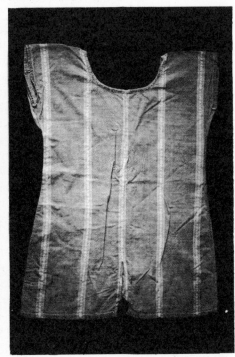

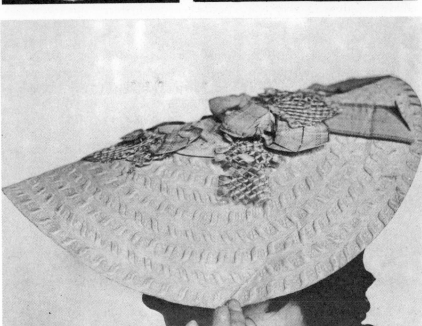

a woven design of ivory curving flowered stripes (428/69). The dress was made in c.1765–70 and altered for use in c.1775–85, the sack pleats being narrowed slightly and the bodice front meeting edge to edge. The original linings remain. The sleeves have tucks stitched down over the sleevehead in the same way as another dress, of c.1785, probably made by the same dressmaker. This is a pink silk lustring *robe à l'anglaise*, with its neckline trimmed with a strip of pinked silk and fly fringe (42/70). The third dress is an ivory figured silk pelisse of c.1815–18 with a small turn-down collar. The hem, fronts and collar edge are trimmed with crossway satin bands and piping, and the cuffs have treble rows of the same decoration. A day dress of c.1903–5 is of an interesting open weave black springy woollen fabric. The bodice is pouched at the centre front, and the sleeves slightly bloused at the wrists (200/70). An evening dress of c.1904–5 was made locally. Labelled 'Gibson Boyce and Co., Bradford', it is made of cream organza, machine embroidered with sprays of flowers in pink, white and green. The scalloped hemline is trimmed with ruched cream chiffon.

There is also a small selection in each of the following categories of women's costume: blouses, bodices, capes, coats, nightwear, shawls, shoes, skirts, stockings and underwear. Accessories include aprons, bags and purses, collars, fans, gloves, jewellery, millinery, parasols, scarves and stoles. There is a large group of babies' gowns and a small selection of children's dresses, footwear, headwear, nightwear, outerwear and underwear.

There are a few items of men's clothes, including a pair of black leather shoes with the edge of the sole and the heel painted red of c.1650–60 (22/30/1), and a scarlet, fine twill weave worsted coat with covered buttons to match, which was worn in the Bishop Blaize procession in 1825 (387/66a). A mid twentieth-century woolsorter's 'brat' or overall is of local interest. The other items are mostly waistcoats and small accessories from the nineteenth and twentieth centuries.

Dresses are stored on padded hangers and covered with polythene bags, except for fragile specimens and beaded dresses which lie flat in a cupboard with long wide drawers.

Each item is entered in an accessions book and then in a card index.

Costume for school projects is dealt with by the schools education service, based at Cartwright Hall, Bradford BD9 4NS. Bona fide students can see the reserve collection by prior arrangement, although numbers have to be limited to not more than two at any one time. Reference books on costume are available for students working in the collection.

In 1973 the Bradford Industrial Museum opened. Housed in a converted worsted mill, it contains machinery and illustrates the development of the wool textile industry.

Far left

188. County Museum, Aylesbury. Bustle dress of c. 1879–81 in blue grey grosgrain with rows of kilting at the hem and dark turquoise velvet used for contrast. (6J49)

Left

189. Bolling Hall Museum, Bradford. Wedding dress of c. 1832–5 in ivory silk alpaca with a matching pelerine cape. The gigot sleeves have wide lapels over the top and are supported inside by a strip of gathered glazed cotton with whale- bone at the edge. The edges of the lapels and cape, and the front skirt are trimmed with cross- way piping and ruched satin thistle motifs. A tasselled silk girdle ties at the centre back waist. (29/45)

BRIGHTON

ART GALLERY AND MUSEUM

Most of the items in this small collection of costume which has been built up in recent years were acquired locally. The majority of the dresses and accessories date from the early nineteenth century onwards. The accessioning system is being revised at the time of writing and there is a card index in which details of every costume are entered.

There are no permanent displays of costume in the museum, but dresses and accessories are often used in other exhibitions.

Small parties of children accompanied by a teacher may see costumes from the reserve collection under supervision and it is usually possible to accommodate up to six advanced students in the store. Appointments should be made well in advance.

PUBLICATIONS AVAILABLE FROM THE MUSEUM

Vanity. Brighton Museum and Art Gallery, 1972

A catalogue of an exhibition for the Brighton Festival which included many engravings, caricatures, drawings and actual specimens of fashionable accessories from the seventeenth century to the present day.

BRISTOL

BLAISE CASTLE FOLK MUSEUM

Opposite
190. Blaise Castle
Folk Museum,
*Bristol. Palest beige
silk dress with
matching coat of
c. 1868–9. The
petersham band
inside the waist is
labelled 'Madame
Devy's Company
Ltd, 73 Grosvenor
St, Grosvenor
Square' with a royal
coat of arms stamped
in gold. It appears
to be original, not a
later addition. This
is one of the earliest
labelled dresses on
record and is
elaborately trimmed
with crossway bands,
fringe and silk
covered tassels.*
(T.6054)

The items donated by the Harford family who built and lived at Blaise Castle from 1795 to 1924 are of local interest in this collection.

There are nearly two hundred dresses from the mid-eighteenth to the twentieth century. Among them is a pale aquamarine silk crepe dress of c.1818–23 with a woven pattern of acorn sprays. Its sleeves are puffed and ruched with a lattice-work of wide piped stripes of aquamarine satin, and the neck and bodice front are trimmed with satin piping. The material is 46 in. wide and is woven with a deep border pattern which is used at the hemline of the dress. A white muslin dress of c.1834–5 has wide pelerine lapels, bordered with white lace, a deep hem reaching to knee level, with a band of embroidery consisting of curving sprays of flowers and leaves above it. The gigot sleeves have long tucks from the elbow to take in the fullness and fit the arm down to the wrist. There is also an 'aesthetic' tea gown of c.1891–2 in golden yellow plush, labelled *Madame Hodgson, 25 Wigmore Street, Cavendish Square, London W.* A loose panel of figured golden yellow silk falls from the neck to the ground at the front, caught in just above the natural waist level.

The collection also contains a few specimens in each of the following categories: accessories (including bags, buttons, bracelets, brooches and pendants, buckles, canes and umbrellas, ear-rings, fans, hair ornaments, handkerchiefs, jewel cases, necklaces, parasols and umbrellas, pockets, posy-holders, purses, rings, skirt holders, a pair of sleeve puffs of c.1835 in stiff white cotton with cane supports, veils, wedding veils and head-dresses); aprons; bathing costumes; bed jackets; belts and sashes; boas; blouses and bodices; bonnet veils; braces; breeches; bustles; capes and cloaks; caps; ceremonial costume and accessories; chemisettes; children's clothes (including babies' gowns and robes, babies' and children's shoes, children's dresses and suits, christening robes and headgear); coats and skirts (women); coats (men); coats (women) and spencers; collars and fichus; cocked hats; combinations; corsets and stays; cravats and ties; crinoline frames; cuffs and ruffles; drawers and bloomers; dresses; dress fronts; gaiters; gloves; hats, bonnets and uglies; jerseys; jumpers; mittens; muffs; nightdresses; nightshirts; negligées and dressing gowns; nightcaps; pelerines; petticoats and underskirts; powdering cloaks; scarves, stoles and wraps; shawls; shirts; shoes, pattens and boots; skirts; smocks; squares; stockings; suits and court coats; sun-bonnets; top hats; tippets; underbreeches; undersleeves; uniforms and livery; vests and chemises; waistcoats. The selections of fans, parasols and umbrellas, smocks, children's clothing, shoes, pattens and boots are quite large.

Four rooms are devoted to displays of over twenty dresses, a wide range

of accessories and selections of children's costume and men's clothing. Other items are stored in a large room where most of the dresses hang in cupboards.

Each item is entered in a card index. A selection of costume reference books is available. There is space for not more than thirty children at a time, and the schools department of the City Museum and Art Gallery deals with talks on costume. Accommodation in the store is limited; two students can see material in the reserve collection at any one time. Appointments should be made well in advance.

PUBLICATIONS AVAILABLE FROM THE MUSEUM

BENNETT, H. and WITT, C. *Eighteenth century women's costume at Blaise Castle House*. Bristol City Museum, 1972.

A catalogue of the collection, with 19 pages of monochrome plates.

Some colour transparencies of costume are on sale in the museum and more are planned. Others have been taken by the museum and could be duplicated on request. A list of publications and prices is available.

CARDIFF

WELSH FOLK MUSEUM

The collection of costume and accessories reflects the social background of Welsh people, mainly middle-class, from the mid-eighteenth to the early twentieth centuries, and was acquired from donors who lived or had some connections with Wales.

There is a large group of women's dresses from the eighteenth century to the 1920s, the major part being nineteenth-century. Most of the twenty eighteenth-century dresses were given by the Tredegars, a local county family; they include a mantua and petticoat heavily embroidered with silver for wear at Court, dating from *c*.1740. There are several interesting fashionable specimens from the early nineteenth century and a large selection of documented wedding dresses, many of them in coloured silks as well as white. The prosperity brought by increasing industrialisation is reflected in the selection of 1890s dresses; they include a pale pink wool costume of *c*.1890 trimmed with wine velvet, the front of its bodice and hem of the skirt at the front decorated with broad bands of gold and silver embroidery. It was worn by Miss Gwen Jones who married Mr Chitty at Caldicott Church on 12 August 1890. There is a photograph of her wearing the dress with the matching hat, which is also in the collection (38.116/3). A dinner dress of *c*.1893–5 is made of deep mustard-yellow ribbed silk, with the hem of the skirt, the bottom of the bodice, the revers, the bows on the shoulder and the trimmings at the bottom of the short sleeves in rich dark purple velvet. It is labelled *Private Dressmaking Department, Cavendish House, Cheltenham* (62.150/2).

There is a good range of underwear and there are a few items in each of the following categories of accessories: gloves, mittens, hats, shawls, mantles, capes, veils, stockings, muffs, hats and bonnets, habit skirts and shoes. Numerous items in lace include aprons, berthes, blouses, cuffs, canezons, fichus, jackets, mantles, pelisses, shawls and scarves. There is a selection of shawls of different types.

Men's costume includes a very small selection in each of the following categories: coats, among them one in soft grey wool with beautifully designed silver embroidery, lined with twill weave wool, of *c*.1750–60 (56.521/35); suits, underwear, bathing costumes, belts and braces, neckbands, neckerchiefs, ties, stocks, pullovers, sweaters and hats.

Among the children's costume is a riding jacket (56.521/33) of *c*.1750 in soft greyish beige woollen cloth decorated with silver braid and lined with pale blue silk. It would have been worn by a girl of about eight to ten. There is also a very small selection, mainly from the nineteenth century, in each of these groups: capes and cloaks, hats, coats and jackets, pinafores, boots and shoes, gowns and robes, dresses, underwear, sashes, pelisses, bonnets and caps, gloves and mittens, collars, shirts and sleeves, clogs.

Among other accessories of dress in the collection are bags, purses, wallets, pocket books, pipes, ear trumpets, combs and curling tongs, shaving equipment, skirt holders and dress ornaments.

All items are entered in an accessions book and then in a card index.

Temporary exhibitions on a theme, for example 'Wedding Dresses', are mounted in St Fagan's Castle. A new wing of the museum has been built for permanent costume display areas as well as a store and the dresses are packed flat in long drawers without folding the fabrics. Parties of up to twenty children can be accommodated in the temporary display area; the new building has room for up to thirty. Two advanced students may work in the reserve collection; a larger study area is available in the new building. Appointments should be made well in advance.

CHELMSFORD

CHELMSFORD AND ESSEX MUSEUM

The small collection of costume has been acquired mainly from local donors, but specimens are not necessarily of local origin.

The women's costume consists mainly of nineteenth and early twentieth-century items. There are a few dresses, including a teagown of *c*.1879–82, labelled *Worth et Cie London*. The dress and attached overskirt are in peach satin with a woven design of flowers in a deeper shade of

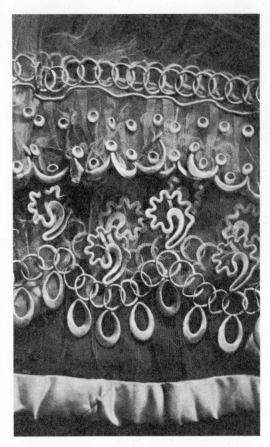 

191, 192. *Welsh Folk Museum, Cardiff. Little circles and ovals of card covered with flossed silk* (left) *trim the hem of a fragile net ball dress, c. 1820–5. (46.336/3) A wedding dress in cream satin, of 1883, labelled 'Phillips and Evans, Merthyr Tydfil'. The front skirt is covered with net encrusted with beads. A photograph shows the bride wearing the dress. (58.297/1)*

yellow and ivory, trimmed elaborately with embroidered net. The design was inspired by an eighteenth-century sack dress (023962:1,2). An evening dress of *c.*1900–2 in lilac silk is labelled *Field of Colchester* (1971:279:1,2).

There are small ranges of underwear and accessories, including four pairs of early nineteenth-century shoes with shoemakers' labels, and a few items of children's clothing. Several men's suits and liveries of the nineteenth and twentieth centuries, as well as military uniforms, are of local interest.

All the dresses are hanging, covered with polythene bags, except for fragile items which are in boxes.

Each item is entered in an accessions register and then in a costume file.

One room is devoted to displays of costume, accessories and uniform.

Groups of up to fifteen children at a time can see items from the reserve collection by arrangement. There is no schools service at the time of writing. Two students can work in the store at a time. Appointments should be made in advance.

CHERTSEY

CHERTSEY MUSEUM

The Olive Matthews Collection of Costume is administered by a Trust and housed in Chertsey Museum. There are small ranges of late eighteenth-century and early nineteenth-century dresses, eighteenth-century men's suits and waistcoats, with a selection of children's and babies' clothes. The accessories include over fifty fans, shoe buckles, jewellery, snuff-boxes, vinaigrettes, lace, parasols, shoes, bags, purses and needlework tools. There is some very good quality material in the collection.

There is only space for two visitors to see the reserve collection at any one time, so appointments should be made in advance.

CHESTER

GROSVENOR MUSEUM

Chester Museum has a small collection of costume and accessories. Among the women's dresses, which date mainly from the mid-Victorian and Edwardian periods, is one of c.1830–5 in lilac and green printed cotton on a white ground, with a front bodice which can be unbuttoned on either side of the bust for breast-feeding (35 L 1959) and a brilliant blue silk dress of c.1868–70, trimmed with stone-coloured silk fringe (11 L 60). A wedding dress of c.1893–5 in white satin has the label of a local dressmaker *Madame Hamley, Chester* on the petersham waistband inside the bodice (82 L 1967).

There are very small selections from the following items, mainly from the nineteenth and twentieth centuries: men's suits and waistcoats, women's underclothes including camisoles, petticoats, nightgowns, drawers and combinations; shawls, scarves and wedding veils; women's bodices, coats, jackets and blouses; capes and mantles; adults' pattens, boots and shoes; children's boots and shoes; children's and babies' clothes; accessories including hairpins, hat-pins, combs, belts, collar stiffeners, hair-bands, buttons, button-hooks, muffs, ostrich feathers, wig stands, fans, bags, purses, stockings, gloves, mittens, umbrellas, parasols, handkerchiefs, bonnets and a bonnet box. Among the hats are three dating from c.1760. One is a girl's hat of blue silk with a small woven pattern, trimmed with lace round the edge of the brim and still with its cream satin ribbons (67 L 52). Another, for a woman, is of straw, lined with pink silk (69 L 52).

The costumes are stored in a small room on dress rails, and are divided into two groups. One contains the best specimens which are reserved for exhibitions and for advanced students to study; the other group of less important items is used as teaching material. Children are allowed to handle some of these things carefully, under supervision.

A card index contains a description of each item under separate categories for dresses, underclothes, children's dresses, etc.

There are a few items of costume on display in the museum. These are in period settings and are frequently changed.

There is room for a group of fifteen children or three advanced students at any one time. Appointments should be made well in advance.

CHRISTCHURCH

THE RED HOUSE MUSEUM AND ART GALLERY
This museum is a branch of the Hampshire County Museum Service. Most of the costume collection was acquired locally, but it does not necessarily reflect local taste as many of the donors retired to the area from other parts of the country.

There are over seventy, mainly nineteenth-century dresses, including an ivory satin wedding dress of c.1879, labelled *Swan and Edgar, Regent St London*, decorated with white feathers down both sides of the centre front panel and all round the fishtail train. The centre front panel is covered with ruched silk net divided by cream corded moiré ribbon bows. Kilted satin trims the hemline and there is a large bow of corded cream moiré silk at the centre back below the waist (α10.55). A plaited straw bustle is labelled *Trade mark Thomson's Corymbus Patented 1873. no 1*, and an inflatable gutta percha or rubber bustle of c.1872–5 is covered with red paisley printed cotton.

There are small ranges of underwear, accessories (including over eighty fans), and children's clothes, among them a large group of christening robes. Men's costume consists of a few suits including a black wool cloth coat of c.1830, military uniforms of local interest, and a small number of accessories.

Each item is entered in an accessions book and then in a card index which is in the process of compilation.

The Druitt collection of over two thousand fashion plates, mounted in albums, is of particular interest. The collection is very comprehensive and contains examples from many different journals throughout the nineteenth century. A few costume reference books are also available for students working in the collection.

Small displays of costume with related material are mounted in the museum and changed annually. There is space for a group of thirty children to work in the display area, or ten college students in the students' room at any one time. Advance notice of intended group visits should be given.

CLAYDON

CLAYDON HOUSE

Claydon House was built by the Verney family and is now a National Trust property. Several seventeenth-century costumes which belonged to the Verneys have been preserved and they are on display.

Items of special interest include a bodice of c.1660–5 in ivory silk, trimmed with crossway strips of ivory satin, pinked in rounded shapes, with ivory braid mounted on top. The whole bodice is mounted on top of a stiff boned corset made of two layers of linen with whalebones stitched between them. The wooden busk has been removed from the linen casing at the centre front. A corset of c.1670 in pink and white silk over a heavily boned linen foundation was probably for maternity wear. It laces at the centre front over a rounded stomacher and there is a rigid metal support at the centre back.

Men's wear includes a nightgown of c.1615–20 worn by Sir Francis Verney, in purple silk damask with a grey silk shag lining, which looks like fur. A cream satin doublet of c.1630 is pinked all over the surface. The breast and the sleeves are slashed and silver braid is sewn all round the edges. There is a strip of satin inside the waist with metal rings, to which the breeches would have been hooked. A cloak, doublet and breeches of yellowish beige silk with a woven pattern of stylised foliage date from *c*.1660. The ends of the sleeves and the petticoat breeches are trimmed with yards of satin ribbon.

Claydon House is open daily from March to October and by appointment only from November to February.

COLCHESTER

THE HOLLYTREES (LATER ANTIQUITIES)
The collection of costume in this branch of the Colchester and Essex Museum is stored and displayed at a large house, The Hollytrees, in the High Street near the main Museum. Many of the items were acquired from local donors.

There is a fairly representative selection of over a hundred dresses from the late eighteenth century to the present day, among them a caraco jacket of *c*.1775–80, in pink chiné silk lined with pink glazed wool, still fastening at the centre front with the original hooks; the cuffs are missing (D42). A pink silk pelisse of *c*.1820 has a detachable cape collar and padded hemline. The original cylindrical clip fasteners are still in position (2016.55). There is also a cream satin wedding dress of *c*.1898, embroidered on the yoke with pearls and tiny sparkling glass beads, with a spray of orange blossom attached to the bodice beneath the chin. It is labelled *Kate Tarrant, Modes et Robes, Lichfield* (46.1968).

The range of accessories includes hats, collars, capes, shoes, aprons and caps, mainly from the nineteenth and twentieth centuries. Underwear consists of chemises, nightgowns, corsets, petticoats and drawers. There is a small group of children's clothes, babies' christening robes, gowns and caps, and a particularly interesting layette of *c*.1660 which belonged to the Tabor family of Colchester.

There are men's coats, suits, several from the eighteenth century and a few from the nineteenth and twentieth centuries, a selection of over thirty waistcoats, and a small group of eighteenth and nineteenth-century smocks. Military uniforms, including helmets, hats, sashes, boots, Sam Brownes and swords, mainly from Essex regiments, and ceremonial and police uniforms are of local interest.

Dresses hang on rails in one small room, protected by polythene bags, with fragile beaded 1920s dresses packed in flat boxes. Underwear and accessories are stored in boxes or polythene bags in a second room with rows of shelves, and men's clothes hang on rails, protected by polythene bags, in a third room.

Each item is entered in an accessions book and then in a card index.

One room is devoted to costume displays and there is a large case in which six dresses are mounted in a period setting. Hats and other accessories, embroidery, waistcoats, and babies' clothes are shown in other cases.

A second room is used for small displays of military uniform.

Groups of not more than ten children at any one time can be accommodated in the display area, and advance notice of an intended visit should be given. As space is limited, it is not normally possible for more than one advanced student at a time to work in the reserve collection. Appointments should be made at least two weeks in advance.

COVENTRY

HERBERT ART GALLERY AND MUSEUMS

This small collection of costume was acquired mainly from local sources and is of predominantly middle-class origin.

The major part of the collection consists of some 160 nineteenth and twentieth-century women's dresses. There are a few specimens dating from the early years, with increasing numbers in each decade from the 1840s onwards. Over eighty of the dresses date from c.1890–1940. There are a few wedding dresses, blouses, aprons, bodices, capes, cloaks, mantles, coats, jackets and uniforms, including a nurse's uniform of c.1910. The selection of underwear also dates from the nineteenth and twentieth centuries and consists of a few nightdresses, camisoles, chemises, combinations, corsets, bustles, brassières, petticoats and drawers. Accessories date from the same period and include sashes, belts, fans, parasols, fichus, buttons, stoles, shawls, cuffs, collars, stockings and shoes. There are a few paper patterns and photographs.

As in most museums there is less men's costume. There are a few twentieth-century suits, a small range of eighteenth to twentieth-century waistcoats, some nineteenth-century shirts, a few twentieth-century overcoats, jackets and blazers and four smocks. A few civil and military uniforms are of local interest. An interesting selection of hats and smoking caps includes an A.R.P. warden's hat and a ratting hat.

The collection of children's and babies' clothes dates mainly from the late nineteenth and twentieth centuries. It includes christening robes, nightdresses, shirts, coats, bonnets, hats, footwear and a few school uniforms.

Most of the costumes are individually protected by polythene bags and hang in date sequence in wardrobes. There is a semi-permanent display of costume, and dresses are sometimes incorporated with other exhibitions, for example a display of bicycles and one on silk ribbon weaving – a local industry.

All items are entered in the accessions register and then in a card index.

The costume department deals with all age groups. It can accommodate two advanced students, or school parties of six to ten fifteen to eighteen

year olds, or fifteen under-fourteen year olds. There is no schools service at the time of writing. Appointments should be made in advance.

PUBLICATIONS AVAILABLE FROM THE MUSEUM

There are a few slides of costumes and a publication on costume is planned for the near future. Further information is available from the museum on request.

DUMFRIES

BURGH MUSEUM

The museum contains a small collection of costume and accessories of local interest, as almost all were acquired from Dumfries and Kircudbrightshire and were either made or worn in this area. They are mainly clothes worn by well-to-do farmers' families and middle-class townspeople, with a few items of occupational costume. There is a small selection of local military and civil uniform.

Of interest are milliners' model bonnets of the 1840s–50s from a shop in Thornhill. There are also twenty-five photograph albums dating from c.1860–1900, *cartes-de-visite* showing costume, mainly of local people, and a collection of several hundred postcards of the late nineteenth and early twentieth centuries, many of which show costume.

All the costumes are hanging on rails covered with polythene bags. with underclothes packed in trunks and boxes. A small selection of accessories is on show in the museum and a few costumes are displayed in period settings at the Old Bridge House, Dumfries.

Each item is entered in an accessions book. Dress is catalogued under folk material with other items; there is no separate costume index.

Up to six advanced students can be accommodated at any one time. The schools service caters for parties of up to ten children at a time. Appointments should be made well in advance.

Opposite

195. Colchester and Essex Museum. White muslin dress of c. 1850–4 with three flounces embroidered 'à disposition'. The sleeves are long and ruched horizontally, ending in double flounces. The bodice is gathered at the front and fastens at the centre back with pearl buttons and worked loops. (116.1964)

DUNFERMLINE

CARNEGIE DUNFERMLINE TRUST, ABBEY PARK HOUSE;
PITTENCRIEF HOUSE MUSEUM

The costume collection is stored at Abbey Park House and displayed at Pittencrief House Museum, Pittencrief Park. There is also a small group of late nineteenth and early twentieth-century academic dress, mainly American, and all worn by Andrew Carnegie, displayed at the Andrew Carnegie Birthplace Memorial, Moodie Street.

The main collection now numbers over a thousand items of dress and

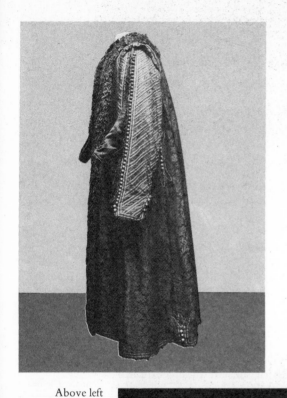

Above left

*196. Claydon House.
Nightgown of
c. 1615 worn by
Sir Francis Verney
in purple damask
with hanging sleeves
fastened with gold
thread buttons and
cord loops. (The
National Trust)*

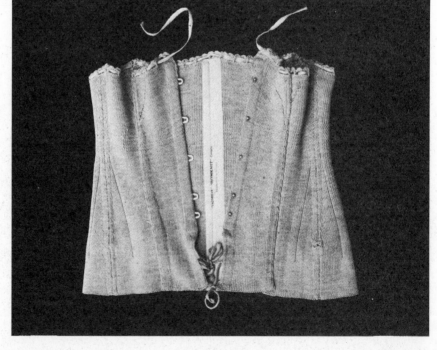

Right

*198. Burgh Museum,
Dumfries. Heavy,
boned, knitted grey
woollen corset of
c. 1910 labelled
'Jacobean Homeknit
Corsets Regd.
Manufactured in
Scotland'.*

accessories from c.1800 to the present day, with the accent on fashionable clothes. Among them is a riding habit of c.1870–80, consisting of a shaped skirt, bodice and breeches (135.71). There are several gifts from the Carnegie family, the majority from Mrs Louise Whitfield Carnegie, Andrew Carnegie's wife, including two dresses of her own. One of these, a day dress of c.1890–1, is labelled *Barrett, 19 East 31st St. N.Y.* (95.68a,b). It has a rich, midnight blue-black velvet, double-breasted bodice with diamond-shaped gunmetal buttons stamped with thistles. The skirt is of pleated silk in the Carnegie tartan. It is arranged rather like a kilt at the front but is gathered at the back into a vestigial bustle. The lace jabot has a thistle motif and is labelled *Haas Bros 27 & 29 West 31st St N.Y.* The other is an evening dress in ivory corded moiré silk labelled *Callot Soeurs Paris* on the waistband and stamped *Paris Hiver 1902 deposée*. (89.68a,b). There is also a dress-stand used for her dresses, still with its label attached: *Ellanem. The L and M Co. Automatic Adjustable Dress Form, Acme Form, 378–388 Throop Avenue, Brooklyn, N.Y. U.S.A.* It has a 1908 patent office mark.

Altogether there are about a hundred dresses, predominantly nineteenth and early twentieth-century, a few wedding dresses, bodices, blouses, skirts, capes, coats and jackets, over seventy shawls, stoles and scarves and about a hundred items of underwear including chemises, petticoats, spencers, combinations, corsets, nightdresses, camisoles and stockings. A small group of clothing accessories with lace trimming or embroidery are filed separately and include chemisettes, handkerchiefs, sleeves, collars, cuffs, jabots, caps, bonnet veils and lappets. The range of accessories dates mainly from the nineteenth century, and consists of aprons, hats, bonnets, belts, combs, fans, gloves, parasols, purses and reticules, shoes and slippers.

All the dresses are hanging in cupboards, protected with polythene bags, except for fragile specimens which are packed in boxes.

Each item in the collection is given an accession number by date of acquisition. The card index is arranged by subject and date within the various categories.

There is a small selection of fashion magazines, fashion plates, paper patterns and photographs.

School parties of up to thirty can work in the costume display area at Pittencrief House, and two college students can work in the reserve collection, where reference books are available, at any one time. Appointments should be made in advance.

PUBLICATIONS AVAILABLE FROM THE MUSEUM

Information sheets on the museum and current displays are available on request; colour transparencies and a catalogue are in preparation.

Opposite right

197 National Museum of Antiquities of Scotland, Edinburgh. A coat of heavy woollen material of c. 1690–1700 from a body apparently carefully buried, found during peat cutting at Gunnister, Shetland. A wool shirt and breeches, two knitted caps, knitted stockings and gloves were also found. (NA1037–1051)

EDINBURGH

NATIONAL MUSEUM OF ANTIQUITIES OF SCOTLAND

This museum is moving to a new building which should be ready in 1976. The costumes have been packed in boxes and put in store until the new accommodation is ready, but specimens can be seen during this time if advance notice is given.

The emphasis in this collection is sociological. It consists of clothes worn by people living in Scotland, made by people working in Scotland, or, if made elsewhere, worn by Scots people; a great many are from Edinburgh. Information is given about the social standing of the wearer, whenever it is known. All strata of society are represented, and there are examples of occupational dress, for example the dresses worn by fishwives (fisherrow).

Some of the most interesting clothes in the collection are the examples of costume made entirely of wool, found by chance in peat bog burials of the late seventeenth and early eighteenth centuries. The bodies and leather objects had completely disappeared, destroyed by the acid in the peat, which preserved the wool. The garments found with one body at Gunnister in Shetland include a shirt, breeches and coat, two knitted caps and knitted stockings and gloves (NA 1037–1051).

There is a large collection of tartan patterns from the firm of Nilson of Bannockburn, with letters relating to the making and selling of tartan from the eighteenth century, as well as garments made of tartan, mainly early nineteenth-century coats.

The collection includes examples of women's dresses, bodices, blouses, underwear, chemises, petticoats, corsets, hoops, bustles, Paisley shawls, Shetland shawls, shawls from other countries, shoes, hats and other accessories; men's suits, waistcoats, underwear, neckwear, nightclothes, shirts, shoes and hats. Among the items of uniform are early nineteenth-century archers' jackets from the Royal Company of Archers. There is also a group of children's dress, babies' clothes and christening robes.

Each item is entered in an accessions book and then filed in a card index with classification letters according to the museum system. A date index is also being organised.

Much of the clothing found in peat bogs is on display at the museum and several articles have been published in the Proceedings of the Society of Antiquaries of Scotland. Costumes from the rest of the collection are shown at the Museum Gallery, 18 Shandwick Place.

Parties of up to thirty children can work in the galleries, but until the new museum is built it is not possible for schoolchildren to see costumes from the reserve collection, and not more than one advanced student or two college students can be accommodated there at a time. Appointments should be made well in advance.

EDINBURGH

Above right

200. Royal Scottish Museum, Edinburgh. A dinner dress of c. 1832 in Old Clan Chattan tartan silk, a large check in red, green and yellow, said to have been worn by Mrs Macpherson of Cluny. The applied bands of white satin are embroidered in light and dark green. (1934.387)

THE ROYAL SCOTTISH MUSEUM

The collection of costume, lace and costume accessories has been built up mainly by the gifts of donors living in Scotland, although some items have been acquired from other parts of the country. The collection aims to trace the development of style from the eighteenth century to the present day and consists mainly of fashionable dress, much of very fine quality.

All items are entered in the accessions register with full detailed descriptions from which the card index is compiled. Female dress, the first and largest category of costume, is subdivided into dresses of the eighteenth century, 1800–1850, 1850–1900 and in decades thereafter from 1900–1960. Some twenty wedding dresses of the nineteenth and twentieth centuries are in a separate category. Other divisions include blouses; coats and capes; jumpers and cardigans; skirts; stomachers and modesty vests; trousers; uniforms; and underwear including petticoats, nightdresses, corsets, stays and drawers.

Over two hundred women's dresses show the changing styles from the mid-eighteenth century to the present day. The collection of couture dresses worn by the Duchess of Portland and given to the museum in 1969 by her daughter, Lady Victoria Wemyss, is of particular interest.

As in most museums there is less men's costume, but there are over eighty waistcoats dating from the early eighteenth to the twentieth century. A Garter doublet and trunk hose of c.1665 in white silk and silver metal tissue trimmed with lace of silver metal threads, with ribbons of white silk damask and silk and silver metal threads (RSM 1947.257) was worn by the sixth Duke of Lennox. The Garter robe may be seen at Lennoxlove.

There is a small group of eighteenth and nineteenth-century coats and a few breeches, smocks and blazers, with a selection of mainly nineteenth and twentieth-century underwear. Military and civil uniform includes several of local interest, particularly those of the Royal Archers, the Sovereign's Bodyguard for Scotland.

A few men's and some fifty items of women's clothes are included in a continental costume category. There are about fifty examples of women's peasant costume from many countries including Iceland, Andalusia and Russia and about twenty of men's dress, including fishermen's clothing from the Faroes.

There is a separate section of sportswear with a few costumes and accessories for tennis, skating and swimming, for both men and women.

Children's dress is a small category, the largest group being of headwear, from the seventeenth to twentieth centuries. A selection of bonnets have Ayrshire embroidery and this work may also be seen in the group of christening robes.

Costume accessories are filed separately from items of costume, under the headings of female headwear, male headwear and peasant headwear, hair ornaments, collars, veils, ties, fichus, shawls (woven and printed), shawls (embroidered and crocheted), cuffs, scarves, sleeves, handkerchiefs, women's gloves, men's gloves, children's gloves, mittens, muffs, purses, bags and pockets, umbrellas and parasols, fans, aprons, feathered accessories, stockings and garters, shoes. There is a fairly representative group in each category. The section of male headwear includes several knitted apprentices' caps dating from the sixteenth century, from archaeological sites in the City of London.

There is a very good selection of lace samples. Some pieces are made as items of clothing, such as cuffs, collars and lappets, while many other pieces have been used as flounces or other costume decorations. Much of this material is on display in the textile gallery, in cases which can be opened out for study purposes.

The Oriental collection contains a wide range of material from the Far East, the Islamic world and the Indian cultural area. The Far East is represented mainly by a large Chinese collection of which an important part is a series of court costumes dating from the late eighteenth and nineteenth centuries. There are also examples of costume worn outside

court circles, chiefly Manchu and Chinese women's gowns. There are accessories to accompany all types of costume and a large group of separate items such as embroidered sleevebands, collars and skirt panels. The Japanese collection consists of kimonos, some priests' robes, hats, shoes, fans and costumes belonging to the Ainu, a race living in the north of Japan with their own distinctive culture. Korean costume is represented by a small group of accessories. The main Islamic costumes are from Persia and Turkey. From Persia there is a group of trousers and coats from the eighteenth century as well as shirts, veils, shawls and a few accessories. Some of the Turkish costume and textiles date from the sixteenth century. There are other Islamic costumes from Syria, Palestine, Egypt and Afghanistan. The costumes of India are both Hindu and Moslem, consisting of tunics, saris and various costume accessories, with a large group of woven and embroidered shawls from Kashmir. There are also examples of costumes from Tibet and Burma. The Tibetan collection has a complete set of costumes and masks worn in the Buddhist 'mystery plays' which are unique.

A large gallery is devoted almost entirely to costume. Over fifty fashionable dresses, suits and accessories are on display, with a small group of peasant costumes which are of ethnographic interest. The costume gallery also includes a small selection of costumes from the Oriental collections divided between the Far East and the Islamic world.

Above right

202. Royal Albert Memorial Museum, Exeter. Riding habit jacket of c. 1760 in firmly woven coarse woollen cloth. The collar is faced with blue satin. (94.1965)

There is plenty of space in the gallery for parties of thirty children, but there is no education service at present, so guide lecturers are not available, nor are there classroom facilities. It is advisable to prepare work and let the museum staff know of an intended visit at least a week beforehand. The costume department can accommodate up to six specialist students at any one time and requests for study facilities should be made at least two weeks in advance.

EXETER

ROYAL ALBERT MEMORIAL MUSEUM

The collection numbers approximately a thousand items of costume and accessories. There is also a large group of lace based on the collection of Mrs Bury Palliser, who wrote *A History of Lace* (1869), and that of Mrs Treadwin, a local lady who owned a business at 5 Cathedral Close, Exeter. She specialised in the making of Honiton lace and also the cleaning, restoration and reproduction of all types of lace. There are examples of many varieties of lace as well as local Honiton lace of various dates. Many of these pieces are made up as items of dress, such as collars, cuffs, lappets, shawls and pelerines. Representative examples from the collection are displayed in frames in the museum gallery. There are Honiton and Devon laces, Italian cutwork, lacis and point lace of the seventeenth century, and laces from the British Isles, Belgium, France, Germany, Denmark, Sweden, Russia and Spain.

The costume collection has been acquired mainly from local, mostly middle-class families, with the addition of the Freda Wills Bequest in 1972. There are a few couture dresses and one or two examples of working clothes, many fashionable wedding dresses and a group of clothes from a family which had some connections at Court in c.1820–60. There is a good representative selection of dresses from the late eighteenth century to the present day; several of these date from c.1840–60 and are made from eighteenth-century silks. There is a sizeable group of underwear including chemises, petticoats, bustles, crinolines and nightwear. Accessories include hats, shawls, aprons, gloves, muffs, parasols and bags. A small but interesting selection of children's dress includes babies' christening robes and gowns. Nearly all the coats and dresses are hanging in cupboards, protected by polythene bags. Fragile specimens, muslin dresses of the early nineteenth century and beaded dresses of the 1920s are packed in boxes.

The small group of men's costume includes suits, coats and waistcoats, a Devon workman's smock and a few uniforms. Most of the collection of military costumes, mainly of local interest, is stored and exhibited at Rougemont House, Exeter.

The displays in the costume gallery are usually mounted for six months. There are over thirty complete outfits on show, with extra accessories. Mention should be made of the ingenious storage arrangements. Metal framework has been used inside a high-ceilinged room to provide a mezzanine floor for easy access to shelves.

There is a small collection of related material, including fashion plates, fashion magazines, a few photographs and some costume reference books, which may be used by students working in the reserve collection.

Parties of thirty to forty children can be accommodated in the gallery and some material is kept in reserve for teaching.

Two advanced students or six older students can work in the store at a time; appointments should be made at least two weeks in advance.

PUBLICATIONS AVAILABLE FROM THE MUSEUM

INDER, P. M. *Honiton Lace*, Exeter Museums Publication No. 55, 1971. 19 monochrome plates.

INDER, P. M. *Costume in pictures. Booklet 1*. City of Exeter Museums and Art Gallery, 1972. Monochrome plates of costumes and accessories from the collection, *c*.1728–1928.

GLASGOW

BURRELL COLLECTION, CAMPHILL MUSEUM
ART GALLERY AND MUSEUM

The main collection of costume and accessories is stored and displayed at Kelvingrove, but there are a few embroidered items of clothing such as nightcaps, dating from the late sixteenth century and early seventeenth century which are kept in the Burrell Collection at Camphill Museum. The collection of dresses ranges from the late eighteenth century to the mid-twentieth century, containing many very fashionable specimens, and is particularly strong in 1850s items, among them a day dress of *c*.1850 in pale mauve-pink challis printed with white flowers, its skirt arranged with three flounces printed *à disposition* (48.145). Another of *c*.1855–8 is in royal blue and brown silk with a woven design of flowers; its bodice is basqued and gathered *à la Vierge* at the front waistline and the wide bell sleeves are lined with pale pink silk (50.69.d). A white silk evening dress of *c*.1850 has flounces woven *à disposition* with a flowered design. The berthe, the sleeves and the heading of the bottom flounce are made of pleated white satin ribbon. There are also rows of ruched white silk net on the berthe (34.26a,b,c).

Among the wedding dresses is one made locally, in 1901, labelled *W. R. Greisch, Glasgow*. It is of white silk crepe with a slightly pouched front bodice trimmed with lace, and a wide swirling skirt with fine tucks over the hips. It is one of the earliest dresses to be neatened with machine stitching (E7023).

An evening dress of c.1904–5 (50.54c) was also made locally; its label reads *Made by Kemp, Buchanan St, Glasgow, for Mrs David MacBrayne, Auchenteil, Helensburgh.* It is in black net embroidered with paillettes and flowers made of strips of ivory gauze. Another black net evening dress of c.1903–5 has a widely gored skirt at the hem, embroidered lavishly with large and medium-sized black paillettes, small sequins and black beads. The black net is mounted over lemon chiffon with acid yellow figured silk beneath. There is a black velvet band round the hem and a black velvet sash. It is labelled *Murray & Co, Montrose, Modes & Robes* (54.52a).

There is also a bustle petticoat in satin weave glazed cotton printed with orange and pale blue flowers on a putty-coloured ground, lined with red cotton. It is labelled *McLintock's Patent purified Russian Down Skirt. No 7–34 inches. Philadelphia 1876 Paris 1878* (E54.85).

There is a sizeable collection of underwear including petticoats, chemises, underskirts, drawers, vests, camisoles, corsets and nightwear. Accessories are catalogued under aprons, bodices and blouses, bags and purses, collars, fans, gloves, headgear, jewellery, parasols, sticks and umbrellas, sleeves, stockings, shoes, shawls, wraps, capes, jackets and dolmans. There are collections of Ayrshire needlework and lace which include many items of dress. Babies' clothing is catalogued under robes, carrying cloaks, bibs, underwear and bonnets. A small group of children's clothes includes dresses, capes, gloves, hats, shoes, stockings and underwear, all from the mid-nineteenth century onwards.

A small selection of men's clothes includes a few coats, shirts and trousers with a group of waistcoats which range from the eighteenth century to the present day.

Each item in the collection acquired from 1875 to 1956 is entered in a general register recording all museum specimens. From 1956 onwards they have been entered in a separate textile accessions register. The card index is undergoing reorganisation at the time of writing.

Dresses hang in glass-fronted cupboards, protected from the light by black curtains, except the fragile specimens which are in boxes.

A few nineteenth and early twentieth-century paper patterns, magazines, fashion plates and books of knitting, netting and crochet instructions are kept with the collection of costume. A few slides of costume can be duplicated on request, and some black and white photographs are available.

There is a small gallery with over fifty items of dress and accessories where groups of up to thirty children may work at a time. Material for schools is kept separate from the reserve collection and is supplied to the education service who show items on request.

There is room for two students to work in the reserve collection at any one time. Appointments should be made in advance.

GLENESK

GLENESK TRUST FOLK MUSEUM

This museum is administered by the Glenesk Trust. The small collection of costume is entirely related to the area and most of the clothes were worn by children and adults of all ages who lived and worked in Glenesk. An interesting selection of photographs, *cartes-de-visite* and newspaper cuttings runs from the mid-nineteenth century to the present day and shows many details of costume in wear.

Women's costume consists of a range of dresses, with a selection of petticoats, chemises, cotton sunbonnets, and other mainly nineteenth and twentieth-century accessories. Many of the dresses may have been made by a local dressmaker who lived and worked in Glenesk from the 1890s to the mid 1920s. Several items in the collection were worn by Queen Victoria, who used to stay eighteen miles away at Braemar.

A group of children's clothes includes a few dresses and a large number of babies' robes, bonnets and gowns. There are a few items of men's clothing, including shirts, stocks, braces, waistcoats, smoking caps and an Inverness cloak.

One room is reserved for displays of costume and accessories; costumes are also shown as part of other exhibits.

All items are entered in a card index.

Space is limited and school parties and students wishing to see items in the reserve collection should make an appointment.

GLOUCESTER

CITY MUSEUM AND ART GALLERY

FOLK LIFE AND REGIMENTAL MUSEUM, BISHOP HOOPER'S LODGING

At present the costume collection is stored in the Folk Museum at Bishop Hooper's Lodging and exhibited in the main museum. There are plans for enlarging the Folk Museum and it is hoped that in the near future there will be space there for more displays.

Much of the collection was acquired locally from donors living in Gloucester or in the county. The dresses date mainly from the nineteenth century, among them a wedding dress of *c.*1827–9 in ivory brocaded silk and a day dress of *c.*1874–7 in pale yellow and blue shot silk taffeta, giving the effect of pale beige (F1138).

There are a few items in each of the following categories of accessories:

Right

*203. Bankfield
Museum, Halifax.
Black georgette
evening dress of
c. 1928–30 with
lace godets from knee
level. The overdress
has a fringe of gold
and jet beads at hip
level. The underdress
is embroidered in
diamond shapes with
gold beads and jet.
(1952.20)*

Far right

*204. Worcestershire
County Museum. A
Colobus monkey fur
coat of c. 1925 lined
with embroidered
grey silk. (The shoes
are modern). (16/21)*

Right

*205. Art Gallery
and Museum, Glas-
gow. Dress of c. 1912
in ivory silk and
wool mixture, with
yoke and sleeves
in tucked spotted net.
The bottom of the
yoke and the inset
skirt panel on the
left side are made of
ivory pleated silk
gauze with a heavier
gauze ribbon chain
stitch machined to it
in stripes, before
pleating. (50.95a)*

aprons, bodices, jackets, mantles, capes, fichus, shawls, veils, nightwear, petticoats, chemises, skirts, gloves, stockings, shoes, parasols, bonnets and hats. One of the hats (86.1965) is of plaited straw lined with ivory silk, the top covered with black silk and trimmed with black lace, of *c*.1760. There are also small items like buttons, spectacles, glove hooks, hand-warmers, fur muffs and châtelaines. There is a small selection of children's clothes, babies' wear and christening robes.

A small group of men's clothes consists of a few coats, breeches, shirts, stockings, hats, shoes, and waistcoats, mainly of the late eighteenth and nineteenth centuries. Uniforms of the Gloucestershire Regiment are of local interest, as are two coachmen's liveries of the 1880s and 1890s. There are a few examples of working dress and occupational costume including thirteen smocks and the uniform of a water bailiff, of *c*.1880–1900 (F379); the boots are labelled *Runciman no 32 Pall Mall London* and the inner linings for the boots *Henry A Murton, Waterproof India Rubber and Gutta Percha depot, Grey Street, and Market Street, Newcastle upon Tyne. Established 1848.*

All items are entered in an accessions book and then in a card index, one copy in the main museum and a duplicate in the Folk Museum. The index gives location numbers of the storage boxes as well as full descriptions of each item. The displays of costume and accessories are changed at intervals of six months.

There is room in the gallery for school parties of up to twenty children; items from the reserve study collection can be produced on request. Advance notice of a visit should be given.

When the new premises are complete up to five advanced students will be able to work in the reserve collection at a time: appointments should be made well in advance.

HALIFAX

BANKFIELD MUSEUM

The museum possesses a large general collection of tools and equipment used in spinning, weaving and cloth-making as well as those used locally for the manufacture of woollen cloth, and samples of raw materials and fabrics are on display. Much of the costume collection relates to this material and has been acquired for the textiles concerned. There are also many specimens given by local donors, reflecting middle-class taste in nineteenth and twentieth-century Halifax.

In the women's costume section there are a few in each of these groups: stays, shifts, brassières, under-bodices, underskirts, modesty vests, knickers, stockings, petticoats, dress frames, blouses, skirts, bodices, jumpers and cardigans. Dresses, a fairly large group, date mainly from the mid-nineteenth century to the present day. Evening dresses and wedding dresses are in separate categories, with a small selection, mainly twentieth-century, in each. Accessories and small items of dress include collars, sleeves, aprons, hats, suits, coats, capes, headscarves, shawls, stoles, boas, day shoes, evening shoes, wedding shoes, boots, gloves, mittens, bags, purses, evening bags, muffs, nightclothes, uniforms, handkerchiefs, jewellery, haircombs, fans and parasols.

A small range of men's clothes is catalogued under shirts, underclothes, ties, suits, waistcoats, spats, shoes, hats, evening dress, nightclothes, jewellery, walking sticks and gloves. Of local interest is a costume of the Halifax Harriers of c.1825–35, consisting of a red cloth coat and waistcoat with cream leather breeches. The waistcoat sleeves are lined with cotton printed with a sepia print of an eagle attacking a bird above a beehive. These were probably cut from a tillot or bale wrapper and used where they would not show (1956.162).

Children's clothes are grouped under christening robes, petticoats, coats, vests, dresses, capes, shoes, hats and nightclothes.

Foreign material has been selected for the textiles, but there are some peasant costumes and accessories among the other items. There are examples from Western Europe, Central and Eastern Europe, Africa, the Middle East, the Far East, the Americas and the Pacific Islands.

There are major displays of weaving, mainly for the woollen industry, but information is also available on silk and primitive weaving. There are exhibits of lace, printed, knitted and woven fabrics, tartans, beadwork, traditional costumes, needlework equipment, netting and tatting, civil uniforms, and Chinese robes and silks. A display of military uniform of the Duke of Wellington's Regiment and the 4th-7th Royal Dragoon Guards, many items of which belonged to the Duke, is of local interest.

There is a large store where almost all the dresses are hanging, protected by polythene bags, and the textiles are stored in boxes. Each item is entered on an accessions card and then in a card index.

Display space for costume is limited at the present time but items from the reserve collection can be produced on request, if sufficient notice is given, for groups of not more than fifteen schoolchildren. Up to three advanced students can work in the costume store at any one time. Appointments should be made well in advance.

PUBLICATIONS AVAILABLE FROM THE MUSEUM

ATKINSON, F. (Editor) *Some Aspects of the Eighteenth Century Woollen and Worsted Trade in Halifax*, Halifax Museums, 1956. This includes extracts from the letter books of Joseph Holroyd and Samuel Hill, two men prominent in the Halifax cloth trade of the early eighteenth century.

INNES, R. A. *Costumes of Upper Burma and the Shan States*, Halifax Museums, 1957. Illustrated with line drawings and five monochrome plates.

INNES, R. A. *Non European Looms in the Collections at Bankfield Museum, Halifax*, Halifax Museums, 1959. Illustrated with seven monochrome plates and line drawings in the text.

ROTH, H. L. *Ancient Egyptian and Greek Looms*, Bankfield Museum, Halifax, 1913. Illustrated with line drawings in the text.

START, L. E. *The Durham Collection of Garments and Embroideries from Albania and Yugoslavia*, with notes by M. E. Durham, Halifax Corporation, 1939. Illustrated with line drawings in the text.

There is a selection of postcards showing spinning and weaving equipment and a list of publications and prices is available on request.

HARTLEBURY

WORCESTERSHIRE COUNTY MUSEUM

The Tickenhill collection forms the nucleus of the whole collection of costume of which approximately half has been acquired from sources in Worcestershire. Items from the Danks family, who lived in Charlton House, Hartlebury, in the 1830s are of particular local interest.

The bulk of the collection dates from the nineteenth and twentieth centuries although there are some eighteenth-century specimens. Women's costume is catalogued under the following headings: footwear; headgear (hats, caps, bonnets, wreaths, veils); nightclothes, underclothes (petticoats, camisoles and underbodices, drawers, combinations, chemises, vests and shifts); dresses, including particularly good ranges for *c.*1800–30 and *c.*1900–30; outer skirts and trousers; blouses and bodices; jackets and coatees; coats, cloaks and mantles; capes and pelerines; shawls, stoles, boas and scarves; stockings and leggings; handbags, purses and pockets; gloves and mittens; muffs; umbrellas and parasols; handkerchiefs and fichus; jewellery and accessories (hat-pins, hairpins and combs, lace pins); crinolines, hoops, bustles, dressing robes, corsets; fans; posy holders; furs; trimmings and fasteners (ribbons, beads, buttons, feathers, flowers, buckles, belts, dress-clips and suspenders, toilet pins, hooks and eyes); collars and cuffs; modesty vests, tippets, ties, sleeves, chemisettes; spectacles and cases; aprons; clothes brushes, buttonhooks, coat hangers, coat racks; châteleines; personalia (*étuis*, pocket knives etc.) riding habits; sportswear;

uniforms (including Red Cross); maternity wear; mourning; jumpers and cardigans; suits and costumes.

The collection of men's clothes is very much smaller, as in most museums. There are a few items in each of the following categories: footwear; headgear; nightclothes; underclothes; suits; trousers; jackets and frock coats; waistcoats; overcoats and capes; scarves, neckerchiefs and handkerchiefs; ties and cravats; stockings and socks; gaiters, spats and leggings; gloves and mittens; collars and dickeys; shirts; smocks; jewellery; umbrellas, canes and walking sticks; wallets, purses; personalia (pocket knives, reading and magnifying glasses, pocket flasks); belts and braces; buttons; sportswear; mourning; vestments and uniforms.

There is a good selection of children's dresses, caps, pinafores, christening robes and capes, mostly nineteenth-century.

The collection is graded into three sections. Grade A contains rare and fragile items; Grade B includes the main bulk of the collection and Grade C consists of expendable material which can be used for schools. There are many dresses which are duplicated in the A and B categories; in some cases specimens are badly damaged, but can be mounted carefully to show one side.

Dresses are hung and boxed in chronological order. Metal framework shelves have been built in all store rooms to take standard size boxes, all of which are very clearly labelled. Accessories are boxed and stored in generic order, e.g. metal buttons, pearl buttons etc., rather than in chronological order.

Costume is displayed in four rooms with related material including fashion plates, accessories, shawls, parasols, embroidery and lace-making equipment. The main displays are changed annually during December and January when the museum is closed. Dresses in bays without glass are changed every three months.

All items are entered on accessions forms and in an accessions book. The collection is still being catalogued in a card index system at the time of writing.

The library contains the Daphne Bullard Memorial Library of costume books donated by the Worcestershire County Museum Society, as well as many general reference works on costume and a variety of nineteenth-century periodicals containing fashion plates. There is also a small selection of nineteenth and twentieth-century paper patterns.

A schools service provides work sheets for costume study to suit different age groups. A group of up to thirty children can be accommodated in the display area or lecture room, and up to six advanced students may work in the reserve collection at a time. Appointments should be made well in advance.

PUBLICATIONS AVAILABLE FROM THE MUSEUM

BULLARD, D. *Catalogue of the Costume Collection Part 1 – 1645–1790*, Worcestershire County Museum, 1966. Illustrated with eight monochrome plates and line drawings in the text.

BULLARD, D. *Catalogue of the Costume Collection Part 2 – 1800–1830*, Worcestershire County Museum, 1968. Illustrated with eight monochrome plates and line drawings in the text.

There is also a selection of colour slides, with continual additions. A list is available.

HEREFORD

HEREFORD CITY LIBRARY AND MUSEUMS

CHURCHILL GARDENS MUSEUM

Most of the costume collection was acquired from local sources and it also includes some of the Cunnington collections. There is a very large selection of dresses dating from the first half of the eighteenth to the mid twentieth centuries with several items in each of the following categories of women's costume: aprons, blouses, bodices, bonnets, bonnets (soft), boots and bottines, bustles, capes, cape shawls, shawl pelerines, cloaks and mantles, coats, collars and cuffs, corsetry, drawers, combinations, crinolines, dressing gowns and jackets, fichus, fronts and shirts, gloves, mittens and muffs, housecaps, jackets and boleros, miscellanea (including bathing dresses and Boots' papier poudré), nightwear, pattens, pelisses, petticoats, riding habits, shawls, shoes, skirts, sleeves, slippers, stockings, underbodices and chemises, veils and hats. Among the hats is one (8231) of straw and fine cane (?), dating from c.1700–25 or earlier, beautifully woven in intricate patterns, and possibly Spanish or Italian. It is reputed to have belonged to Queen Anne. Two similarly shaped hats worn by European ladies are seen in an Indian painting (Mogul style) of c.1670 in the British Museum (1928–8–15.05).

Costume accessories include a few dress patterns, belts, bracelets, brooches, buckles, buttons, card cases, châtelaines, combs, dress holders, ear ornaments, fans, head ornaments, fobs, garters, handbags, handkerchiefs, hat-pins, links and studs, lockets and pendants, materials and trimmings, muffs, necklaces, parasols, pockets, purses, rings, scarves, scent bottles, seals, spectacles, sticks, umbrellas, wig curlers and wig stands, watches, and miscellanea including back scratchers, ear trumpets, glove stretchers, hair curlers, snuff boxes and shawl fasteners.

Some categories have very large numbers of items; there are, for example, numerous nineteenth-century nightdresses and quite a large range of petticoats of the eighteenth, nineteenth and twentieth centuries. In others there are fewer items but they may be of exceptional quality, as, for example, the range of riding habits. One of these is of c.1750–60 in drab wool and silk mixture decorated in front and on the cuffs with passementerie in a slightly yellowish shade (7046).

Men's costume is catalogued under civil uniform, coats, gloves, hats, liveries, neckwear, nightwear, overcoats, shirts, shoes, boots, smocks, socks and stockings, suits, trousers, underwear, waistcoats. There are a few items in each category, a large representative selection of waistcoats, a fine collection of smocks and a few costumes of local industry. The collection of children's costume is catalogued under bonnets, caps, capes, cloaks, coats, dresses, gloves, pinafores, school uniforms, robes, gowns, shoes, boots, stockings, underwear and nightwear. There are sizeable groups of dresses, mainly nineteenth-century with a few twentieth-century, and of underwear and nightwear, again mainly nineteenth-century.

A small category of foreign costume includes Polish and Chinese items.

Each item in the collection of costume accessories and civil uniform is entered in an accessions book and then in a card index. Notes are made of the occasions on which they were worn, if known.

All the items of dress and accessories are packed in cardboard boxes and stored in order of accession. It is necessary to use the file system first and find the accession numbers of the dresses required before selecting the boxes. The large collection of military uniform, mainly of local regiments, is catalogued separately.

Displays of costume, which are usually changed every six months, are mounted in an attractive eighteenth-century house, Churchill Gardens Museum, in Venn's Lane, where the costumes are stored, not far from the main library and museum.

As space is limited, not more than twenty-five children can work in the display area at any one time. It is usually possible to accommodate one advanced student in the reserve collection. Appointments should be made well in advance.

HITCHIN

HITCHIN MUSEUM AND ART GALLERY

Most of the items in this small collection of costume were acquired locally and their provenance is known. In some cases there are photographs of people wearing the clothes.

There are about thirty dresses, mainly nineteenth-century. A particularly good range from the 1830s was given by Mrs Hughes of Offley. They

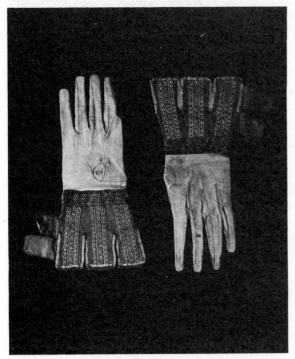

were from the trousseau of Elizabeth Mary Burroughs of Offley Place. Born in 1793, she married her cousin, Sir Thomas Salusbury of Llanwern, in 1833. He died in 1835 and some of the dresses she wore before he died were put away and have therefore survived in good condition. Two dresses of c.1810 probably belonged to her as well.

A black satin evening dress of 1928 is labelled *Jeanne Lanvin Hiver 1928, Paris Unis France*. The number *1889* is stamped on the label. The dress has a V-neckline and is cut in panels to flute out at the hem, which is bordered in net, on which are mounted two rows of box-pleated satin frills. The skirt is slightly longer at the back (H5385). There is a small range of accessories and underwear, a few coats, cloaks and shawls, a selection of babies' and children's clothing and a few items of men's clothing, including a few military uniforms of local interest and one smock.

Each item is entered in an accessions register; a card index and catalogue are in preparation. Other related material includes fashion plates and a few magazines. Most of the dresses are protected by polythene bags and hanging in a cupboard, while all other items are stored in boxes.

A large room devoted to displays of costume and accessories has adequate space for groups of up to thirty children. Material can be produced from the reserve collection if advance notice is given, but groups should not be larger than fifteen. There is room for one advanced student to work in the store. Appointments should be made in advance.

Above right

207. Hitchin Museum and Art Gallery. Pale apple green silk dress of c. 1828–30 with a detachable scalloped pelerine collar, bordered with crossway satin. The dress has a low neckline and a detachable wide vandyked collar bordered with blonde lace for evening wear. The skirt is trimmed with crossway satin piped bands and satin leaves.

HULL

THE GEORGIAN HOUSES
The largest section of this collection is the range of nineteenth and early twentieth-century dresses. There are also a few items in each of the following categories of women's costume: blouses, bodices, bonnets, underclothes, shawls, shoes, stockings, bags and purses, fans and parasols. A small group of children's clothing includes baby clothes, children's dresses, underclothes and shoes, mainly nineteenth-century. There are a few men's suits, shirts and eighteenth-century waistcoats.

The clothes which belonged to William Wilberforce, some of which are on display, are of particular interest.

The file cards of this collection were destroyed during the war, but the provenance of those items which came from local donors after the war is known; each item is now being given an accession number.

The collection had been in store pending the rebuilding of the museum, but has recently moved into a new store, where all the dresses are on hangers, protected with polythene bags, in large cupboards.

A selection of costume is on semi-permanent display and it is possible that a small costume gallery may be added to the museum in the future.

A schools service is attached to the museum and arrangements can be made for talks to small groups of children. As space is limited groups of not more than four students can work in the reserve collection at any one time. Appointments should be made in advance.

IPSWICH

IPSWICH MUSEUMS AND ART GALLERIES
There is quite a large collection of costume and accessories here which has never been exhibited. It is being unpacked, catalogued and moved into new store rooms at Christchurch Mansion and Wolsey Art Gallery at the time of writing. Much of the collection was given by local people, but there are other items from all over the country, many from Suffolk.

The group of around two hundred dresses dates from c.1800 to 1930 and includes wedding dresses. Two dresses belonged to a Mrs Seebohm who came from a Quaker family. They date from c.1904 and c.1912–13. Although by this period Quakers were allowed to wear more fashionable clothes, they still had to be in sober colours. The first (1952.32.41) is in soft mole brown satin, with sleeves ruched over the top, and is labelled *Comley, 3 Bentinck Street, Manchester Square W.* The second is an evening dress (1952.32.39) in ivory satin covered with black ninon. On top of this is a layer of black net embroidered with sprays of leaves in gold and silver

208. Ipswich Museums and Art Galleries. Riding habit of c. 1820 in navy blue doeskin with black braid buttons. The jacket is high-waisted and the sleeves fully gathered over the sleevehead. The long skirt can be tied up for walking. (R1960–125)

sequins and little gold beads. The satin dress hem is bordered with black velvet.

There are a large number of accessories, including shawls, hats, hatpins, dress clips, aprons, shoes, bonnets, veils, caps, collars and berthes, with a wide selection of underwear.

The small range of men's clothes contains several items of considerable interest, including two Vandyke suits of c.1770–85 and a Portman's gown of c.1820. There are also a few civil and military uniforms, court dress, shirts and accessories. An interesting group of shoes, found in walled-up chimneys and roofs, date from the Tudor period to the end of the eighteenth century.

Dresses are hung in large cupboards with sliding doors which are virtually dustproof. Plans have been made for a display area. It will not be possible to accommodate students in the store room until the collection is finally sorted and catalogued, and visitors who wish to see items in the reserve collection should write to make an appointment.

KINGUSSIE

THE HIGHLAND FOLK MUSEUM

This is a small museum which shows a few items of dress mounted as part of the permanent display. There are samples of tiny clothes made by children in the mid-nineteenth century among the exhibits on Scottish education. Various plaids and shawls, with a few nineteenth-century dresses and cloaks, are on show, and a few items of military uniform, mainly of local interest.

There are approximately eighty costumes in store, mostly from one family, dating from the late nineteenth century, but they have not yet been catalogued. It is not possible for students to see the reserve collection during the summer months, as study space is limited.

LEEDS

KIRKSTALL ABBEY HOUSE MUSEUM

In this collection, acquired mainly from local donors, there are a few items in each of the following categories of women's dress: aprons, bathing costumes, belts, blouses, boas, boleros, bodices, bustles, camisoles, capes, chemisettes, collars, coats, corsets, combinations, cravats (ladies'), crinolines, cuffs, drawers, dolmans, fichus, gaiters, gloves, hats, handkerchiefs, bonnets and caps, jackets, mittens, muffs, nightcaps, nightdresses and dressing gowns, petticoats, pelisses, ribbons, pockets, sashes, scarves, shawls, shoes, boots, pattens and slippers. There is quite a sizeable range of mainly nineteenth and twentieth-century dresses.

The small selection of men's dress includes a few pairs of breeches, coats, collars and cuffs, combinations, gaiters, gloves, hats, jackets, puttees, shirts, suits, smocks, ties, trousers and a representative collection of nineteenth-century waistcoats. The baby clothes and children's dress date from the nineteenth and twentieth centuries and include bonnets and caps, capes and cloaks, christening robes, chemises, clogs, coats, collars, dresses, long gowns, gloves and mittens, jackets, nightgowns, petticoats, pinafores, shawls and shirts. Each item is entered in a card index.

A gallery is devoted to costume displays, changed twice a year, for which items of furniture from the museum provide a period background. There is space for a party of up to thirty children to work in the gallery and there is a Leeds schools museum service. Not more than five advanced students can work in the reserve collection at one time as space is limited. Appointments should be made well in advance.

LEEDS

LOTHERTON HALL

Lotherton Hall, the gift of Sir Alvary and Lady Gascoigne, is a branch of Leeds City Art Gallery and Temple Newsam House. Costume is collected in the context of decorative art and the small collection, which ranges from the mid-eighteenth to the early twentieth century, is based on the

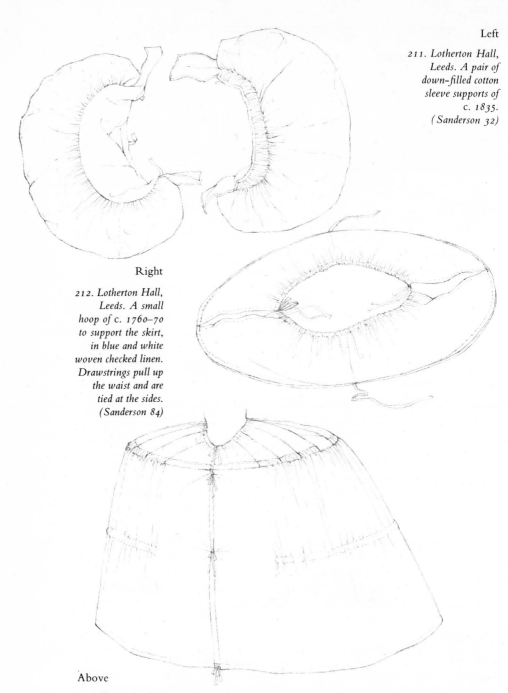

211. Lotherton Hall,
Leeds. A pair of
down-filled cotton
sleeve supports of
c. 1835.
(Sanderson 32)

Right

212. Lotherton Hall,
Leeds. A small
hoop of c. 1760–70
to support the skirt,
in blue and white
woven checked linen.
Drawstrings pull up
the waist and are
tied at the sides.
(Sanderson 84)

Above

213. Laing Art Gallery and Museum, Newcastle-upon-Tyne. White linen petticoat of
c. 1745–55 with hoops of cane and iron (or steel) enclosed in casings to hold it out. On top
there are rows of lambswool padding to soften the line at the hips. Tapes tie across inside to
hold the petticoat in shape. (58.8c)

Sanderson Collection, purchased in 1949. The provenance of each object is not always known.

There are a few items in each of the following categories of women's dress, mainly from the eighteenth and nineteenth centuries: underwear, chemises, skirts, drawers, hoops, corsets, neckwear, sleeves, cuffs, ruffles, petticoats, bodices, outerwear, accessories, headwear, footwear, gloves, aprons, fans, parasols, purses. There are about thirty dresses ranging from the mid-eighteenth to the early twentieth century.

The range of men's costume includes two dressing gowns of c.1825–35; one (Sanderson 180) is in Chinese embroidered ivory satin of c.1780 in a design of butterflies and flowers in variegated colours. The other (Sanderson 179) is in faded aubergine corded silk with a brocaded design of flowers in silver, pinks, blues and greens, dating from c.1740. There are also a few items in each of these categories: underwear, shirts, neckwear, suits, stockings, breeches, waistcoats, coats, outerwear, accessories, headwear, footwear, gloves, canes and swords.

A very small group of children's costume consists of a few specimens of underwear, shirts, chemises, petticoats, breeches, hoops, dresses, bodices, outerwear, accessories, headwear and footwear.

Each item is entered in an accessions book at Temple Newsam and the card index is undergoing reorganisation at Lotherton Hall at the time of writing.

Specially designed costume display areas have just been opened and two more rooms are planned for this purpose. At the moment the area holds a dozen costumes, with fashion plates and accessories. There is adequate space for groups of up to ten students. Costume for schools is dealt with by the schools service at the City Museum.

Three rooms are planned for storage, with a students' room, but at present there is space in the reserve collection for up to six students to work at any one time. Appointments should be made well in advance.

LEICESTER

WYGSTON'S HOUSE (COSTUME MUSEUM)

The collection of costume and accessories is quite large and contains many items of knitwear, which are of particular interest as this is a local industry. The Elliot and Hardy collections of knitwear form the basis of the range. Elliot was a manufacturer in Swanwick, Derby, with a small shop employing six assistants. He kept a sample of each new range of underwear and hosiery, and items for special orders, such as underclothes for Princess May of Teck, later Queen Mary's, trousseau. All these garments were knitted on the hand frame. Embroidery was done by outworkers near Swanwick. There is a large selection of sample patterns of knitting for

Opposite left
214. Wygston's
House Museum,
Leicester. Two
machine-knitted
woollen stockings
dated 1862. Left, a
red, black and white
striped one
(358.1955/8). Right,
a purple and red
striped one.
(358.1955/18)

clothing, some dated, mainly from the first half of the twentieth century, acquired in 1968 from the Benjamin Russell factory. A wide range of stockings includes samples for the 1851 and 1862 Exhibitions with the dates woven into the welts.

The costumes are almost all from local donors, reflecting county and middle-class taste in Leicestershire during the nineteenth and twentieth centuries. Many of the 1890s and 1900s dresses are labelled *Joseph Johnson* and *Adderley*, the names of two local stores. Johnson's is still in existence, but is now in the Fenwick group. Among the Adderley's dresses is a day dress in purple corded silk of *c.*1898. The bodice is based on a sateen foundation; the purple silk is cut in a bolero shape and the front is made of ivory satin covered with machine embroidered net. There is a deep purple doeskin cape worn with this dress, also made at Adderley's. It is decorated with lines of machine stitching and has a high curving shaped collar (671.1962).

Women's clothing is catalogued under dresses, modern wedding dresses, skirts, bodices, jackets, bathing costumes, hunting outfits, hats, coats, uniforms, capes, shawls, fichus, collars, undersleeves, veils, underwear, jewellery, fans, gloves, muffs, aprons, handkerchiefs, bags, parasols, spectacles, shoes and accessories, and stockings. There are nearly five hundred dresses ranging from the eighteenth century to the present day. There is a small group of eighteenth-century dresses and a representative selection of Regency, and early and mid-Victorian dresses. The 1870s and 1880s are very well covered with over eighty specimens and there are nearly fifty from 1890–1910. Fewer dresses survive from the First World War years but there are nearly seventy 1920s dresses, many of them beaded. Similar numbers survive from the 1930s and from the period 1940–70. The shoe collection contains over four hundred specimens ranging from the sixteenth century to the present day. There are over two hundred pairs of stockings and over a hundred and fifty hats. There are fewer specimens in the other categories.

As in most collections the range of men's clothing is smaller than the women's. There are a few eighteenth-century suits, over fifty nineteenth-century suits and thirty dating from the twentieth century, with ten hunting outfits. There are ten bathing costumes, eleven smocks and a range of over fifty waistcoats, with small groups of industrial clothing, underwear, shirts, accessories, hats, hose, shoes and smoking caps. There are specimens of civil and military uniform which are of local interest.

Children's clothing is catalogued under girls' dresses, boys' clothes, hats, shoes, underwear, and babies' robes and bonnets, with several items in each category.

A new museum of technology is planned, where there would be displays devoted to the history of the local hosiery industry, showing the

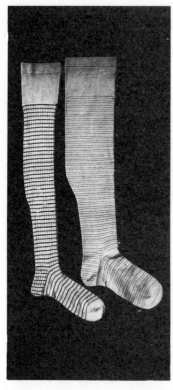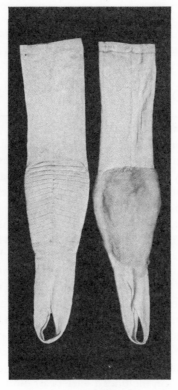

development of machinery from the cottage industry to modern times.

A range of shoes dating from the sixteenth century to the present day is shown in the Costume museum, as shoemaking is another local industry. Costumes are mounted in cases with a few items of furniture to give a sense of period style. There are also displays of purses and handbags, fans, embroidery and lace making.

The costumes are stored in one room on metal racks with wheels which can be moved to allow space for working. Most of the costumes are hanging, protected by polythene bags, except for fragile specimens and heavily beaded 1920s dresses which are packed in boxes. All the accessories are also in boxes. The storage area in the costume museum is air-conditioned, and there is extra storage room in the Newarke Museum. All items are entered in an accessions book and then in a card index.

The museum education service caters for children up to sixteen and borrows expendable items from the costume collection. There is space for a group of thirty to work in the display area. Groups of up to six older students can see items in the reserve collection, where there is also a small collection of fashion magazines, fashion plates and some costume reference books which they may use. Appointments should be made well in advance.

Above centre

215. City of Liverpool Museum. White knitted silk under-stockings with lamb's wool padding for the calves. One (right) is inside out. The stockings were found with a court suit of c. 1790–1800 and are probably of that date. (50.104.5)

Above right

216. City of Liverpool Museum. Afternoon dress of c. 1912–14 in brown chiffon over yellow satin and turquoise silk. (54.61.1)

PUBLICATIONS AVAILABLE FROM THE MUSEUM
There is a small selection of slides, with more planned. A list is available.

LIVERPOOL

CITY OF LIVERPOOL MUSEUM
The collection of women's dresses here includes a few specimens from the
1780s, which have been remodelled from earlier silks. There are not
many dresses from c.1790–1840, but there are a few good items from the
1850s and 1860s. Among the larger number from 1870 onwards is a day
dress of c.1895 (61.175.2) made of soft sage green wool cloqué; the surface
has a ruched appearance, resulting in an almost uncrushable material. An
afternoon dress of c.1898 in black satin with a lilac satin yoke covered
with passementerie, bordered with black chiffon pleated frills, is labelled
By Special Appointment to Her Majesty the Queen. Jays, Regent St. London W
(55.26.6). A black velvet coat of c.1903 (1969.250.1) has lines of black
cross-cut ribbed silk machined on both edges, with a vivid crimson satin
lining and similar colour velvet sleeve ends (one missing); the original fur
collar and cuffs have been removed. There is also a very good selection
of evening dresses for c.1910–14, a rare period. From c.1930–1970 there
are fewer items.
    The collection includes a variety of blouses, capes and dolmans, mainly
from the late nineteenth and early twentieth centuries.
    The range of underwear includes chemises, petticoats, nightgowns and
a few corsets. Among the collection of shoes are some from the eighteenth
and early nineteenth centuries and many more from c.1890. There are
approximately fifty hats and bonnets dating from the mid nineteenth
century onwards. A small group of children's costume includes two
items from the eighteenth century.
    There are ten eighteenth-century specimens of men's costume, several
blazers, smoking jackets, dinner jackets and civil uniforms, mainly from
the late nineteenth century, and waistcoats from the mid eighteenth to the
early twentieth century. A pair of white knitted silk stockings which have
their own lamb's wool padding for the calves woven in at the back, dating
from c.1790–1810, are of particular interest (50.104.5). A large collection
of military uniforms is catalogued and housed separately.
    The recently acquired Tinne collection (also catalogued separately) is
of sociological interest. This collection of about a hundred dresses, seventy-
five hats, twenty-five pairs of shoes, underwear, baby clothes, children's
clothes, maids' caps and aprons and a bathing dress, were bought by a
local doctor's wife, during the period 1914–45, for herself and her family.
Many of the items were unworn and had been purchased in sales, as the

labels were still attached.

Each item in the collection of costume and accessories is entered in the accessions book with a full description. The provenance of each specimen acquired since 1945 is known; all records before that date were destroyed in the war. There is no card index system at the time of writing, but the costumes are stored in date sequence in large wooden wardrobes. Fragile items and heavily beaded dresses of the 1920s are packed flat.

Costume is displayed in the galleries in conjunction with other exhibits, such as 'Musical Instruments' and 'The History of Liverpool'. At the time of writing there is no separate costume gallery. It is possible for up to four advanced students to work in the costume section and groups of up to ten C.S.E. or O-level students and sixth formers can be accommodated. The education department deals with groups of children aged eight to fifteen in groups of twenty to thirty, using costume as illustration of a theme, such as *The Age of Victoria*. As space is limited, appointments should be made well in advance.

LONDON

BETHNAL GREEN MUSEUM

This museum is a branch of the Victoria and Albert Museum and does not have a reserve collection of costume. Examples of nineteenth-century children's costume, women's clothes from *c*.1750–1960 with a section devoted to wedding dresses, and a few men's suits from the eighteenth century are on display.

There is a large group of dolls and dolls' clothing, much of which is useful for costume study. Displays of fashion plates, paper patterns, needlework accessories and the tools and fittings from a village shoe-maker's shop from Honington, Warwickshire, founded in 1729, provide background material for the costume displays. Of particular interest is the material on the local Spitalfields silk industry, with examples of eighteenth-century silks and designs on paper, a scale model of a hand loom with a Jacquard machine, and many photographs of looms.

There is adequate space for several groups of thirty children to work in the display area, but the schools service should be notified in advance of intended visits.

LONDON

BRITISH MUSEUM

The Department of Prints and Drawings houses the Schreiber collection of fans and fan leaves. There are over six hundred specimens, dating

Right

217. Bethnal Green
Museum, London.
Court suit of
c. 1790–1800 in
purple cut velvet em-
broidered in several
shades of green,
yellow, white and
pink silk, with
matching buttons.
(875–1894)

Far right

218. Bethnal Green
Museum, London.
White muslin gown
of c. 1800–5 with
a long train, em-
broidered in white
cotton. (T.124–1913)

Right

219. British
Museum, Depart-
ment of Prints and
Drawings. Detail of
an unmounted fan
leaf, c. 1785, 'The
Ladies Hatter'
painted in body
colour on silk.
(Schreiber Coll.
Book 4, no. 368)

mainly from the eighteenth and nineteenth centuries. The catalogue
indicates a wide variety of subject matter: historical, biblical, classical,
pastoral, fancy, social and instructive. The fans are of both English and
foreign origin; there are examples from France, Italy, Spain, Germany,

Holland and America as well as some Oriental specimens. Almost all the
fans are decorated, by one or more of the following processes: etching,
stipple engraving, line engraving, lithography, chromolithography,
drawing or hand painting. Some have extra decorations in the form of
sequins, feathers and ribbon.

They are catalogued in: CUST, L. *Catalogue of the Collection of Fans and
Fan Leaves Presented to the Trustees of the British Museum by the Lady
Charlotte Schreiber*, Longmans 1893.

LONDON

THE MUSEUM OF MANKIND (BRITISH MUSEUM)
The collections of the Ethnography Department cover an extremely wide
field of tribal and village cultures of the world. There are textiles and
some weaving equipment from most areas which are covered by the
Department, but the majority of made-up costumes are in the Asiatic
section of the collections. There is a selection of Arab costumes and the
recent acquisition of a group of peasant costume from Bulgaria comple-
ments a small number of South-East European examples already in the
collections. There are also a few North American Indian pieces.

As well as textiles and costume, there is a good collection of African
masks and many examples of jewellery. A selection of these items is often
on display in the newly designed exhibition areas at 6 Burlington Gardens,
where there is space for groups of up to thirty children to work. Notice of
intended visits should be given. All the textiles and costumes will
eventually be stored in this building and will be available to students who
make an appointment.

PUBLICATIONS AVAILABLE FROM THE MUSEUM

WEIR, S. *Spinning and Weaving in Palestine*, The British Museum, 1970.
25 plates in monochrome and colour of weaving equipment and local
people at work.

LONDON

CITY OF LONDON POLICE MUSEUM
The museum houses a small collection of police uniforms dating from the
mid-nineteenth century to the present day. Among the earliest are an
inspector's greatcoat of 1863 and a police hat of 1851. A criminal records
album of the 1860s and 1870s provides an interesting if somewhat unusual
source of photographs showing occupational and working costume.

Visitors should telephone or write in advance to: The Commissioner,
City of London Police, 26 Old Jewry, London EC2R 8DJ. Tel: (01) 606 8866

LONDON

THE GUILDHALL MUSEUM

This museum will shortly be amalgamated with the London Museum to form the Museum of London in a new building to be erected at the junction of London Wall and Aldersgate Street within the City of London. The two collections of costume and costume accessories are described separately, but will eventually be under one roof.

The Guildhall Museum has an interesting collection of excavated material dating from Roman times to the beginning of the seventeenth century. New material is constantly being added when foundations for large buildings are excavated in the City of London. There are fragments of Roman costume (mainly shoes), medieval shoes, fragments of sixteenth and seventeenth-century costume and shoes, all of leather. Fragments of silk and larger pieces of woollen cloth and linen also survive, with several knitted sixteenth-century apprentices' caps.

There are a few uniforms, both civil and military, connected with the City of London, and a small collection of leathercraft, showing examples of work carried out by the City Guilds and Companies, including many items of dress.

The museum also houses, on behalf of the Worshipful Company of Glovers, the Spence collection of gloves. This comprises over two hundred superb pairs of gloves, from the fifteenth to the nineteenth centuries.

All the items are entered in an accessions book, then in a card index, and are stored in boxes. A selection of material is on display in the museum.

Until the new museum is built it will be difficult to deal with large school parties, as space is limited in the museum. Much of the material is too fragile to be handled, but may be examined closely under supervision. Parties of twelve older children, aged sixteen to eighteen, can see items in store on special request. Both collections are of considerable interest to specialists and up to two can be accommodated in the reserve collection at any one time. Appointments should be made well in advance.

LONDON

HORNIMAN MUSEUM AND LIBRARY

This museum houses a large collection of ethnographic costume from all over the world. There are specimens of African, American, Asian and Oriental costume as well as European peasant costume. The earliest specimens date from the early nineteenth century and additions are still being made to the collection, although Western influences are now permeating many cultures.

There are many examples to show the techniques used for printing, dyeing, tie-dyeing and weaving, with the equipment used. Beads, head-dresses, feathers and other items for personal adornment are also included in the collection.

Specimens of costume are on display and many more will be exhibited eventually. Items can be produced from the reserve collection if a request is made well in advance.

There is a schools service which caters for parties of up to thirty children in the galleries. A group of up to twelve older students can work in the store at any one time. Appointments should be made in advance.

LONDON

THE LONDON MUSEUM

This museum will shortly be amalgamated with the Guildhall Museum to form the Museum of London in a new building to be erected at the junction of London Wall and Aldersgate Street within the City of London. The two collections of costume and costume accessories are described separately, but will eventually be under one roof.

The collection of costume at the London Museum is one of the largest in the country and can be divided into four sections: royal costume, theatrical costume, ordinary dress, fashionable and unfashionable, associated in some way with London, and excavated material from the City of London. It is comprehensively catalogued, each item being listed first in the accessions book and then entered on one or more cards for the card index, which is extensively cross referenced.

Large items of women's clothing are sorted into the following categories: brides' and bridesmaids' dresses; ceremonial dresses; cloaks; coats and pelisses; dresses; fancy dresses; riding habits; skirts with jackets; suits; veils. The range of eighteenth-century dresses is particularly fine and many of the nineteenth and twentieth-century specimens are labelled with their makers' names. Smaller items are sorted into these sections: aprons and overalls; bathing costumes; blouses and jumpers; bodices and spencers; capes and pelisses; fichus, berthes and kerchiefs; jackets and mantles; neckwear; sashes and belts; scarves and boas; shawls; skirts and slacks; sleeves and cuffs; stomachers. There are several very rare jackets and bodices from the seventeenth and eighteenth centuries. A large collection of accessories is filed under bags and purses; caps, bonnets and hats; hat pins; combs and hair ornaments; fans; parasols; gloves; muffs; shoes. The underwear collection is very large and contains specimens of brassières; camisoles; corsets; chemises and vests; chemisettes; combinations; dressing gowns; jackets and negligée wear; garters; hoops and bustles; night and boudoir caps; nightgowns; pantalettes and knickers; petticoats; pockets; sleeve puffs; stockings.

Children's clothing is divided into babies' wear and clothes for boys and girls. There is a small selection of each of the following: babies' bodices, caps, coats, dresses, gloves, shoes, socks, underwear, with accessories like cot covers, baskets and pillows. Children's clothes are represented by a selection in each of these categories: bodices and waist-coats; caps and hats; coats and cloaks; dresses and skirts; gloves; neckwear; pinafores; shoes; socks and stockings; underwear and general items including parasols and purses. The collection comes up to the present day to include a 1967 gymslip and 1950 bathing dresses.

Each item which is associated with royalty or a theatrical personality is filed in the personalia section. The many items for royalty are catalogued under the following headings: state garments; suits; umbrellas; shoes; hats; dresses; accessories; bodices and skirts; handkerchiefs; headwear; parasols; shawls and scarves; stockings; underwear. There are also miscellaneous items including the paper pattern for a body belt worn by George IV, dated 8 October 1824. Many royal personages are represented in the collection, some by state robes and dresses, others by no more than a handkerchief, a nightcap or a fan. There are numerous items from George IV, Princess Charlotte and Queen Victoria and her descendants, as well as the coronation robes of King George V and Queen Mary (1911) and Princess Margaret's wedding dress, a particularly lovely gown in white silk organza (on permanent loan).

The theatrical personalities represented include Sir George Alexander, Sir Frank Benson, Sarah Bernhardt, Gordon Craig, Sir Johnston Forbes-Robertson, David Garrick, Grimaldi, Sir Henry Irving, Edmund Kean, Henry Kemble, Dame Madge Kendal, Marie Lloyd, Sir John Martin-Harvey, Adelina Patti, Anna Pavlova, Sir George Robey, Ellen Terry, Bransby Williams and Martita Hunt. The majority of the items are theatrical costumes, for which there is a published catalogue. This collection may eventually be housed at the Museum of Performing Arts, when this is built.

The selection of men's costume is much smaller than that for women as in most museums. Among the larger items it includes breeches and trousers, coats and capes, and a few complete suits. There is a wide range of waistcoats from c.1700–1945, particularly good from c.1750–1850, but with fewer specimens from the earlier and later years. There is an interesting group of civilian uniform of the city and county of London including court wear, coronation wear (not worn by royalty) a fireman's uniform, footmen's livery, legal dress, police uniform, items worn by various orders, and articles from the royal household. There are a few items of military uniform. Smaller pieces of costume and accessories are catalogued under: bags and wallets; gloves; ecclesiastical gloves; hats and caps; shoes and boots; umbrellas and canes; wigs and wigstands; bathing

Left

*220. London
Museum. A skirt in
natural linen of
c. 1700–15 with
a geometric linear
pattern, embroidered
in brown silk with
back stitch. The
foliage and birds of
paradise are em-
broidered in pink,
red, turquoise,
brown, yellow and
green. The back
panel of the skirt is
missing. Very few
items from this period
have survived.
(63.125)*

costumes; braces and belts; dressing gowns; stockings; neckwear; nightcaps and nightshirts; sleeves and cuffs; smocks; shirts and underwear.
Mention should also be made of the artist's lay figure with both men's
and women's clothes, used by the sculptor, Roubiliac (1695–1762), of
considerable interest for costume detail.

Right

*221. Guildhall
Museum, London.
A glove (one of a
pair) of c. 1600 with
a deep cuff heavily
embroidered with
silver-gilt thread and
silk, bordered with
silver-gilt lace and
spangles. (23343)*

A useful collection of textiles includes soft furnishing linens, banners,
lace, patchwork, tapestries and twenty-four rolls of velvet, the majority
cut on the cross, which were unused stock from a draper's shop kept by
Mrs Jardine of East Croydon from c.1890–1930. There are examples of
beadwork, samplers and Berlin woolwork, as well as the implements
used in their manufacture. These are grouped under embroidery silks,
housewives and others; industrial spinning and weaving implements;
sewing clamps; embroidery scissors; straw splitters; needles, needlebooks,
pins and pincushions; patterns for dressmaking and knitting; silk winders
and holders; tape measures including a cloth-worker's measure marked
with quarters from the early eighteenth century; thimbles and a sailmaker's
seam presser.

Among many other miscellaneous items related to dress are shoe
buckles, of which there are a large selection from the eighteenth century;
buttons; favours and rosettes, several from 1863 commemorating the
wedding of King Edward VII and Queen Alexandra; riding accessories,
dress boxes, bonnet boxes, fan boxes and a muff box, mainly of nineteenth-
century origin; dress supporters (clips for holding up skirts at the end of
the nineteenth century) and sachets and cases for gloves, cards and letters.
Some of these items are fascinating: a seventeenth-century shaving
brush (A6113), a mirror decorated with stump work of c.1640 (A12227);

boot warmers of porcelain stamped *By Her Majesty's Royal Letters Patent – Health comfort Patent Bootdrying and warming last* (A1969.70); a muff warmer with a paper cartridge of *c*.1894 (64.43); curling irons and goffering irons; a *Keptonu* treasure garter (64.103.30); an electric massage roller (for reducing wrinkles) of the early twentieth century (66.82.3.); an early twentieth-century travelling iron (69.160.1); an Elegan hairnet of *c*.1920–30 (64.103.36).

The section of excavated material is catalogued under bags and purses, shoes, belts, straps and caps, with some very interesting sixteenth-century knitted ones. There are also fragments of material and leather Roman sandals and shoes, a few medieval and several sixteenth-century shoes. All this material is very fragile.

Many of the eighteenth and nineteenth-century dresses are hanging in cupboards but the major part of the collection is packed in boxes, in category and date sequence, until the new storage space is available.

A selection of fashion plates, and a few contemporary photographs and magazines are kept with the costume collection. There is also a useful file of photographs of paintings and portraits showing costume. All these are most helpful for dating material.

A large selection of costumes and accessories is on display in the museum. A schools service caters for children from eight to eighteen and can help with project work, such as 'Costume in the Victorian Era'. Advance notice of intended visits should be given. Groups of up to five art students or College of Education students, or two advanced students, can be accommodated in the reserve collection at any one time. Appointments should be made well in advance.

PUBLICATIONS AVAILABLE FROM THE MUSEUM

CRUSO, T. *Costume. A Catalogue.* 1936. 57 monochrome plates, also diagrams and line drawings.

HALLS, Z. *Women's Costumes 1600–1750.* H.M.S.O., 1969. Catalogue of costume with 21 monochrome plates and two folding patterns.

HALLS, Z. *Men's Costume 1580–1750.* H.M.S.O., 1970. Catalogue of costume with 21 monochrome plates.

HALLS, Z. *Women's Costume 1750–1800.* H.M.S.O., 1972. Catalogue of costume with 24 monochrome plates.

HALLS, Z. *Men's Costume 1750–1800.* H.M.S.O., 1973. Catalogue of costume with 24 monochrome plates.

HOLMES, M. R. *Stage Costume and Accessories.* H.M.S.O., 1968. Catalogue with 28 monochrome plates and one colour plate.

A range of monochrome and colour postcards is also available.

Further publications on costume including one on royal costumes in the collection are in preparation. A detailed list is available on request.

LONDON

METROPOLITAN POLICE MUSEUM

The museum contains a collection of over two hundred police uniforms of all ranks, from 1829 to the present day, with accessories, including helmets, medals and buttons.

At the moment the collection is used for police instruction only, but it is hoped that a museum will be established in the future with a permanent display open to the general public.

All enquiries should be addressed to The Publicity Branch, New Scotland Yard, Broadway, London SW1H 0BG.

LONDON

NATIONAL ARMY MUSEUM (WITH A BRANCH AT THE
ROYAL MILITARY ACADEMY SANDHURST)

The displays in the uniform gallery are largely grouped in chronological order, the story of British and Indian Army uniforms being the most important feature. With them are shown headgear, weapons, buttons, buckles, badges, decorations and many other items of equipment. Contemporary drawings and paintings, showing many of the uniforms and accessories in wear, are displayed as part of the exhibition. An additional display of Indian Army uniforms from the collection may be seen in the Indian Army Memorial Room at the Royal Military Academy Sandhurst, which is open to the public.

A reserve collection of considerable size is stored at Camberley. It is the largest collection of military costume in the country, comprising several thousand items, covering regular army uniforms dating from the mid eighteenth century and auxiliary uniforms from the Napoleonic Wars to the present day.

The reading room has a large collection of books, prints, drawings and photographs; it is available to students, who should have a reader's ticket. Many of the items in the large collections of prints and drawings could be described as ethnographical, as they show people of many other countries in ordinary dress, as well as in uniform. There are over 13,000 photographs, some of them nineteenth-century originals. Others show objects in the museum and students may use these for study or purchase copies.

There is space for groups of up to thirty children to work in the Uniform Gallery at Chelsea. Serious students can see items in the reserve collection at Camberley.

Appointments should be made well in advance.

PUBLICATIONS AVAILABLE FROM THE MUSEUM

Postcards and colour transparencies of uniforms are available. The bookstall has a large range of publications on military uniform. A list will be sent on request.

LONDON

NATIONAL MARITIME MUSEUM

This museum houses a sizeable collection of naval uniform, biased towards the executive branches, although there are examples from the civil branches such as pursers', surgeons', paymasters' and those of others providing specialist services. There are also a few examples of Merchant Service and East India Company uniforms.

One of the earliest uniforms, on permanent loan from the Ministry of Defence, is part of one of the two sets of uniforms which were made up in 1748; the regulations were not printed. The collection continues to the 1960s.

Very little is on display at the time of writing as much of the material is undergoing conservation and will be put on exhibition in the near future. Appointments to see the reserve collection should be made well in advance.

PUBLICATIONS AVAILABLE FROM THE MUSEUM

MAY, W. E. *The Dress of Naval Officers*. H.M.S.O., 1966. 69 monochrome plates of costume and of contemporary portraits from the collection.

LONDON

PERMANENT EXHIBITION OF JUDICIAL AND LEGAL COSTUME,
ROYAL COURTS OF JUSTICE

A permanent exhibition of legal costume will be established in the near future. A temporary exhibition was mounted in July 1971, showing a selection of historic and contemporary legal costume and accessories. This will form the nucleus of the collection. Enquiries should be addressed to The Trustees of the Permanent Exhibition of Judicial and Legal Costume, Royal Courts of Justice, Strand, London WC2A 2LL

LONDON

VESTRY HOUSE MUSEUM OF LOCAL HISTORY AND ANTIQUITIES

This museum is primarily concerned with local history and the majority of the items in the small costume collection have been acquired locally or from donors living in Essex. There is a small collection of photographs

showing local people in working–class dress and occupational clothing;
many show schoolchildren.

In the women's collection there are about twenty nineteenth and
twentieth-century dresses, a small range of underwear, including nightdresses, drawers, chemises, petticoats, and nightcaps, and a few coats,
skirts, blouses, bodices, mantles, parasols, capes, fans, handbags, feathers,
shoes and hair ornaments. Men's costume consists of a few military and
civic uniforms of local interest, with a smock, a few sticks, watch-chains
and other accessories.

At present the costumes are being re-catalogued while new storage is
arranged.

There is room in the display area for a group of not more than twenty
children and items can be produced from the reserve collection on request.
Advance notice should be given.

LONDON

VICTORIA AND ALBERT MUSEUM

The collection at this museum is probably better known than any other
in the world. It forms part of the Department of Textiles with embroidery,

Right

*224. Victoria &
Albert Museum,
London. An evening
outfit of 1967 by
Balenciaga of black
pure silk Zibeline
(Staron) worn by
Mrs Loel Guinness.
The dress is high-
necked and sleeveless,
cut with a single
seam, flaring from
the shoulders to the
knee at the front
and the ground at the
back.*

Far right

*225. Victoria &
Albert Museum,
London. A suit of
c. 1740–60 con-
sisting of coat,
waistcoat and breeches
in deep crimson and
ivory woven silk
with a diamond
pattern. (T.137–1932)*

woven and printed fabrics, lace, tapestries and carpets. Costume was originally collected for the textile used, as a form of decorative art, and as a result there are particularly good examples of small embroidered items of the late sixteenth and early seventeenth centuries as well as many eighteenth-century dresses made in superbly designed woven silks.

The museum is fortunate in possessing an extremely fine range of men's suits, many of them in woollen cloth, although these are normally very rare. A representative range dating from *c.*1600 until the mid nineteenth century is exhibited in the Costume Court. Many of the seventeenth-century items came from the Isham family. There is a fine group of over a hundred and fifty waistcoats dating from *c.*1700–1930.

The collection concentrates on fashionable dress, both English and Continental, and includes many couture specimens. Some of them were worn by Heather Firbank, sister of the novelist, between *c.*1908 and 1921, and were shown in *Lady of Fashion*, an exhibition held in 1961.

The acquisition in 1971 of over two hundred couture dresses and accessories (representing about seventy couturiers) for the exhibition *Fashion: an Anthology by Cecil Beaton* has enriched it considerably. The dresses were generously donated to the museum through Sir Cecil Beaton, by the many people who had preserved them. Most of these items are fully documented. Some of them were worn by well-known people on public occasions; they may be examples of extravagant cut or lavish decoration typical of a particular period. They were all made by eminent couturiers, whose labels are still in most of the dresses, among them Balenciaga, Balmain, Chanel, Courrèges, Dior, Fath, Givenchy, Grès, Poiret, Schiaparelli, Vionnet and Worth.

There is a good representative selection of accessories; the range of over four hundred fans is particularly fine, the specimens dating from the late seventeenth to the early twentieth century with a large group from the eighteenth century. The shoe collection was enlarged in 1971 by eighty fashionable pairs dating from c.1914–1960 bequeathed by the late Leonard Ernest Bussey.

There are over a hundred and twenty dresses and suits, with a selection of approximately five hundred accessories, arranged in chronological sequence in the Costume Court, which is specially lit to prevent damage to the fragile textiles on display. At the sides of the cases are photographs of paintings, engravings and other primary source material showing dress in its contemporary setting. Around the outer walls of the court are selections of fashion plates in movable frames. Cases are also reserved for small temporary displays. The large collection of jewellery in the Department of Metalwork should be noted.

All items in the Department are entered in accessions registers. The costume entries are duplicated for handlists and since 1970 it has been the policy to take small black and white photographs of all new acquisitions for them.

The dresses are mainly stored flat, with as few folds as possible, in specially designed cupboards, with large shallow drawers which can be pulled out easily; the items are immediately visible without handling. Men's suits of the seventeenth century are also stored in this way; those from the eighteenth century onward are hanging on padded hangers in cupboards. Most small items of lace and some other accessories are kept in cellophane bags for easy visibility and to prevent damage when being handled.

Oriental textiles and costumes are kept in three departments; the Indian Section and the Far Eastern Section with the Middle Eastern items in the Department of Textiles.

The library contains a very large collection of books on costume and textiles, and there are examples of almost all the primary sources already described, on display in the museum, as well as in the reserve collections.

The Circulation Department arranges displays of textiles, including costume, which go to museums, colleges and libraries all over the country. The Education Service deals with parties of up to forty children accompanied by an adequate number of teachers; talks can be arranged and groups can work in the Costume Court.

Students wishing to work with material from the reserve collection should make an appointment; items can be put in cases in the textile study room on request to be worked on at any time. There is space in the store for not more than eight students at any one time, and during periods when there is a shortage of staff the visit may have to be limited to forty-five minutes. Visitors who wish to take photographs must write in advance to the Keeper of the Department.

PUBLICATIONS AVAILABLE FROM THE MUSEUM

ANTHONY, P and ARNOLD, J. *Costume*, the Victoria and Albert Museum in association with the Costume Society, 1966. A general bibliography of over four hundred books on costume. (Revised edition in preparation.)

BLUMSTEIN, M. (GINSBURG, M.) *Dolls*. Victoria and Albert Museum, small picture book, H.M.S.O., 1959.

GIBBS SMITH, C. H. *The Fashionable Lady in the Nineteenth Century*, H.M.S.O., 1960. Monochrome plates of fashion plates for each fifth year from 1800–1900.

GINSBURG, M. *A Brief Guide to the Costume Court*, H.M.S.O., 1962. Gives an outline of the display with notes on contemporary fashions.

GINSBURG, M. *Fashion: An Anthology by Cecil Beaton*, Introduction by Cecil Beaton, H.M.S.O., 1971. A catalogue of the exhibition, with line drawings and monochrome photographs of couturiers and dresses *c*.1900–71.

KING, D. 'Three Spanish Cloaks', in *The Victoria and Albert Museum Bulletin*, no 4, 1968, pp 26–30.

Black and white charts showing the changing line of fashion and a selection of postcards of costumes from the collection in both black and white and colour are available from the publications counter. Booklets listing publications and prices are available.

Lists of picture sheets and postcards depicting costume and dolls, a bibliography of books on costume and corsetry, a list of textile bibliographies and a photograph list are available from the Department of Textiles.

LUTON

MUSEUM AND ART GALLERY

The collection of costume is mostly of local provenance, hats and lace being the two strongest areas. There are about a hundred women's dresses dating from the late eighteenth century to the 1950s, and nearly as many bodices, capes and jackets, from the late eighteenth century to the

Far left

*226. Victoria &
Albert Museum,
London. An evening
dress of* c. *1893 in
palest creamy lemon
grosgrain with a
narrow striped moiré
effect. The bodice is
trimmed with orchid
pink chiffon and
velvet. The em-
broidery is carried
out in silver cord,
sequins and beads.*
(T. 47–1973)

Left

*227. The Museum
and Art Gallery,
Luton. A display
which shows a range
of straw hats in the
collection.*

1920s. The range of footwear dates mainly from the nineteenth century, as does a small selection of stockings including several particularly fine specimens. There are a few pairs of nineteenth-century gloves, a good selection of fans from the eighteenth to the twentieth centuries and a range of underwear. One large room is devoted to displays of costume. Three cases contain dresses, and there is one case each for parasols, jewellery, fans, shoes and stockings, bags and purses and children's clothes. A wall bracket provides a selection of fashion plates.

Straw hats are the main feature of the large collection of hats, as straw plaiting was a local cottage industry. Displays in the museum show the different types of straw, the varieties of plaiting, hat blocking, stitching, straw flattening, straw splitters, dyers' shade cards, machinery and several examples of straw hats.

The lace collection is a very large one, as lace making was also a local industry. One room is devoted to displays of lace making and shows East Midlands pillow lace, Buckinghamshire point ground lace, Bedfordshire Maltese lace, the interior of a lace maker's cottage, bone and wooden bobbins, bobbin winders, lighting appliances, pillows set up for lace making and pincushions. A large reserve collection contains numerous specimens of lace, both hand and machine-made, carefully mounted and covered with cellophane so that students can see them easily.

There are a few items of men's clothes and uniforms, with a particularly good group of smocks, both adults' and children's.

All items are entered in an accessions book and then in a card index.

There is room in the museum for parties of thirty children with two teachers. The schools service will provide work sheets for any age groups between eight and fifteen. There is space for six college students or two advanced students in the reserve collection. Two weeks' advance notice of a visit should be given.

PUBLICATIONS AVAILABLE FROM THE MUSEUM

FREEMAN, C. E. *Pillow Lace in the East Midlands*, 1958. 52 pages, 17 monochrome plates, 10 text illustrations.

FREEMAN, C. E. *Luton and the Hat Industry*, 1953. 36 pages, 17 monochrome plates, 10 text illustrations.

There are also nine photographs of smocks, and a small selection of black and white postcards and colour transparencies. A list will be sent on request.

MAIDSTONE

MUSEUM AND ART GALLERY

Most of the items are from local donors although there are some from further afield. The collection, which dates mainly from the nineteenth century, with some earlier items, includes over fifty women's dresses, among them a sack dress of *c*.1765–75, with a wide hooped skirt, in terracotta silk (badly faded) with large sprays of flowers in white, pinks, yellows and greens. The petticoat is trimmed with a deep flounce of silk gimp worked into a net with a large open mesh, which is also used for serpentine curves on the robings and down the sides of the skirt and on the stomacher front. Among other items of women's clothing are a riding habit of *c*.1740–50 in cream twill weave fustian (badly stained) with a brown velvet peaked hat, and a bathing dress of *c*.1930 which is labelled *R. H. Forma British Patent no 10466. Made in Saxony size 46.* It is made of fine black cotton stockinette with a built-in brassière in black cotton stockinette beneath the loose shape. The bathing dress has a skirt panel cut on the cross at the side and back, from the waist, with a zig-zag edge trimmed with white braid. This covers the short legs of the suit.

There are also a few items in each of these categories: aprons, blouses, bodices, boleros, bustles, caps, capes, chemises, cloaks, coats, châtelaines, collars, corsets, crinolines, combinations, fans, feathers, gloves, habits, handkerchiefs, hats, jackets, lace, mantles, nightdresses, pantaloons, pattens, petticoats, pinafores, purses, ribbons, robes, scarves, shawls, shirts, shoes, skirts, sleeves, smocks, socks, stoles, stockings, suits, trousers, veils and waistcoats. Among the hats is one of c.1800 in straw-coloured satin with panels of ivory (discoloured) crimped georgette over it. Each panel is bordered with silk twisted cord to conceal the stitching.

There are a few items of men's clothing in the collection and several military uniforms of local interest which are kept in the local regimental room in the museum. A small selection of coaching liveries are also on display at the Tyrwhitt Drake Museum of Carriages, Mill Street, Maidstone.

Crayford was a centre for printed fabrics in the 1840s and the museum has several pattern books from Messrs George, P & J Baker of Crayford, Kent, which provide some very interesting samples of printed woollen dress fabrics for 1841–3, and some of the printing blocks.

Each item in the collection is entered in the accessions book and there is a card index which is being reorganized at the time of writing.

Most of the collection is in store, packed in boxes, but more accommodation will shortly be available. More than thirty dresses, a few suits and a range of accessories are displayed in a large room which is devoted to costume.

Groups of up to thirty children or students can work in the gallery or up to two students in the reserve collection at any one time. Appointments should be made in advance.

MANCHESTER

THE GALLERY OF ENGLISH COSTUME

The Gallery of English Costume, which is a department of Manchester City Art Galleries, is in an eighteenth-century house on the outskirts of Manchester. It was established when the Cunnington collection was purchased by public subscription (with a contribution from Manchester Corporation) for the City of Manchester in 1947; it is so well known that it needs little introduction.

The main part of the large collection consists of women's clothing, with a sizeable range of babies' and children's dress and men's wear. There are just over 1,500 dresses, from the mid-eighteenth century to the present day. Many of the eighteenth-century dresses have been remade during that century, providing a most interesting survey of the re-use of silks at that time and at certain periods in the nineteenth century (see pages 129–146). The collection concentrates on the dress of the middle-class Englishwoman and there are examples from all over the country, as well as clothes bought in France and worn in England, but it also includes a few couture specimens and some examples of working dress. Many of the dresses retain their dressmakers' labels. A large and comprehensive collection of accessories includes particularly good ranges of corsets, shoes, gloves and hats.

The whole of Platt Hall is used for costume displays and storage. Over two hundred items of dress and accessories are exhibited in five rooms to give a continuous sequence from the eighteenth century to the present day. The examples in this chronological display are changed at intervals, but the exhibition is a permanent one. Five other rooms are devoted to displays of different aspects of the history of costume. They have included 'Fashions for One Lifetime, 1800–1870'; 'The Heads of Englishwomen', which showed the changing styles of hats and head-dresses from c.1700 onwards, 'The Changing Shapes of Fashion, 1700–1910', a selection of corsets which provided the sub-structure of the dress; 'The Shop Windows' with selections of haberdashery of 1830–50, 1860–80 and 1890–1910; 'Borrowed Plumes' which showed feathers in fashionable dress from 1770–1950 and 'Fashion in Miniature', a display of dolls.

Many items of seventeenth-century dress are on display, including men's embroidered linen caps, women's embroidered coifs, bobbin lace and linen collars of the 1630s, plain linen collars and cuffs of the 1640s, gloves and a falling band of c.1620.

All the items in the collection are entered in a very comprehensive card index, cross-referenced for easy access to the store. The costumes are hung in date sequence in large cupboards on padded hangers. Fragile specimens and beaded dresses are stored flat in drawers and boxes. Most of the conservation work is done on the premises.

The reference library contains a large selection of books on costume and accessories with many specialised works, trade catalogues, fashion journals, patterns, books of textile samples, photographs and other records. School parties of up to forty children with an adequate number of teachers can work in the exhibition area; they should always give notice of an intended visit. Students wishing to work with material from the reserve collection or the library should make an appointment.

For further information on the collection see an article by Anne Buck 'The Gallery of English Costume, Platt Hall, Manchester', in *Costume* The Journal of the Costume Society no. 6, 1972, which contains a general description with some black and white illustrations.

PUBLICATIONS AVAILABLE FROM THE MUSEUM

Manchester City Art Galleries Picture Books
    1. A Brief View. 1949
    2. Women's Costume in the 18th Century. 1954
    3. Women's Costume, 1800–35. 1952
    4. Women's Costume, 1835–70. 1951
    5. Women's Costume, 1870–1900. 1953

6. Women's Costume, 1900–30. 1956
7. Children's Costume. 1959
8. Costume for Sport. 1963
9. Fashion in Miniature. 1971

Each booklet contains twenty pages of illustrations of costume and accessories from the collection, with descriptive notes.

A selection of black and white and colour postcards and colour transparencies of costumes in the collection are also available. A detailed list of publications and prices may be obtained free of charge from the museum.

MARKET HARBOROUGH

THE SYMINGTON MUSEUM OF PERIOD CORSETRY

The firm owns approximately three hundred samples of foundation garments, comprising corsets, brassières and children's corsets from *c.*1850 to the present day. At the moment the collection is in store while a museum is being established on the premises. Each item is to be catalogued and there will eventually be a range of postcards and a publication on the history of the collection. Visitors should make an appointment in advance.

For photographs and further information on the collection see 'The Symington Collection of Period Corsetry', the text of a lecture by Chris Page, in *High Victorian*, the proceedings of the annual conference of the Costume Society, March 1968.

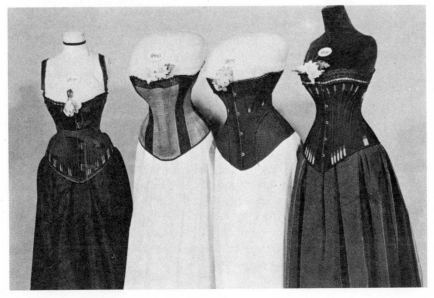

228. The Symington Museum of Period Corsetry, Market Harborough. Four corsets from the second half of the nineteenth century, dating left to right from 1856, 1860, 1875, and 1890.

NEWCASTLE-UPON-TYNE

LAING ART GALLERY AND MUSEUM

Some of the costumes in this collection were gifts from the Joicey collection but many are of local interest, acquired from donors living in Newcastle and the surrounding area.

Most of the small group of eighteenth-century dresses have been remodelled or altered from earlier silks. There are a few dresses from the end of the eighteenth century to c.1830 and a fairly representative selection of dresses from the mid-nineteenth to mid-twentieth centuries. A sizeable collection of mainly nineteenth and twentieth-century underwear includes nightdresses, chemises, drawers and petticoats.

Among the accessories are a representative selection of over fifty pairs of shoes from c.1700–1960 and a small number of parasols, umbrellas, fans, gloves, purses and other small accessories, mostly nineteenth-century.

The collection of men's costume consists of a few eighteenth and early nineteenth-century suits, with a group of waistcoats of the same period. There is a shirt (58.36b) in white linen with a high collar and frills at the front opening. It is T-shaped with gussets under the arms and three buttons fastening the neck. The letters *4 WG 1803* are marked in red cross-stitch near the hem. There are also a few civil and military uniforms.

A small selection of mainly nineteenth-century children's clothes includes christening robes and babies' wear.

Plans for the future expansion of this museum and reorganisation of storage space include rehousing the costume collection. At the time of writing most of the dresses are on padded hangers covered with cellophane bags and hanging in chronological order in two large cupboards. Accessories and fragile dresses of the 1920s and 1930s are in boxes.

All items are entered in an accessions register and then in a card index which is being reorganised at the time of writing.

The displays in the costume gallery are changed every twelve to eighteen months. About ten dresses and suits are on display arranged in chronological order, with an indication of period background. Other cases show a selection of different types of accessories. There may be displays of costume in the new Joicey Museum in the future.

Space is limited but a group of twenty children can work comfortably in the costume gallery. A few expendable items are reserved for older children to handle, under strict supervision. Groups of not more than ten children aged fourteen to eighteen or two advanced students can be accommodated at any one time in the reserve collection where a small selection of reference books on costume is available.

NORTHAMPTON

ABINGTON PARK MUSEUM
CENTRAL MUSEUM AND ART GALLERY

Costume and accessories are stored at Abington Park Museum and items are on show both there and at the Central Museum where the large collection of shoes is stored and exhibited. There is also a selection of tools and machinery used in the shoe trade, many given by local industry. Shoes are the most important section of the whole costume collection, with over three thousand pairs. There are approximately five hundred pairs of shoes, boots and pattens on show, ranging in date from a few Roman and medieval fragments, some specimens of 1509–47 excavated in the City of London, and one pair of very early seventeenth-century shoes, to an increasingly large selection through the eighteenth, nineteenth and present centuries. They include prize boots and shoes for exhibition, and apprentices' pieces from the late eighteenth to the twentieth century. These show superb craftsmanship and were not intended for wear, so they are in perfect condition. There are shoes made by Yantorny and ballet shoes worn by Nijinsky. The display of shoes is semi-permanent but a major reorganisation of the exhibits is planned for the near future. The costumes displays at both the Central Museum and Abington Park Museum are changed approximately twice a year.

Much of the costume collection was acquired from local donors but it does not entirely reflect local taste as a large number of items were given by Osborne Robinson, of the Northampton Repertory Theatre, who collected items from all over the country. Among the representative selection of nineteenth and twentieth-century dresses is a dinner dress of c.1830–6 in palest dove-grey moiré taffeta, with gigot sleeves. Its skirt is decorated with grey taffeta piping in a design of thistles and leaves (D29/36). Three other dresses are of interest because they were made locally: a pale grey doeskin two-piece dress of c.1898–1900, trimmed with black velvet ribbon and lace has the label of *Adnitt Brothers, Costumiers, Northampton*, a store which still exists (D129/56–7). The other two dresses have the label *Mrs Lodge, Northampton*; one is a deep mauve silk dress of c.1908–12, trimmed with embroidered muslin and lace and the other a wedding dress of c.1912 in ivory satin covered with fine embroidered silk gauze (D186/1962 and D154/1962).

The selection of underwear includes drawers, petticoats, chemises, camisoles, mantles, veils, handkerchiefs and parasols. There is a small range of children's clothes with a large quantity of babies' gowns, bonnets and christening robes.

A few men's suits date from the eighteenth and nineteenth centuries with a representative selection of eighteenth, nineteenth and twentieth-

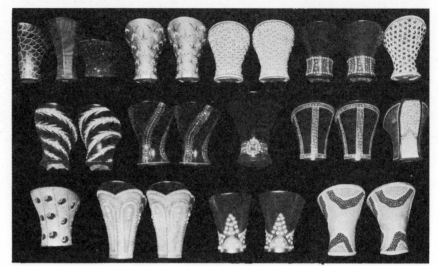

229. Central Museum and Art Gallery, North-ampton. A glittering selection of richly decorated shoe heels made by Fernand Weil, Emil Petit et Cie. of Paris, and imported as samples by the Bective Shoe Company in 1925. They were presented to the museum in 1943 with the original illustrated catalogue and price list.

century waistcoats and a number of nineteenth and twentieth-century hats.

The costumes are stored in a small room hanging on rails, covered with polythene bags, except for fragile items, underwear and accessories which are in boxes.

Every item in the collection is registered in the accessions book and then in a card index. The shoe collection is catalogued separately from the costumes and other accessories, as it is so large.

There is a schools service which caters for groups of up to thirty children, and costumes are borrowed from the reserve collections for them to study under close supervision. Typical subjects for talks are 'Shoe Styles', 'Use of Materials for Shoes', and 'Shoemaking in Northampton-shire'. Space is limited but up to fifteen advanced students can be accommodated in the shoe reserve collection and two at Abington House to study at any one time. Appointments should be made well in advance.

PUBLICATIONS AVAILABLE FROM THE MUSEUM

Shoe and Leather Bibliography
SWANN, J. M. *Picture Book of Boots and Shoes*, Northampton Museum, 1964.
SWANN, J. M. *Shoes Concealed in Buildings*, Northampton Museum, 1970.
    Illustrated with ten monochrome plates.
There are several monochrome postcards of shoes in the collection.
    The museum has a selection of publications dealing with footwear, many of them offprints from journals, which are most useful for students.
    A list of publications, a shoe and leather bibliography and a list of photographs available to order may be obtained free of charge from the museum.

NORWICH

The main collection of costume is stored and displayed at Strangers' Hall where one room has recently been completely fitted for costume displays. These are usually related to social background, sometimes in room settings of the same period or with other material. Accessories are also displayed with the tools and machinery for their manufacture at the Bridewell Museum. The displays of local leathercraft show various stages and processes in shoemaking, with shoes from the seventeenth to the twentieth century. Norwich shawls and crape can be seen near the Jacquard hand loom used in Norwich for weaving patterned silk, with cloth-workers' tools and early sewing machines.

Archaeological finds displayed at Norwich Castle Museum include Roman costume accessories.

Among women's costume there is a good representative range of dresses, beginning with a small group from the eighteenth century, almost all of which have been remodelled or altered, mainly during the eighteenth century. Some of the early nineteenth-century dresses are of very fine quality, as are a pair of dresses from c.1879–80. One is a wedding dress in white figured satin trimmed with plain satin down the front panel, with beautifully embroidered buttons. It is labelled *Taylor and Co Milliner and Dressmaker Shanghai* (1.105.1961). The other is the going-away dress of the same woman, also probably made in Shanghai. It is in palest pink silk gauze with white silk gauze draped over the skirt, trimmed with lace and kilted trimmings.

There are several coats, bathing dresses, riding habits and some examples of occupational costume including a W.V.S. uniform and a nurse's uniform, all from the twentieth century. The wide range of underwear includes a few eighteenth-century corsets, a selection of wrappers and powdering gowns from the eighteenth to the twentieth century, a large range of mainly nineteenth-century chemisettes and a few bustles and crinoline petticoats.

The twentieth-century collection of 128 items, both dresses and accessories, which belonged to Lady Fairhaven, the wife of the shipping magnate, is of particular interest. She bought her clothes from couturiers and large stores in France, America and England. Many of the dresses still retain the labels *Stern Bros New York*, *Reville, London and Paris*, *B. Altmann & Co., Paris and New York*, *Jays London* and *Maison Pendoux et Cie, Paris*.

Left

230. Strangers' Hall
Museum of Domestic
Life, Norwich.
White muslin dress
of c. 1808–10
embroidered with
silver gilt, gold
thread and gold silk.
It is a simple shape
and relies on the
superb embroidery at
the neck, round the
ends of the sleeves,
and across the front
for its effect.
(75.944)

Right

231. The Bowes
Museum, Barnard
Castle. White
muslin lingerie dress
of c. 1908–9,
elaborately trimmed
with fine tucks, lace
and embroidery
insertion, worn by
the Countess of
Liverpool.
(CST 708/1963.702)

There is a large selection of infants' and babies' wear with a good range of children's dresses of the nineteenth and twentieth centuries.

The range of men's costume is limited; there are three eighteenth-century suits, some dinner jackets and lounge suits from the nineteenth and twentieth centuries, and a representative selection of about forty waistcoats from the eighteenth to the twentieth century. A man's coat of c.1700 in a Bizarre silk with a brown ribbed ground, brocaded with two kinds of silver gilt thread is illustrated in plate 32A of *Baroque and Rococo silks* by Peter Thornton.

A collection of ecclesiastical, religious and clerical dress was started in 1970; there are already some specimens in each category. The collection will be as broadly based as possible under the following headings: habits and orders, societies and congregations, clerical dress, vestments, lay participating dress, such as Salvation Army suits and bonnets, choristers' dress; additional documentary material.

The collection of shoes dating from the seventeenth to the twentieth century is only a part of the large collection of accessories which includes a fine group of approximately 250 shawls, mainly nineteenth-century, almost all acquired locally and a certain number of Norwich origin. The Strangers' Hall also houses a collection of over fifty pattern books of Norwich stuffs, mainly dress textiles, dating from 1757 to 1890. These are from several different firms and include samples of many named calimancoes with the prices in code.

Each item of costume is entered in the accessions book and then on a file card. The cards are indexed alphabetically and in date sequence according to the category. There are a considerable number of sub-divisions. Women's neckwear, for example, is divided into berthes, collars, cravats, fichus, jabots, neckerchiefs and half handkerchiefs, stoles, scarves and tuckers.

For further information on the collection see an article by Pamela Clabburn, 'The Costume Collection in Strangers' Hall Norwich', in *Costume*, The Journal of the Costume Society, no. 3, 1969.

There is space for twenty children in the costume gallery and items from the reserve collection can be seen by special arrangement, under supervision. Groups of not more than four advanced students can be accommodated at any one time in the store where a small selection of reference books on costume is available. Appointments should be made well in advance.

PUBLICATIONS AVAILABLE FROM THE MUSEUM

A free handlist of the categories of costume in the collection, compiled by Pamela Clabburn, is available for students on request. Other publications will include *The Norwich Shawl Industry* (in preparation). Please write for further information.

NOTTINGHAM

CITY OF NOTTINGHAM MUSEUM AND ART GALLERY

The museum contains a fairly large collection of costume, costume accessories and lace.

A selection of small items of seventeenth-century costume on display in the galleries includes embroidered coifs, nightcaps, a woman's embroidered bodice of c.1600–10, a man's doublet of c.1610, a woman's court bodice of c.1670 and a man's suit of c.1700. These are changed at frequent intervals.

Most of the main collection was acquired from local donors, although there are some specimens from further afield. Women's costume includes aprons, a few bathing costumes ranging from c.1890–1946 and a small selection in each of the following groups: belts, blouses, boas, bodices, bonnets, boots, bustles, camisoles, caps, capes, chemises ranging from the eighteenth to nineteenth centuries, chemisettes from c.1800–1900 including nine for mourning, cloaks, coats, collars, combinations, corsets, crinolines, cuffs, drawers, dressing gowns, dressing jackets, fans, fichus, frills, furs, gaiters, gloves, hats, hoods (both eighteenth and nineteenth century), jackets, jumpers, lappets, mantles, mittens, necklets, nightdresses, overalls, pattens, pelisses, petticoats, riding hats, sashes, scarves, shawls, shoes, skirts, sleeves, slippers, squares, stockings, sunbonnets, teagowns, ties, trains, underbodices, undersleeves, veils, vests and waistcoats. A sizeable range of dresses dates from c.1730 to the 1950s. There are not many eighteenth-century specimens but the collection is representative from the early nineteenth century to c. 1947. An ivory satin evening dress of c.1893, trimmed with a long fringe of pearls and gold beads on the bodice, with short puffed sleeves in velvet, was made locally, being labelled on the waistband *Jessop, Nottingham, Robes and Confections* (62.483).

The large lace collection, with the Alderman Spalding lace collection, includes samples of every kind, both hand and machine made. Examples of machine-made Nottingham lace are of local interest. Many of the pieces of lace are made up as cuffs, collars, sleeves, flounces and bonnet veils.

The small group of occupational costume consists of a few smocks, maids' dresses and livery.

There is a large selection of babies' clothes, christening robes and capes, dating mainly from the mid and late nineteenth and early twentieth centuries, and a small group of children's dresses and suits, caps, shoes and underwear of the same period.

The displays of costume in the gallery usually have a theme and are changed once in six to twelve months. There is a large group of frames containing labels with relevant information beside mounted embroidery and lace samples, specimens of bodices, eighteenth-century ruffles and other dress accessories to show construction, woven and printed textiles, baby clothes. These are used for exhibition in the gallery and can also be studied in the store. At the time of writing the collection of dresses is being reorganised to hang in cupboards in a store leading from the display galleries, so that they will be more easily accessible for students. Fragile items, accessories and lace are packed in cardboard boxes. A small selection of books on costume, lace and textiles is available for anyone working in the collection.

Each item is given an accession number, entered in a day book and then in a card index.

As study accommodation is limited, school parties have to be restricted to not more than fifteen, if they wish to see costumes which are not on display. Ten college students or two advanced students can work at any one time in the store. Appointments should be made at least two weeks in advance.

PUBLICATIONS AVAILABLE FROM THE MUSEUM

HALLS, Z. *Machine-made Lace in Nottingham in the Eighteenth and Nineteenth Century*, Nottingham Museum and Art Gallery, 1964. Monochrome plates.

A few slides of costume are available, and a list can be obtained from the museum.

232. Nottingham Museum and Art Gallery. Wedding dress of c. 1873–4 in eau de nil corded silk with diagonal pleated trimmings on the skirt. (68.405)

OXFORD

ASHMOLEAN MUSEUM

The department of Eastern Art has a small costume collection including a few Chinese and Japanese robes. One item of historical interest is the Arab costume with a large cloth of gold cloak which belonged to T. E. Lawrence.

Visitors should write or telephone in advance to see the reserve collection.

PADIHAM

GAWTHORPE HALL

This collection of textiles, intended for the use of students, was formed by Miss Rachel Kay-Shuttleworth. Formerly a private collection, it is now administered by a group of trustees under the auspices of the National Trust and the Nelson and Colne College of Further Education. A small fee is charged for the use of the collection on the same principle as those charged for adult education classes. Students and teachers in the area will find the collection most useful for study purposes, since there are many specimens of material related to dress as well as over forty costumes. There are printed and woven materials, pieces of embroidery and lace, with a range of the tools used for dressmaking and lacemaking.

A new catalogue system is being arranged at the time of writing, since the collection has been in store for a number of years.

Appointments to work in the collection should be made well in advance.

PAISLEY

MUSEUM AND ART GALLERIES

The three collections of shawls here are of major importance. These are the Whyte collection, the MacIntyre collection and the Museum collection, which was built up by gifts from various donors, the majority living locally, and through purchases. Altogether there are about five hundred shawls covering the whole range of the Paisley industry, as well as specimens from Norwich and India. There are woven, printed and embroidered specimens in rich ranges of colour.

The Paisley Museum was founded in 1870, in the declining years of the shawl industry, and for this reason acquired many examples of the designs, looms, printing blocks and products of the factories which closed down then and later on. There are about seventy design and sample books which give dates and manufacturers' and designers' names. There are English and French as well as local designers, but all the products were woven in Paisley. The whole process of designing and weaving can be seen from many different samples, although so far there is not one complete sequence of design, weaving diagram on squared paper and final woven shawl. In addition to the sample books there are many technical works on weaving and pamphlets about weaving inventions, such as patent net, which were printed in the early nineteenth century.

The small collection of costume includes a few mainly nineteenth-century women's dresses and a sizeable group of underwear including petticoats, chemises, vests, drawers, corsets and corset covers and drawers. Small ranges of hats, bonnets, caps, hoods, shoes and gloves also date mainly from the nineteenth and early twentieth centuries, as do very small groups of children's and men's clothing.

There is no permanent display of costume but items are occasionally put on show. One large room is devoted to the display of Paisley shawls, shawl designs and looms. An extension is now being added to the museum and the costume collection will be more readily accessible when the large collection of shawls has been rehoused and many specimens put on display.

There is an accession book for all objects entering the museum, but there is no card index for costume at the time of writing. All items are noted in a costume and costume accessories handlist.

The schools service does not cater for costume study but, if adequate notice is given, dresses can be mounted in cases for school parties working under supervision. Space and facilities are limited and not more than thirty children or six college students or two special students can be accommodated at any one time. Appointments to work in the collection should be made well in advance.

PUBLICATIONS AVAILABLE FROM THE MUSEUM

ROCK, C. H. *Paisley Shawls*, Paisley Museum and Art Galleries, 1966.
A useful handbook with seventeen monochrome plates of shawls, looms and weavers.

PETERBOROUGH

MUSEUM AND ART GALLERY

This small collection of costume was acquired mainly from local donors, although some material has come from outside the county. All the costumes are stored in boxes.

The card index is divided into the following categories, and there is a small selection of items in each, mostly dating from the nineteenth century, but with a few from the eighteenth and some from the twentieth century: women's clothing – dresses; bodices and skirts; capes; shawls and pelerines; aprons and pockets; sleeves and collars; hats and caps; underwear; stockings, garters and gloves; shoes; handkerchiefs; fans and muffs; parasols and umbrellas; jewellery. One elaborate afternoon dress of embroidered black chiffon of *c*.1902–4 is from the Mills family of Tansor Court near Peterborough. It is labelled *Doucet, 21 Rue de la Paix Paris* and the model number *17886* is on the waistband of the dress. Children's clothes include a few dresses and coats, shoes, hats and underwear with a larger group of robes. The very small group of men's clothes includes two smocks and a young man's suit in natural doeskin of *c*.1750–60. The fronts and collar of the frock and waistcoat are embroidered in silver and sequins, with silver buttons and the buttonholes have been cut in curved shapes to suit the embroidery (D.394.74/51). A late eighteenth-century riding cloak in red woollen cloth with a buttoned front flap is also of interest (D.395).

There is no costume on show at the time of writing as the museum is undergoing reorganisation and structural alterations, but displays are planned for the future. Advanced students may work in the collection by appointment and there is space for two at any one time.

PRESTON

HARRIS MUSEUM AND ART GALLERY

The museum has a sizeable collection of costume and accessories, much of which was in store at the time of writing while alterations were in progress in the museum and library. The major part of the collection dates from the early nineteenth to the twentieth century, and is very useful for local students.

Each item is entered in an accessions book and in a card index under the following categories: dresses, capes, jackets, dolmans, blouses, bodices, coats, skirts, shoes, hats, gloves, parasols, underwear, ties, cravats, waistcoats, trousers. There are several interesting bustles in the collection. One labelled *New Phantom, patent applied for* (741) dating from *c*.1885, has a collapsible frame and fastens with a buckle at the waist. *The American Braided Wire Co* bustle of *c*.1886 has two rows of springs (742). A collection of over 2,000 fashion plates and cuttings from magazines which date from 1789 to 1940 is invaluable.

Mention should be made of the paintings by Arthur Devis in the Art Gallery. These are most useful sources of information for mid-eighteenth-century costume.

There are displays of costume and accessories in the museum, which are large enough for groups of up to twenty children to work from. Space is limited in the store and not more than two advanced students can be accommodated at any one time. Appointments should be made well in advance.

READING

MUSEUM AND ART GALLERY

The costume collection is a small one consisting mainly of nineteenth-century material, acquired from local donors within recent years. The museum tries to collect specimens to show the development of styles in dress as well as providing an aspect of local history.

There are about eighty dresses from the nineteenth-century with a few eighteenth and twentieth-century specimens. A turquoise figured silk dress of c.1818, with ivory crimped gauze long sleeves caught in with piped bands, is too fragile to be handled (27.62). A servant's dress in blue denim with a white linen apron of c.1890–1900 is a rare specimen of working dress (91.69). An ivory twill weave woollen dress dating from c.1890–1 has a draped skirt and slightly puffed sleeves. The bodice is boned and at the back is one bone in a casing stamped in gold *Leather capped regd 143206*. There are small ranges of underwear and accessories, including a collection of thirty-four fans of Chinese, Japanese and European origin.

Men's clothing consists of a few suits, waistcoats, smoking jackets, items of underwear and smocks. There is a small range of children's clothes, babies' gowns and christening robes. A school uniform consisting of a very dark green wool dress with a white linen collar, apron, sleeved mittens and black bonnet was made and worn by a girl who attended the Green School of Reading (1782–1922) between 1903 and 1907.

The dresses are hanging in glass-fronted cupboards protected from the light by curtains. The accessories are packed in boxes. At the time of writing each item is entered in a card index and filed by order of accession.

The schools service has some expendable items of costume and dolls which children may handle under supervision, and they are building up a collection of replicas of period costume that they can wear. There are occasional temporary displays of costume in the museum but arrangements can be made for students to see items from the reserve collection if there is nothing on show. There is space for up to fifteen children in the gallery and not more than four students at any one time in the reserve collection.

Provision has been made in the capital programme for 1974–7 for building a new museum and art gallery to form part of the civic centre site, where there will be larger stores and exhibition areas.

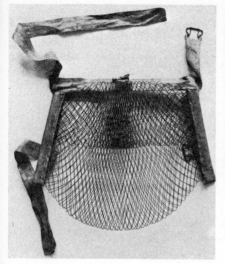 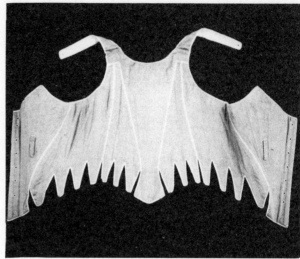

READING

Above left

233. Harris Museum
and Art Gallery,
Preston. 'The Myra
Patented Health
Dress Improver',
c. 1887, made by the
American Braided
Wire Co., which can
be adjusted to shape
with tapes and
buckles. (740)

Above right

234. Museum and
Art Gallery, Peter-
borough. Brown
twill weave cotton
corset of c. 1785–90,
lightly boned, with a
plain weave linen
lining. (D454)

MUSEUM OF ENGLISH RURAL LIFE

The small collection of costume consists of a few items of country people's clothing, some examples of lace and lace-making equipment, a few sunbonnets, shoes and pattens, and over forty smocks, ranging from nineteenth-century working smocks to those made during the 1920s. The general collection contains pieces of equipment for laundry work. In the small exhibition area some of these items and examples of smocks are on display with photographs of country people using them.

All the items are entered in a card index, with a photograph of each.

The museum has a large library of negatives and prints. It contains at least one photograph of every object in the collection as well as those of comparative material in other collections. Other photographs date from the nineteenth century and early twentieth century and show country people at work.

There is space for parties of fifteen school children in the display area and not more than ten students in the library to see objects in the reserve collection. Advance notice of an intended visit should be given as space is limited.

PUBLICATIONS AVAILABLE FROM THE MUSEUM

Free leaflets on information resources, the photographic collection and the use of the collection are available. Black and white photographs of items in the collection may be purchased. An index of contact prints may be consulted during office hours.

RUFFORD

RUFFORD OLD HALL

This National Trust property contains a small collection of costume which has not yet been catalogued. One room is fitted with cases for displays of between five and ten costumes.

SALISBURY

SALISBURY AND SOUTH WILTSHIRE MUSEUM

Most of the items in the costume collection were acquired from donors living in or near Salisbury and reflect local taste to a certain extent. The main part of the range of women's clothing is the collection of about a hundred dresses. There are a few eighteenth-century specimens, but most are from the nineteenth century, the largest group being from c.1800–1820, and a few from the twentieth century. Among them is a morning dress of c.1798–1805 with a high stomacher front opening, in white cotton with a small regular geometric pattern printed in dark purple. The long sleeves are detachable and the dress can be worn with short sleeves only (D2 17/46). A pelisse-robe of c.1824–7 in acid green silk, lined with fine white silk, has a padded hem with a deep band of black, acid green and white flossed silk set above it (D10 2/44).

There are a few items of women's underwear and a small selection of accessories including aprons, fans, bags, reticules and parasols. The group of men's clothing consists of a few suits, coats, breeches, hats and a dozen smocks, with a representative selection of waistcoats, several from the eighteenth century. A few military uniforms are of local interest. There is a large collection of babies' robes, caps, bonnets and christening robes.

Each item has an accession number and costume catalogue number in the card index.

At the time of writing there is a small area for display and the costumes are stored in one small room on hangers beneath polythene bags. Re-organisation will shortly make a larger store available and there will be space for groups of up to ten children to see items from the reserve collection or for one advanced student to work in the store at any one time. Appointments should be made well in advance.

PUBLICATIONS AVAILABLE FROM THE MUSEUM

Postcards and other publications are planned, and details will be sent on request.

SHREWSBURY

BOROUGH MUSEUM AND ART GALLERY

This small collection consists of approximately forty items acquired from local sources. Most are fairly simple clothes, worn by local people, and are mainly nineteenth-century women's and children's wear. There are, however, four particularly noteworthy specimens. A mantua of c.1708–9, in sap green brocaded silk with a pattern in white, tan, pink and bright yellow with a greenish tinge, is a very rare and perfect specimen of the style which first began to appear for informal wear at the end of the seventeenth century, pleated to fit from a simple T-shape.

There is also a pelisse robe in beige wool of c.1805–12. Two men's black beaver hats, both made locally are also of interest. One is a top hat of c.1795–1820 with a double row of tarnished metal ribbon. The cream satin lining is stamped *J Forth 8 Pride Hill Shrewsbury* with the royal coat of arms. The other is a round hat of c.1795–1820 with a paper label printed *Jones, Hat Manufacturer Shrewsbury* stuck to the brown glazed cotton lining. A piece of brown leather is stitched beneath the brim at the back of the hat.

The costumes are stored in boxes; each item is entered in an accessions register and there is a handlist of the contents of each box. A few items, including a collection of uniforms of the Queen's Dragoon Guards, are displayed at Clive House Museum, College Hill, Shrewsbury.

There are facilities for two advanced students to study in the store; school parties should be limited to fifteen at any one time to allow adequate space to work. Appointments should be made at least two weeks in advance.

SNOWSHILL

SNOWSHILL MANOR

This collection of costume was formed by Charles Wade who left it, with the seventeenth-century manor house in which it is stored and where a few items from it are displayed, to the National Trust. Lacemaking and weaving equipment are also on display.

The collection includes a range of over forty eighteenth-century women's dresses and eighteen eighteenth-century jackets, a representative selection of silk, muslin and printed cotton gowns of c.1800–20 and a small group of dresses dating from c.1820 to the early twentieth century. Many of the eighteenth-century dresses have had slight alterations and some are very fragile. A small but interesting range of outerwear includes pelisses and cardinal capes dating from the early and mid-nineteenth century. There are a few items, mainly from the eighteenth and early

Far left

235. Salisbury and South Wiltshire Museum. A gown of c. 1780–5 in ivory silk, block printed with a dark green curving design of leaves and flower sprays down the centre of each width. The details were completed by hand-painting. The skirt can be looped up 'en polonaise'. (D22 29/48)

Left

236. Castle Howard. A white satin fancy dress made in Paris in c. 1912. 'The Empress Josephine' has a skirt embroidered with a design of bees (the emblem of Napoleon) in gilt metal thread.

nineteenth centuries, in each of the following categories: aprons, chemises, chemisettes, corsets, drawers, gloves, headwear, mittens, scarves, shawls, squares, shoes, sleeve ruffles, petticoats, parasols and umbrellas. Although small, each of the categories includes several interesting and well-preserved specimens.

The group of men's suits, dating from the mid eighteenth to the early nineteenth century, is particularly fine. There are over thirty heavily embroidered silk and velvet coats and a few in plain wool and silk; many have survived with matching breeches and waistcoats. There are nine well-worn overcoats, cloaks and caped coats in heavy woollen cloth dating from the late eighteenth and early nineteenth centuries, which have fortunately been preserved. Other examples of men's clothing include waistcoats, breeches, trousers, hats, uniforms, hunting coats, liveries and underclothes. There are a few examples of babies' wear and children's clothes.

There is no complete catalogue or card index at the time of writing. All the dresses, suits and coats are hanging in cupboards on padded hangers, protected from the light. Since many of the specimens are very fragile and should not be handled, the collection is suitable for advanced students only. There is space for two people to work in the store at any one time, and appointments should be made at least three weeks in advance.

STOKE BRUERNE

WATERWAYS MUSEUM

The museum contains a small collection of bargees' costume and several items are on display. They are of particular interest as few examples of this type of costume have survived.

Visitors should write or telephone in advance to see the reserve collection.

TAUNTON

SOMERSET COUNTY MUSEUM

The collection consists mainly of costumes given by local people but these are not necessarily of local origin except for some smocks. There are approximately three hundred items of women's clothing including dresses, bodices, skirts, jackets and underwear. The majority date from the nineteenth century, but there are a few eighteenth and twentieth-century specimens. There are a small number of men's clothes, mainly from the nineteenth century.

A small group of dresses is on display in the museum. It is planned that the local Regimental Museum, with a sizeable group of uniforms, should move into the Castle in the near future.

Students are advised to write or telephone well in advance if they wish to see any part of the reserve collection.

TRURO

ROYAL INSTITUTION OF CORNWALL COUNTY MUSEUM AND ART GALLERY

The small collection of costume has been acquired almost entirely from local donors. Costume accessories are occasionally put on display as part of other exhibits. There are a few eighteenth-century children's clothes, a group of uniforms, mainly of local interest, and several women's dresses of the eighteenth and nineteenth centuries.

Small groups of children and students are usually able to see the costumes on request, although it is best to telephone or write in advance.

Opposite below

239. Snowshill Manor. White silk bonnet of c. 1828–30 with pale turquoise blue gauze ribbons.

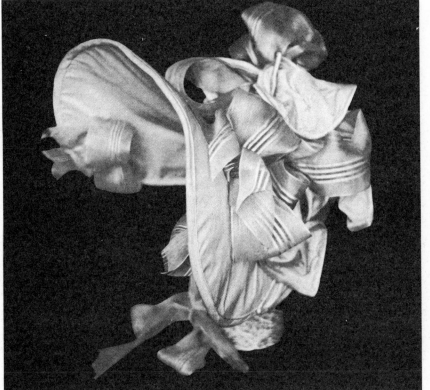

Above left

237. County of
Warwick Museum.
Detail of a white
linen shirt, em-
broidered in red silk,
made in the second
half of the sixteenth
century. (37/1962)

Above right

238. Borough
Museum and Art
Gallery, Shrewsbury.
Black low-crowned
hat of c. 1790–
1810, the forerunner
of the top hat, with
a double row of
metal ribbon. The
cream satin lining is
stamped 'J. Forth
8 Pride Hill,
Shrewsbury' with
the royal coat of arms.
The paper lining and
a layer of stiffened
cotton are visible
inside.

WARWICK

ST JOHN'S HOUSE, COTEN END (BRANCH OF COUNTY OF WARWICK MUSEUM)
The County of Warwick Museum collection has mainly been acquired
from donors living locally or with Warwickshire connections and is
stored and displayed at St John's House. Among the selection of about a
hundred mainly nineteenth and twentieth-century dresses are an extremely
good group of 1930s evening dresses, all worn by the late Lady Beryl
Graeme Thomson. A black velvet evening dress of *c*.1932–4, cut on the
cross with a trailing skirt at the back, and a low-cut back bodice with
three *diamanté* buttons, is very elegant (101/1961/5). Another evening
dress, of *c*.1934–6, is also made of black velvet cut on the cross. It has one
floating sleeve lined with grey chiffon and one *diamanté* shoulder strap.
There are weights to hold the bodice draperies in position (101/1961/10).
There is also an exquisite dinner dress of *c*.1935–8 of grey chiffon over a
grey silk slip, which fastens down the centre back with tiny bobble
buttons. It is finely tucked over the hips, falling out into the skirt at the
back (101/1961/3).

The collection also includes some interesting twentieth-century
women's uniforms; one dating from *c*.1917–18 is a white linen land army
uniform with a green armband, worn during the First World War
(89/1964/A). There are also groups of items in each of the following
categories: accessories, aprons, bathing costumes, blouses, bodices, capes,
caps, corsets, collars, cuffs, cami-knickers, chemises, combinations,
drawers, fans, fichus, gloves, hats, jabots, nightwear, parasols, petticoats,
slips and vests.

Men's costume includes four seventeenth-century buff coats, a few
eighteenth-century waistcoats, a selection of nineteenth and twentieth-
century coats and suits, fourteen smocks, underwear, hunting coats and
uniforms. The Royal Regiment of Fusiliers' collection which includes
many uniforms is also displayed at St John's House.

A range of mainly nineteenth-century children's clothes includes
several dresses for older girls, as well as christening robes and babies'
gowns.

All items are entered in an accessions register and then in a separate card
index for costume and accessories. Dresses hang in cupboards, protected
with polythene bags, and accessories are stored in boxes. A collection of
about eight dresses with accessories and four smocks, changed twice a
year, are always on exhibition in the small display area.

A party of up to thirty children can see items from the store by prior
arrangement, and there is space for not more than six advanced students
at a time to work in the reserve collection. Appointments should be made
well in advance.

WESTON-SUPER-MARE

PUBLIC LIBRARY AND MUSEUM

The collection of costume has been acquired mainly from local donors, a gift from the Addis family providing many specimens from c.1870 to the 1930s, with the main emphasis on the 1890s. The collection includes a range of over sixty dresses from c.1800 to the mid-twentieth century, the largest section from c.1870–90. There are small ranges of underwear, a few men's suits, several smocks and a small range of children's clothing including one boy's suit of c.1760 and another of c.1810.

Until very recently the collection was in store but a new costume gallery has just been opened, showing costume in a social background with other items from the museum for local history displays. New storage units have been built, the reserve collection is now accessible, and the accessions register and the card index are complete.

There is room for groups of up to thirty children to work in the gallery and items from the reserve collection can be seen by special arrangement, under supervision. Space is limited in the store and not more than one advanced student can work there at any one time.

Appointments should be made well in advance.

WEYBRIDGE

WEYBRIDGE MUSEUM

This is a local history museum which collects material to give a comprehensive picture of the history of Weybridge and north-west Surrey. The main part of the collection was acquired from local donors, and documentary evidence about the wearer is collected wherever possible.

Women's clothing includes a small selection of skirts, dresses, wedding dresses, underclothes, petticoats, blouses, bathing costumes, coats, capes and nightclothes, all mainly from the nineteenth and twentieth centuries. Among the accessories there are a few of each of: lace, hats, bonnets, caps, aprons, purses, scarves, belts, buckles, shawls, gloves, fans, shoes, ornaments, ribbons, buttons, collars, handkerchiefs, flowers and feathers, stockings and muffs, parasols and umbrellas.

The group of children's dress includes babies' clothes, among them a 'Babygro' of 1968 and a few other items. Men's clothing includes a few waistcoats, trousers, shirts, cricketing flannels, ties and smoking caps, almost all from the late nineteenth and twentieth centuries. There are also a few pieces of occupational costume and uniforms.

Each item is entered in an accessions card which is duplicated for the donors' file and subject classification file. A small selection of costume reference books are available for students working in the collection, and

a free educational service guide is available for teachers organising visits
to the museum.

The schools service will arrange for groups of up to forty children to
have a slide lecture on costume. There is space for up to twenty children
to work from the displays of costume in the gallery or ten sixth-formers
to see reserve material, or two advanced students to work in the store at
any one time. Appointments should be made in advance.

WINCHESTER

HAMPSHIRE COUNTY MUSEUM SERVICE

At the time of writing the Hampshire County costume collection, which
includes material from the Curtis Museum at Alton and the Willis
Museum at Basingstoke, is in store at Chilcombe House, the headquarters
of the Hampshire County Museum Service. It contains over two hundred
dresses and a very large group of accessories. The card index is undergoing
reorganisation and there are future plans to establish a costume gallery in
or near Winchester.

Further information can be obtained from Hampshire County Museum
Service.

WOODSTOCK

OXFORD CITY AND COUNTY MUSEUM

There are two collections of excavated leather objects totalling over a
thousand items altogether, of which over four hundred are shoes or parts
of shoes. They were all found in the Barbican ditch of Oxford castle and
will probably be added to in the near future as more excavations are in
progress. The earliest group consists of Saxon leatherwork and probably
dates from the early tenth century. It includes offcuts of leather, a complete child's shoe, and an adult's shoe. The second group, from $c.1216$–
$c.1400$, consists of 291 soles, 93 uppers, four semi-complete shoes, fragments of leather including seven decorated pieces, seven knife sheaths and
two fragments of gloves.

These objects will eventually be on display but at the moment can only
be seen by serious students. Colour transparencies of some of the objects
can be supplied on request.

All enquiries should be addressed to:

The Director

Oxford Archaeological Excavations Committee

c/o Oxford City and County Museum

WORTHING

MUSEUM AND ART GALLERY

The collection of costume and accessories, which was acquired mainly from local donors, consists predominantly of nineteenth-century speci-mens, with a small group of eighteenth-century material and a rapidly increasing selection from the twentieth century.

Although small, the eighteenth century section is interesting and contains, among other items, a circular full-length cloak and separate hood of camlet and mohair, dating from c.1770, and a pair of white kid gloves, with hand-painted decorations, dated 1796 on the inside.

There are over five hundred dresses and a selection of items in each of the following categories: aprons, over twenty bathing costumes, bed jackets, belts, blouses, bodices, bustles, chemises, chemisettes, capes, cloaks, coats, drawers, fans, fichus, gloves, hats, jewellery, nightdresses, parasols, petticoats, stockings, shoes, scarves, shawls, skirts and suits.

Babies' and children's clothes include a large group of christening robes, caps, bonnets, dresses, capes and suits, mostly nineteenth-century.

A small group of men's clothing includes a few nineteenth-century suits, shirts, waistcoats, a demob suit, a few 1950s and 1960s suits, some examples of underwear and over twenty smocks.

Each item is entered in an accessions register and then in a card index. Most of the dresses hang in wardrobes but fragile specimens are packed in boxes.

There are four displays of costume in the gallery, in which about ten dresses with accessories are exhibited and changed at frequent intervals, with space for groups of up to thirty children to work in the display area.

The costume store is being moved to temporary accommodation during the building of the new library and museum. As space will be limited for several years from the time of writing, students wishing to work in the reserve collection should make an appointment in advance.

PUBLICATIONS AVAILABLE FROM THE MUSEUM

Catalogue of the Costume Collection, Part 1, Eighteenth Century, compiled by D. Bullard, Worthing Museum Publications No. 6, 1964.
Catalogue of the Costume Collection, Part 2, Early Nineteenth Century 1800–1830, Worthing Museum Publications, 1968.
Catalogue of the Costume Collection, Part 3, Mid-Nineteenth Century 1830–1860 in preparation.
Each booklet is illustrated with eight monochrome plates of items in the collection. A few colour transparencies of costumes in the collection are also available.

YORK

CASTLE HOWARD

The costume galleries at Castle Howard were founded by Mr George Howard in 1965. The collection is based on that of Miss Cecile Hummel, which numbers some two thousand catalogued items, to which a further five thousand have been added.

The collection of dresses starts in *c.*1750 and runs to the present day but there are more from the mid and late nineteenth century than any other period. About three-quarters of the costumes are of Yorkshire provenance and a quarter come from the rest of the country (excluding Miss Hummel's collection). There are a number of labelled dresses, including some from Worth, Jeanne Lanvin, Castillo, Chanel and Victor Stiebel, as well as some of Yorkshire shops and dressmakers. There is a good range of wedding dresses from the early nineteenth century to the present day. A large selection of underwear of the same dates includes nightdresses, chemises, combinations, stockings, petticoats and drawers, with a few corsets, cage crinolines and bustles.

A representative group of shawls from the end of the eighteenth to the twentieth centuries includes Norwich, Paisley and Indian examples. The lace collection is very large, and many of the specimens are made up as costume accessories, such as collars, cuffs and lappets. The selection of children's clothes is small but representative and there is a very large group of christening robes and babies' clothes.

There are fewer men's than women's clothes, as in most museums, but they are fairly representative, from the mid-eighteenth century to the present day, including several liveries, some connected with Castle Howard, and military uniform, mainly of Yorkshire regiments.

There is a good range of hats and a collection of shoes from the eighteenth century onwards, more women's than men's. A small group of sportswear includes a few nineteenth- and twentieth-century bathing costumes and riding habits.

Perhaps some of the most charming items in the collection are the late nineteenth-century fancy dress costumes, some from Lady Cecilia Howard's family. There are also over a hundred items of theatrical costume, the most important being those designed by Bakst for the Diaghilev ballet *The Sleeping Princess* produced in 1921.

Collections of paper patterns, magazines, *cartes-de-visite*, group photographs and fashion plates are stored with the costumes. A variety of general costume reference books are available for students working in the collection.

All items are entered in an accessions book and filed in a Rotadex index under the donors'/lenders'/vendors' names.

Over fifty costumes are on display in galleries which cover a large area on the ground floor of the eighteenth-century stable block. Dresses are mounted in period settings often with furniture from Castle Howard, with titles for each tableau, for example, *A Wedding reception of the 1870s*, *Off to the Ball in 1830*, *A Nightclub in 1927*, *A Victorian Kitchen in the 1860s*. A new storage and conservation area opened recently. The displays are changed during the winter months when Castle Howard is closed. Conservation work is also carried out at this time. Duplicated guide sheets are prepared each year for the new display.

The collection is used as a centre for the study of period costume by schools and colleges. School parties of up to thirty children can be accommodated. There are guide lecturers to conduct tours, and time is allowed for sketching in the galleries. These visits take place when the collection is closed to the general public. Space in the reserve collection is limited but up to six advanced students can be accommodated at any one time. In the future it may be necessary to charge a small fee to cover this service as the collection is self-supporting. For further information on the collection see an article by Cecile Hummel 'Castle Howard, A Costume Museum in a Stately Home', in *Costume*, the Journal of the Costume Society, No. 2, 1968.

YORK

CASTLE MUSEUM

The museum houses a very large collection of costume which has been acquired mainly from local donors. There are items from all over the county, mainly eighteenth and nineteenth-century, although the twentieth-century group is being enlarged.

Women's costume consists of a few eighteenth-century dresses, over a hundred spencers, dresses, pelerines, bodices and skirts from c.1800–50, over three hundred dresses, bodices, blouses and skirts from c.1850–1900 and over two hundred dresses, blouses, skirts and suits from c.1920 to the present day, including uniforms from the Second World War. Many of the dresses have undergone slight alterations as they were once used for theatrical purposes.

There are over two hundred items of underclothing, mostly nineteenth and twentieth-century, including bustles, bed-jackets, chemises, chemisettes, corsets, crinolines, nightdresses, petticoats and stockings. There are over fifty shawls, stoles and scarves and about two hundred items in the category of capes, coats and dolmans, dating from the late nineteenth and early twentieth centuries. Other accessories include small groups of fans, gloves, lace, ribbons, aprons, parasols, umbrellas, handbags, purses, footwear, hats, bonnets, hatpins, châtelaines and needlework equipment.

Babies' clothing consists of about a hundred items, including robes, bonnets, christening gowns, bootees and cloaks, a few from the eighteenth but most from the nineteenth and twentieth centuries. A group of over eighty children's dresses, underwear and suits dates mainly from the nineteenth century.

A small group of men's clothing consists of about eighty items, including shirts, suits, breeches, neckwear, waistcoats and livery. The large collection of uniform from local regiments ranges in date from the eighteenth century to the Second World War; most of it is on display.

All items in the collection are entered in the accessions register and then in a card index.

Several rooms in the museum are devoted to costume display. The dresses are related to period background, and accessories are exhibited separately as well as with the costumes.

A separate schools department deals with costume for groups of children aged from eight to eighteen, working in the display area. It has not been possible to accommodate students working in the store since 1969 and it is unlikely that the reserve collection will be available for some time, owing to reorganisation, although items can be shown to visitors if requests are made well in advance.

240. Gawthorpe Hall, Padiham. A selection of nineteenth-century needlework equipment, including a needlebook, a tape measure, a folding pocket-knife, a pin-cushion, a needle-case and a small sewing-case containing a thimble, a stiletto and two mother-of-pearl thread winders.

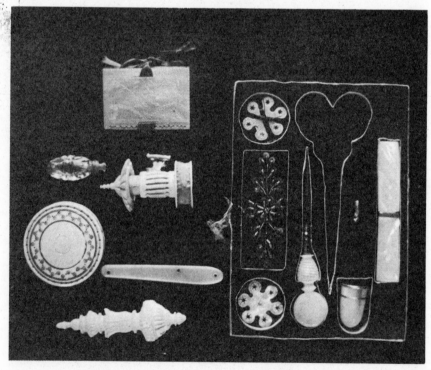